ARMITAGE'S
GARDEN PERENNIALS

ARMITAGE'S
GARDEN PERENNIALS

Second Edition, Fully Revised and Updated

ALLAN M. ARMITAGE

Timber Press
Portland • London

First edition published in 2000 by Timber Press.

Published in 2011 by Timber Press, Inc.

The Haseltine Building
133 S.W. Second Avenue, Suite 450
Portland, Oregon 97204-3527
www.timberpress.com

2 The Quadrant
135 Salusbury Road
London NW6 6RJ
www.timberpress.co.uk

ISBN-13: 978-1-60469-038-5

Designed by Christi Payne
Printed in China
The Library of Congress has cataloged the previous edition as follows:

Armitage, A. M. (Allan M.)
    [Garden perennials]
    Armitage's garden perennials: a color encyclopedia / by Allan M. Armitage
        p.   cm.
    Includes index
    ISBN 0-88192-435-0
    1. Perennials Encyclopedias.   2. Perennials Pictorial works.
  I. Title. II. Title: Garden perennials.
SB434.A755 2000
635.9'32!'03—dc21   99-30800
                                                                 CIP

A catalog record for this book is also available from the British Library.

This edition is dedicated to the Armitage family –
to my saintly wife, Susan
to Laura and Ray, and Hampton and Mary Grace
to Heather and David, and Kate, Will, Ben, and Drew
and to Jonathan.
Susan and I continue to be blessed to watch them grow.

CONTENTS

PREFACE

Gardening is one of those things that gets in one's blood—a thing that is difficult to explain, even to people who have been so transfused. Gardening, however, is rather abstract and is many things to many people. Rock gardens, alpine gardens, bog gardens, butterfly gardens, water gardens, woodland gardens, and native plant gardens are nirvana to some and meaningless to others. But all gardeners and their garden themes are tied together by the one glue that binds: the plants. And regardless of the real job they hold, when gardeners get together, the language of plants cuts through all other spoken baloney.

Plants are the common denominator of gardeners. Gardeners love plants, more than water features, or bird feeders, or anything else in their garden, and will go to incredible lengths—and expense—to secure them. By definition, gardeners are collectors. Numismatists and philatelists have nothing on them. And perennials include many fabulous, collectible plants. To talk about perennials often inspires passion, but to see them can incite lust and rioting among otherwise conservative, law-abiding citizens. So, to stir things up, I have provided in this book photos of some of my favorite perennials, hoping to share the diversity of plants that can make up a garden. If a picture is worth a thousand words, then considerable trees have been saved.

The plant palette has been expanded significantly since the first edition of this book was published in 2000. You will find many new selections not available at the turn of the 21st century, but I have also retained many of the great plants that will be with us for another decade or so.

Come join me as you turn these pages for a magical ride through some of the treasures of the perennial plant kingdom, and the joys of being a gardener. Simply remember the Armitage credo of gardening, "This is gardening, not brain surgery. Gardening should always provide far more pleasure than pain." Have fun.

Phlox divaricata and woodland friends in Ed and Donna Lambert's garden

PART ONE
Armitage's Garden Perennials, A to Z

Acanthus mollis

Acanthus mollis

Acanthus mollis

Acanthus mollis 'Hollard's Gold'

Acanthus
BEAR'S BREECHES

The two common forms are common bear's breeches, *Acanthus mollis*, and spiny bear's breeches, *A. spinosus*. Both have similar tall spikes of purple and white flowers, which arise from leafy plants in late spring. Each white flower on the flower stem is surrounded by a spiny purple sepal-like bract. The bracts provide the color and, when mishandled, considerable pain. Mature clumps produce six to twelve flowers, providing a wonderful contrast to the dark green foliage. The difference between the two species is found mainly in the leaves. The leaf of common bear's breeches is much fuller and more rounded than that of spiny bear's breeches, which is sharply lobed. Spiny bear's breeches sounds painful, but the leaves are pussy cats.

A number of cultivars and hybrids have been produced. *Acanthus mollis* 'Hollard's Gold' has been around for some time

Acanthus mollis 'Tasmanian Angel'

Acanthus spinosus

Acanthus dioscoridis

Acanthus spinosus

Acanthus spinosus 'Spinosissimus'

Acanthus hungaricus

and produces chartreuse leaves. Unfortunately I have never seen much vigor, and plants have either ended up struggling or on the compost pile after a few years. Another potentially quite beautiful type is the variegated 'Tasmanian Angel'. It's spectacular where it thrives—it simply hasn't thrived for me in the Southeast. Pinkish flowers arise from the white and green leaves. Excellent on the West Coast, but a little slow elsewhere. If you really want "spiny" in spiny bear's breeches, try *A. spinosus* 'Spinosissimus'. It's a true man- and woman-eater, and it's a well-known fact that many a small pet has inadvertently wandered into a patch of breeches, never to be seen

Achillea 'Moonshine'

again. 'Summer Beauty', a hybrid between the two species, is vigorous, grows 4 to 5 feet wide in a couple of years, and bears shiny deep green leaves and spires of white flowers surrounded by purple bracts. An excellent choice for the beginning breeches.

There is a good deal of debate and confusion as to the identity and differences among these plants and similar species, such as Hungarian bear's breeches, *Acanthus hungaricus*, and smooth bear's breeches, *A. dioscoridis*. The former is quite similar to *A. spinosus* but a little more cold hardy and with pinker flowers, while the latter is significantly shorter.

If one thinks about the names of the plants people buy for their gardens, a bystander would be convinced that we are a bunch of zookeepers, not plantkeepers. We can hardly grow herbaceous plants and not wonder how plantspeople even had time to

think about plants. We have pigsqueak, hogweed, leopard's bane, pussytoes, rattlesnake master, toad lily, and snakeroot, just to name a few. Some of those names make sense because the plants actually resemble such fauna, but what in the world are the breeches of a bear? What were these people smoking? Of course, it really doesn't matter, since we are growing the plant, not the name. And, without doubt, bear's breeches include some wonderful garden plants. Full sun to partial shade, zones 5 to 9.

Achillea
YARROW

Visit any garden, and there will probably be some yarrow. From plants 5 feet tall to ground huggers, and with flowers in nearly all the colors of the rainbow, the genus provides great diversity and many fine

garden plants. The genus name commemorates the warrior Achilles, and plants have been put to many herbal and medicinal uses. Most yarrows are easy to grow and provide excellent foliage and years of color. All yarrows may be cut and brought inside fresh, or hung upside down for dried flower arrangements.

Fernleaf yarrow, *Achillea filipendulina*, is one of the most useful plants for the spring and summer garden. Its usefulness arises from its functionality: it is prized for color and form in the garden, for fragrance as an herbal plant, and as a cut flower with outstanding longevity. Plants bear large (about 3 inches across), flat yellow flowers on top of 3- to 4-foot-tall plants. The leaves are deeply divided, giving them a somewhat fernlike appearance, thus accounting for its common name. A number of older cultivars, such as 'Gold Plate', are still around,

Achillea filipendulina 'Gold Plate'

Achillea filipendulina 'Coronation Gold'

Achillea filipendulina 'Coronation Gold'
cut stems from the garden

Achillea 'Anthea'

Achillea 'Credo'

but few differences in appearance or garden performance between the yellow-flowered forms are obvious. The grand dame of the group is 'Coronation Gold', developed in 1953 to commemorate the coronation of Queen Elizabeth of England. Plants have large yellow flowers and handsome gray-green foliage on 2- to 3-foot-tall plants, and the cultivar has lost little of its original popularity with her subjects. As a garden plant or as a cut flower, 'Coronation Gold' is outstanding, and after five decades continues to be a mainstay among gardeners.

A number of additional choices are also out there; most are hybrids, in which fernleaf yarrow is one of the main parents. They tend to be vigorous and usually more compact. Generally they are not as tall as 'Coronation Gold' and the tones are softer.

'Moonshine' is shorter and has been a bright standby for many years. 'Anthea' is just a youngster compared to the previous selections, but was rapidly accepted by gardeners. The full pale yellow to sulphur-yellow flowers on a 2-foot-tall frame quickly made her a favorite. 'Martina' provides yet another excellent yellow and bears many flowers, but the flowering stems are not quite as upright as the previous selection. All cultivars are reasonably easy to locate in American nurseries. Full sun, zones 3 to 8.

As ubiquitous in some areas as turf, common yarrow, *Achillea millefolium*, is generally low to the ground and can double as a ground cover as well as a garden plant. The green foliage is finely cut in what appears to be a thousand leaflets (thus "millefolium") and quickly fills in large

areas as the plants spread. Flowers occur in spring and early summer, and the plants retain reasonably good green foliage the rest of the season. They can be used as fresh cut flowers, but they persist for only two or three days, not nearly as long as fernleaf yarrow flowers. Another common name of yarrow, soldier's woundwort, stems from the fact that Achilles made use of this species at the siege of Troy to heal the wounds of his soldiers. Apparently, the leaves and flowers have been used for almost every ill imaginable, including nosebleeds, and the green leaves are still used as a styptic in fresh cuts and wounds and to help heal bruises. And if that is not enough, yarrow is used for making beer. Gerard's *Herball* (1633) also suggests the leaves as a remedy for toothache. Having tasted some of the

Achillea 'Martina'

Achillea 'Appleblossom'

Achillea 'McVitie'

Achillea 'Fireland'

Achillea 'Pomegranate'

Achillea 'Summer Berries'

Achillea 'Pink Grapefruit'

Yarrows arranged with Culver's root and statice

concoctions of my beer-making friends, no ingredient in homebrew surprises me!

The popularity of common yarrow has declined in recent years, perhaps because so many new plants, from new genera, have appeared on the gardening scene. That is not to say that new cultivars do not continue to appear, simply that their development is slowing down. This is really not a bad thing, as so many cultivars had been developed that no one could keep up with them anyway. I like some of the older hybrids like 'Appleblossom' and 'Kelwayi', which have large pastel and bright rose-red flowers, respectively, and spread well. 'McVitie' (white) is well established and provides excellent performance. For small yellows, I recommend 'Credo', and for an all-around tough plant with exceptional performance, it is still hard to beat 'Paprika'. For oohs and aahs, nothing trumps the earth tones

Achillea 'Kelwayi'

Achillea tomentosa 'King Edward'

of 'Fireland', but it grows close to 3 feet; while the height and vigor are outstanding, plants can fall over after a rain or heavy winds. As for me, I want less maintenance, so I choose some of the shorter cultivars. The deep red of 'Pomegranate' immediately catches the eye, while more pastel colors found in 'Summer Berries' and 'Pink Grapefruit' are softer and easier to combine with other plants. They are all easy to maintain throughout the season. Although they don't make long-lasting cut flowers, I have seen them in outstanding arrangements with other perennials like Culver's root and statice. All selections prefer good drainage and full sun. Hardy in zones 3 to 8.

As a substitute for snuff, sneezewort, *Achillea ptarmica*, probably works quite well, if one is still into that sort of thing. If you feel so inclined, put some leaves up your nose and you will quickly understand the root of the common name. However, the flowers are a bit more useful in the garden. They are excellent cut flowers, acting as fillers in cottage bouquets, and the white flowers are easy

Achillea ptarmica 'The Pearl'

Achillea ptarmica 'Ballerina'

Achillea 'Paprika'

Aconitum carmichaelii 'Arendsii' with *Leonotis leonurus*

to combine with almost any stronger hue. Plants are at their best in northern areas or in gardens where cool summer nights are the norm. In gardens south of zone 6, plants get leggy and performance is marginal. The thick, dark green leaves are not cut like other species but have entire margins. The blooms are always white and double. In general, plants are 1 to 2 feet tall but with rich soil conditions and cool nights can easily grow to 3 feet.

Most of the selections are similar, so using the old-fashioned 'The Pearl' ('Boule de Neige') or 'Perry's White' is approximately the same as using 'Angel's Breath' or 'Ballerina'. The latter are somewhat more compact and shorter, but the flowers are about the same. Full sun, hardy in zones 2 to 7.

If I had a rock garden and lived in a moderate climate with cold winters and cool summers, woolly yarrow, *Achillea tomentosa*, might be one of my first choices. Growing less than 6 inches tall, sporting handsome densely hairy foliage and then producing brilliant golden yellow flowers, this is an easy choice. Further south where evenings don't cool down significantly or where evening rains are common, plants tend to melt out. Occasionally the species is available, and there is nothing wrong with it at all; however, the only plants you are likely to find are those of 'King Edward', an old but reliable filler. Full, sun, hardy in zones 3 to 6.

Aconitum
MONKSHOOD

Classic plants for the late summer and fall garden, monkshoods add bold accents to northern gardens. Flowers are usually in shades of blue or purple, but ivory, yellow, and bicolors can also be found. The hood on the flower resembles your favorite monk's hood and is responsible for the common name of the genus. For certain, they are poisonous (they are also

Aconitum napellus

Aconitum carmichaelii 'Pink Sensation'

known as wolfsbane), but for people with half a brain, that is not a problem. Simply don't eat them—any part of them. Don't worry about your pets: most dogs and cats are smarter than the average gardener. All monkshoods do far better in the northern states and Canada than in the South.

Some of the most popular are the purple and blue-flowered forms like *Aconitum carmichaelii*, azure monkshood, and *A. napellus*, common monkshood. Azure monkshood grows 4 to 6 feet tall and has thick, dark green leaves, which are divided about two-thirds of the way to the midrib. In late summer and early fall, dozens of individual hooded flowers make up each 5- to 6-inch-long flower spike. Some of the selections of azure monkshood are among the latest of the genus to flower (the species is also known as the late-flowering

Aconitum carmichaelii var. *wilsonii*

Aconitum ×*cammarum* 'Eleanor'

Aconitum napellus 'Alba'

Aconitum ×*cammarum* 'Bicolor'

monkshood). My favorite is 'Arendsii', because of the large deep blue flowers held on 3-foot-tall, compact, well-branched plants. If I could purchase but one aconitum, it would be this. 'Pink Sensation' offers the vigor of monkshood with light pink flowers on plants only about 2 feet tall. Taller forms (up to 6 feet tall) such as 'Barker's Variety' and var. *wilsonii* may also be planted.

Common monkshood (*Aconitum napellus*) is the one you would most easily find in retail or mail-order catalogs. Plants have handsome blue flowers, which open a little earlier than azure monkshood, but as far as gardeners are concerned, there is little difference between the two. 'Alba' provides white flowers; 'Carneum' is a beautiful pink-flowered selection. 'Bicolor', a selection of *A.* ×*cammarum*, is well worth looking for. Plants grow about 4 feet tall on straight

Aconitum napellus 'Carneum'

Aconitum 'Ivorine'

Aconitum napellus

Aconitum lycoctonum

erect stems and provide flowers in an exotic combination of azure blue and white. 'Eleanor' provides creamy white flowers on strong upright flower stalks. Place all monkshoods in full sun to partial shade and moist soils. Useful in zones 3 to 6.

A wonderful white to light yellow-flowered cultivar I always enjoy seeing is 'Ivorine', a hybrid involving a little-known species, *Aconitum septentrionale* (which itself is well worth trying to locate in

catalogs during the winter). I have seen it successfully grown in the wonderful garden of Donna Hackman, near Warrenton, Virginia. Zones 4 to 6(7). Yellow wolfsbane, *A. lycoctonum* (*A. lamarckii*), has long stems with light green, deeply divided leaves and bears yellow flowers in late summer and fall. The thing can barely stand up straight. Grow it so the stems scramble over other plants, and it is not at all bad. The soft yellows complement just about any other

color and fit well into many gardens. Cool temperatures, full sun, zones 3 to 6.

Adiantum
MAIDENHAIR FERN

There is no debate: ferns have made a great comeback with American gardeners. In many gardeners' minds, ferns had been thought of as just some "green things," but this notion has been dispelled over the last

Adiantum capillus-veneris

Adiantum pedatum

Adiantum pedatum with hostas

Adiantum pedatum with sword ferns

ten years. The realization that ferns are as garden worthy as their flowering counterpoints has rekindled interest in these tough plants. Of course, once curiosity about ferns is piqued, it quickly becomes apparent that the diversity of color, size, and form they offer is remarkable. One of the most distinctive groups is the maidenhair family, consisting of the northern and southern maidenhairs.

Only gardeners who live in the southern one-third of the country are fortunate enough to appreciate the beauty of the southern maidenhair, *Adiantum capillus-veneris*, in their gardens. The light green fronds are doubly or triply divided and arch over thin wiry stems. The dark purple stems are handsome in themselves, rising 6 to 8 inches

Adiantum capillus-veneris

from the ground and then branching into a horseshoe shape at the top. The horseshoe is characteristic of the maidenhair ferns but is not as obvious in the southern form as in the northern because the inch-long pinnae (individual "leaflets") are so numerous as to hide the shape. However, closer inspection will easily reveal the horseshoe. Plants require mild winters, basic soils, and excellent drainage and are not nearly as easy to grow as many of the coarser ferns commonly found at retailers. They are at their best tumbling from containers; they look wonderful in shaded rock gardens or arching over walls. Some of the finest plantings I have seen are in the Birmingham Botanical Gardens, where optimal conditions occur for rampant growth. Plants don't do well in highly acid conditions, and in areas of pine or oak growth, lime should be added. Native throughout the south temperate and subtropical regions in Europe, Africa, India, China, Japan, the Americas, and Australia. Reliably cold hardy in zones 7b to 10.

Southern maidenhair may be little known in the garden, but northern maidenhair, *Adiantum pedatum*, suffers no such lack of recognition. In the spring, the plant is characterized by thin deep black stems and grayish pinnae that form an obvious, almost perfect horseshoe on top of them. As plants mature, the pinnae change from gray to light green to dark green and they top out at about 12 inches tall. The dark color of the stems is continued in the branches of the horseshoe, making this fern one of the most distinctive and easily recognized in gardens. Plants move around freely in loose soils and a few plants can quickly form significant colonies. The distinctive shape and garden "feel" of the lacy, airy fronds and black stems, combined with its toughness, have made this a most useful, must-have fern for the shady moist woodland garden. For me, this is on my top ten no-brainer list, associating with everything

Adiantum pedatum subsp. *subpumilum*

Adiantum pedatum 'Imbricatum'

from lowly oxalis to hostas. Similar to southern maidenhair, lime is useful for best growth but seems to be less important than with its southern cousin.

It is hard to beat this species for overall garden performance, but those who wish to walk on the wild side of the northern maidenhair path might want to try some of the modifications that have occasionally occurred with the species. 'Imbricatum' has crowded stiffly erect fronds that are rather blue-green. Its long sweeping foliage makes it appear almost shrub-like. The opposite is true in subsp. *subpumilum*, in which the fronds are dwarf and congested; the plants grow in a 6- to 9-inch-tall mound. Partial shade, good drainage, performs well in zones 2 to 7b.

"Buglelawn"

Ajuga reptans 'Burgundy Glow'

Ajuga reptans 'Black Scallop'

Ajuga reptans 'Toffee Chip'

Ajuga
BUGLE WEED

Some groups of plants simply perform too well for their own good, and bugle weed may be one of these. Of the forty species known, only common bugle weed (*Ajuga reptans*) is used extensively, and although a couple of others (*A. genevensis*, *A. australis*) are excellent garden plants, common bugle weed is by far the most diverse, offering all sorts of leaf and flower variations. One of the strengths of this plant is its ability to colonize large areas of the garden. Many a gardener has started by putting out a few plants only to turn around a few years later to find a sea of the stuff. When planted near lawns, plants creep relentlessly into the turf, and the result of such restlessness has been coined "buglelawn."

Ajuga reptans, common bugle weed, has become popular due to its tenacious ability to settle large areas of the garden. It is planted as small rosettes of foliage that quickly search out new ground. Not all selections are as fast-growing, and intelligent cultivar selection can help curb their appetite for territory. Common bugle weed is grown mainly for the colorful foliage, but a large splash of purple-blue flowers can be breathtaking in the spring.

Some of my favorite cultivars are 'Burgundy Glow', with multicolored foliage, and 'Catlin's Giant', with big dark green leaves and large spikes of blue flowers. For

Ajuga reptans 'Chocolate Chip'

Ajuga reptans 'Blueberry Muffin'

Ajuga genevensis 'Pink Beauty'

Ajuga genevensis 'Pink Beauty' thinking about spilling into a lawn

Ajuga reptans 'Sparkler'

dark leaves, I have been most impressed with the shellacked black leaves of 'Black Scallop'; it looks good anywhere. Its only problem is that it's so dark, it tends to disappear if brighter plants aren't close by. 'Chocolate Chip' has darker leaves and quite outstanding flowers, even when planted in a container. I also think the variegated 'Toffee Chip' is really quite wonderful and brightens up the shade. 'Sparkler' is certainly interesting, but for me it looks like it is sick rather than handsome. For even more compact plants, try the bright leaves of 'Blueberry Muffin'. The names of the bugle weeds are enough to make you want to go out and have them for a snack. Partial shade, hardy in zones 3 to 9.

Another fine garden plant is Geneva bugle weed, *Ajuga genevensis*, with its light green wavy leaves and handsome flowers. 'Pink Beauty' is the best available cultivar, producing good looking flowers on moderately aggressive plants. Partial shade, hardy in zones 4 to 9.

Lastly, if you are a collector, find Australian bugle weed, *Ajuga australis*. Plants do

Ajuga australis

Allium aflatunense 'Purple Sensation'

Allium aflatunense 'Purple Sensation' with tulips

Allium cristophii

not run, and flowers are quite impressive. Hardiness is unknown, but I doubt it would survive winters north of zone 7b or 8.

Allium
ORNAMENTAL ONION

One of the great joys of gardening is that there are no rules. I suppose planting rusty cars in the lawn and calling them garden art, or experimenting with the number of ways teal-colored tractor tires can be used as planters might raise the wrath of a few neighbors. However, the term "ornamental" is used everywhere in gardening. What other activity embraces sweet potatoes, herbs, fruits, and vegetables as part of the ornamental landscape? Ornamental onions are reasonably edible, if not particularly tasty, but their beauty is seldom in question. The number of choices is mind-boggling, and plants are wonderful playthings for the bold and inquiring gardener. Most members of this large genus are bulbous and are easily planted in spring or fall.

Allium aflatunense, purple ornamental onion, is one of the most common ornamental onions, providing a brilliant purple scene in the spring. While the species itself is occasionally available, the main selection is 'Purple Sensation'. Plants grow 3 to 4 feet tall, and the rounded heads, usually dark purple, particularly in the cool nights of the spring, are quite sensational, especially in the North. They are early to flower, popping up through the tulips in the spring. Further south, they are still wonderful but will not be as dark. Bulbs are inexpensive;

Allium cristophii

Allium 'Globemaster'

Allium 'Globemaster' seed heads

plant at least ten together, no more than 6 inches apart. Hardy in zones 4 to 8.

Persian onion, *Allium cristophii*, produces 10- to 12-inch-wide, deep purple flower heads, one of the largest flower heads of any onion. Each head consists of hundreds of star-shaped flowers on a 1- to 2-foot-tall stem. Flowers open in the spring and persist for about three weeks. The flower is the most obvious part of the plant, not only because of its size but also because there are only two to three leaves produced at the base. This is a lovely onion, persistent and long-lived in many areas of the country. Full sun, not great in hot climates, performs best in zones 4 to 6 but is hardy in zones 4 to 8.

I have tried at least a dozen different types of ornamental onions in the Armitage garden, and 'Globemaster' is absolutely one of the best. The three to four leaves emerge in early spring, and soon a fat flower bud or two can be seen at the base. The flowers force their way through the foliage and emerge as 6-inch-wide lavender softballs. Even the seed heads are ornamental, persisting for weeks after the flower has passed on. Great plants, about 3 feet tall, perennial as any onion I have grown. Full sun to partial shade, hardy in zones 4 to 8.

Allium karataviense, Turkestan onion, and *A. giganteum*, giant onion, are the Mutt and Jeff of the onion world—these two species are obviously onions (just smell the leaves) but differ significantly in flower color, leaf color, and height. The two gray-

Allium karataviense foliage

Allium karataviense

Allium giganteum

Allium giganteum seed heads

green leaves of the Turkestan onion lie on the ground and are mottled with purple. The fat flower buds emerge through the base of the leaves and then form perfectly round silver-lilac flower heads on 4- to 6-inch-tall stalks.

Compared to these pixies, the 6-foot-tall giant onion is an absolute behemoth. The large, straplike gray leaves emerge early but die back even before the flowers are fully developed. The flower heads consist of hundreds of purple flowers arranged in neat 4-inch-wide globes. After the flowers have fallen off, and the leaves have disappeared, the ghostly white remains of the flower heads are themselves quite striking, and provide another month or so of value. Both species are excellent cut flowers; giant onion is a staple in the cut flower trade and may be purchased at all good flower shops.

Both are summer dormant, prefer full sun and are cold hardy to zone 4. Giant onion is more heat and humidity tolerant than Turkestan onion. Persistent for about two years only.

Anemone
WINDFLOWER

As a gardener, I admit to a certain degree of laziness. Okay, as I get a little older, I admit to a lot. Being a tad indolent I am always on the lookout for plant groups that can provide a great deal of pleasure for as many seasons as possible. There are a number of genera whose members flower at different seasons, but one of the most rewarding has to be the genus *Anemone*. This grand group of plants consists of spring-flowering plants arising

Anemone blanda 'Radar'

Anemone blanda 'White Splendor'

Anemone blanda 'Blue Star'

Anemone coronaria 'De Caen Blue'

from tubers (like a potato) as well as fibrous-rooted plants that mostly flower in the fall, with one or two spring-and-summer-bloomers thrown in. From the time the snow is melting to the time the snow is falling, anemones can be a gardener's companion. Cut flowers, shade and sun lovers, and heights from ankle to waist, this fine genus offers something for everybody, especially lazy folks like me.

In the late fall, I have my trowel in one hand, the tubers of the Grecian windflower (*Anemone blanda*) in the other, and confusion as to which end is up. With real plants, any dummy knows to plant the green part up, but anemone tubers simply look like shriveled-up rocks. It turns out that it doesn't really matter which end is up—the plants will find the proper orientation. When you are ready to plant them, toss the tubers in a pail of water and allow them to absorb the water for about four hours. It is fascinating to watch them plump up to about four times their original size. Doing this jumpstarts the germination process.

Put about a hundred of the tubers around the garden, preferably in groups of at least twenty. They are cheap enough to do this without spending all the Christmas money. Once you have tossed them in their respective shallow trenches (6 to 8 inches deep), you can expect wonderful springtime flowering, unless the squirrels, chipmunks, gophers, voles, or dogs get at them. That is why you plant a hundred. The flowers consist of 1- to 2-inch-wide daisies in colors of blue, purple, red, white, and pink over finely cut fernlike foliage. Plants are available as single- or double-flowered forms. They are only about 8 inches tall, but if they naturalize, they are outstanding components of the woodland garden. If they don't naturalize and become food for your garden fauna, you have not spent a great deal of money. Open woodland conditions are recommended, but since plants go dormant in late spring, full sun is fine. Hardy in zones 4 to 7.

Anemone coronaria 'De Caen Rose'

Anemone hupehensis 'Richard Arends'

Anemone 'Pamina'

The only real differences between cultivars is flower color, such as the bicolors of 'Radar', the white flowers of 'White Splendor', and the lavender-blue of 'Blue Star', to name but a few.

Another tuberous form, even more ornamental than the Grecian windflower, is the poppy anemone, *Anemone coronaria*. Equally confusing as to head and tail, equally useful to put in the water bucket, and equally tempting to hungry creatures—nevertheless, they are so beautiful that they are well worth planting in the fall. My good friends Ed and Donna Lambert, in Athens, plant some every year, and it is always a terrific exercise to take my students to their garden to view the clumps of windflowers. The 2-inch-wide flowers open in early spring atop stems that may be anywhere from 6 to 18 inches tall. They are excellent in the vase and have become an important cut flower throughout the world. Plant in full sun, protect from critters if possible. Hardy in zones 6 to 9.

Although a number of hybrids have been bred, the best are the popular double-flowered De Caen hybrids, available as mixes or as single colors.

Regardless of how excited one gets about the spring flowerers, the crowning jewels of the anemone group remain the fall-flowering forms of the Japanese species. And with good reason! The Japanese anemone *Anemone hupehensis* includes some wonderful 3- to 4-foot-tall selections, such as the rosy red semi-double flowers of 'Richard Arends'. The Japanese hybrids, *A.* ×*hybrida*, are similar but more common and better adapted to North American gardens. If provided with a little shade and ample moisture, plants can reach 5 feet in height and 3 feet across in two to three years. The flowers begin to open in late summer to early fall and remain in color for three to five weeks, depending on the temperatures. Dozens of selections are available in white, pink, rose, and

Anemone 'Margarete'

Anemone 'Serenade'

Anemone tomentosa 'Robustissima'

Anemone 'Honorine Jobert'

Anemone 'Honorine Jobert'

lilac, with single, semi-double, and double flowers. Some of my favorite hybrids are the semi-double pink-flowered 'Pamina', the single pink 2½-inch-wide flowers of 'Serenade', and the rosy red of 'Margarete'. However, if I had but one to choose, I would probably show my true populist colors and choose the old-fashioned but timeless single white flowers of 'Honorine Jobert'.

Southern gardeners who have had less success in establishing the hybrids should use the indestructible grape leaf anemones (*Anemone tomentosa*), with their pale pink

or white flowers in late summer and early fall. The toughest of them all is 'Robustissima'—handsome, adaptable to sun or shade, and disease- and insect-free. Plants bear 2-inch-wide, mauve-pink flowers in late summer. I grow them in full sun in the Trial Gardens at UGA, where they remain in a fairly compact clump, but in the shady Armitage garden, plants move around with abandon and fill up space in no time. The hybrids are hardy in zones 4 to 7, grape leaf anemone in zones 5 to 8.

Most early anemones grow from tubers, but gardeners cannot live by tubers alone.

Some of the finest garden plants in this group are the spring-flowering snowdrop anemone (*Anemone sylvestris*). I enjoy this plant because of its habit of providing beautifully clean white flowers with yellow stamens in early spring. In fact, in areas of late winters, one can often see them piercing the snow, thus its common name. The 2-inch-wide flowers are only part of the delight of this 1- to 2-foot-tall plant, since after flowering, the woolly fruit persist into the summer. On the downside, it can be outrageously aggressive, reseeding freely where it is happy. It is happier in the North than in the South, where inconsistent winters and hot summers take their toll. While some gardeners consider it a bit of a weed, not me; I accept anyone's snowdrop anemone weeds with pleasure. Full sun, hardy in zones 4 to 7.

Anemone sylvestris

Aquilegia chrysantha

Anemone sylvestris

Aquilegia vulgaris 'Treble Pink'

Aquilegia
COLUMBINE

Columbines are among the best known and most popular groups of plants almost anywhere gardening is enjoyed. The Armitage garden would be but a shell of itself without columbines welcoming spring. Since there are over sixty-five different species of columbine and dozens of named varieties from which to choose, trying one or two should not be difficult. The garden requirements for all columbines—whether they originate from the East Coast, West Coast, Europe, or Asia—are essentially the same: partial shade and reasonably rich well-drained soils.

The plants are distinguished from most other genera by having petals with spurs, ranging from those with spurs over 4 inches long (Texas columbine, *Aquilegia chrysantha*) to those whose spurs are essentially nonexistent, such as some of the double- and treble-flowered hybrids of granny's bonnet, *A. vulgaris*. Spur size and shape are helpful clues to the identity of many of the species. The spurs of the alpine columbine (*A. alpina*) and fan columbine (*A. flabellata*) are hooked (like a fishhook), while those on the Rocky Mountain columbine (*A. caerulea*) are nearly always straight. The alpine columbine has some of the finest blue flowers, and even though they are native to the cool mountains of Austria, they tolerate heat as well as any species. The fan columbine, *A. flabellata*, is usually found in the white form ('Alba'), and the blue cast to its foliage, plump flowers, and low stature make it a favorite among columbine lovers. The fine blue and white flowers of the Rocky Mountain columbine persist for years, especially in areas of cool summers.

Flower colors vary tremendously, but the most diversity is found in the selections of hybrid columbine, *Aquilegia* ×*hybrida*. As a seed-propagated mix, they can be striking, providing a festival of colors for the color-hungry eye in the spring. The

Aquilegia alpina

Aquilegia alpina

Aquilegia flabellata 'Alba'

Aquilegia 'Dove'

Aquilegia 'Blue Bird'

Aquilegia caerulea

Aquilegia 'Spring Magic White'

Aquilegia 'Spring Magic Blue and White'

Aquilegia 'Swan Pink and White' with snapdragons and alyssum

Aquilegia 'Swan Pink and Yellow'

Aquilegia 'Spring Magic Rose and Ivory'

well-established Song Bird series remains an excellent choice; it includes the white flowers of 'Dove' and the fine blue of 'Blue Bird'. The Swan series and the Spring Magic series are relatively new, bringing more compact habits along with a diversity of colors. 'Swan Pink and Yellow' and 'Swan Pink and White' are very impressive, while the choices in Spring Magic would be welcome in my garden any time.

While large gaudy flowers appear to be the norm, one of my favorites has always

Aquilegia canadensis

Aquilegia canadensis

Aquilegia canadensis 'Little Lanterns'

been the delightful red and yellow flowers of the Canadian columbine (*Aquilegia canadensis*). Just like citizens of that northern neighbor, the plants are quiet, conservative, and do their job without bluster. Columbines can be promiscuous, and natural hybridization occurs with ease. The resulting seedlings are usually as handsome as any of the parents and leave many a gardener scratching his or her head as to where they came from. Depending on how long the cool temperatures of spring persist,

Aquilegia canadensis 'Corbett'

Leaf miner damage on columbine foliage

plants will remain in flower for three to six weeks. One of the neatest things that has occurred in the new millennium is that breeders are introducing hybrids of our native plants, otherwise known as "nativars." I have always loved 'Corbett', a natural, light yellow, short selection from Corbett, Maryland, but I am really pleased to recommend 'Little Lanterns', brighter and shorter than the species, and 'Pink Lanterns', a larger plant with similar nodding flowers in pink. Both are great choices for the perennial area of the garden.

The leaves of all columbines are ternate (in threes) and unfortunately are susceptible to the bane of all columbines, the leaf miner. Leaf miners burrow just beneath the surface of the foliage and leave scars like a crazed gopher. All columbines seem to be fair game for these marauding tunnelers, although some forms and some years are better than others. The best way to deal with them is to clean up all leaf debris in the fall and winter and dispose of it. However, if miners disfigure your plants to the point that they're too ugly to look at, cut them back to the ground, dispose of the foliage, and allow the plants to regrow. The leaf miner life cycle is finished by the time the new foliage emerges. Partial shade, zones 3 to 8.

Aquilegia canadensis 'Pink Lanterns'

Arisaema triphyllum

Arisaema dracontium

Arisaema ringens

Arisaema triphyllum

Arisaema ringens

Arisaema heterophyllum

Arisaema
JACK-IN-THE-PULPIT

I used to think it was only a male thing, but it seems every gardener, regardless of gender, likes to grow weird plants. Weird is relative, of course, but some of the jacks are definitely in that category. I first became enamored with jacks when I discovered our most common native, *Arisaema triphyllum*. This species is relatively easy to find in plant catalogs, but once you discover it, you won't stop there. Dragons, cobras, candy jacks, and bloody jacks await. Jack fever is upon you.

The word "triphyllum" refers to the three leaflets found on *Arisaema triphyllum*; however, plants may often be found with five, or occasionally four leaflets. Similarly, variability in height can be present, with plants ranging from 1 to nearly 3 feet. Flowers, which occur in spring to early summer, consist of a straight narrow stalk (spadix) surrounded by a thin white membrane (spathe). This arrangement of flowers was dubbed jack-in-the-pulpit, and similar flowers are found on dieffenbachia, philodendron, arum lily, and taro (*Colocasia*). Plants are generally purchased in small containers and should be placed outside in the fall or early spring. They multiply by small corms which, if planted in the spring, will flower the second year. The corms can become quite large and were cooked and eaten by native Indians, becoming known as Indian turnip.

Arisaema dracontium

Arisaema sikokianum

Arisaema tortuosum

Once I noticed this jack, I quickly became aware of the wonderful dragon jack, *Arisaema dracontium*, another of our fine native plants. The plant grows 3 to 4 feet tall and bears a long skinny green spadix, which protrudes from the green spathe like a snake's tongue or a dragon's tail. Both tolerate partial shade and are hardy from zones 4 to 8.

An astounding number of jacks, mostly from Asia, are being offered by mail-order nurseries for collectors and shade gardeners. Little needs to be said about the makeup of these plants; they are all somewhat bizarre, and plants that definitely set you aside from mainstream gardeners. They are also often expensive, so a collection may result in the depletion

Arisaema consanguineum

Ariseama candidissimum

Arisaema taiwanense

Arisaema fargesii

Arisaema fargesii

of significant retirement savings. One of the easiest of the foreign jacks to grow is cobra jack, *Arisaema ringens*. Visitors always ooh and aah at the cobra-like pose of the spathes. Two other relatively easy-to-grow jacks are the green-flowered *A. heterophyllum* and the wonderful bloody jack, *A. consanguineum*, a large member with deeply cut leaves and flowers atop long stems. I think the candy jack, *A. candidissimum*, with wonderful white spathes blushed in pink is also terrific, but I have had little success in growing it in my garden. I have had the Taiwan jack, *A. taiwanense*, in the garden for at least ten years, and the umbrella-like leaf canopy and the interesting flowers are always fun. *Arisaema fargesii* is not very well known, but the large leaves and the deep

purple spathes are quite something. If you can find it, give it a go.

You can tell I had jack fever, as I kept spending my money on these weird and wacky plants. I finished the last of my kids' college fund on the gaudy jack, *Arisaema sikokianum*, whose wonderful purple pulpit embraces the rounded ball-peen spadix. However, the most elegant of the jacks has to be *A. tortuosum*, which can be spotted in Kew Gardens in England. Beyond my talents, and beyond my finances.

Arisaemas should not be planted or viewed by people with heart problems, as any of these is enough to give one cardiac arrest. Plant jacks shallowly in moisture-retentive, well-drained soils rich in organic matter in the shade garden. Hardy in zones 4 to 7.

Artemisia
MUGWORT

For plant designers, landscape contractors, and the everyday gardener, the gray hues of artemisias are excellent to calm down screaming colors or to provide a cool contrast to a sea of green. Not all are long-lived perennials, and some may leave us after two or three years, but the good selections are worth every square inch of space.

The genus was named after Artemis, the Greek goddess who was thought to be the daughter of Zeus and Leto and the twin sister of Apollo. She was the Hellenic goddess of forests and hills, childbirth, virginity, fertility, the hunt, and often was depicted as a huntress carrying a bow and

Artemisia ludoviciana 'Silver King'

Artemisia ludoviciana 'Valerie Finnis'

Artemisia ludociviana var. *latiloba*

Artemisia 'Powis Castle' along wall

arrows. Like most mothers, she was an excellent multitasker. The common name mugwort is often said to derive from the word "mug" because it was used in flavoring drinks. However, more reliable sources say the name is derived from the Old Norse *muggi*, meaning "marsh," and Germanic *wuertz*, meaning "root," which refers to its use since ancient times to repel insects, especially moths. Still with me?

White sage, *Artemisia ludoviciana*, has been around for many years and was the most commonly used large artemisia for gray foliage. The species is seldom sold, but you can still find one of the popular selections, 'Silver King'. This plant looks terrific for a couple of years, lulling you to sleep, but then pops up all over the place.

Its vigorous nature made it a popular cut stem for fillers in arrangements and it is sometimes produced by cut flower growers for that purpose. However, in the garden, they develop into dozens of in-laws who never go away, and they bring the aunts and cousins with them. The deciduous leaves are gray-green, entire (not cut) and insignificant yellow flowers are produced. They grow 3 to 5 feet tall and 3 to 4 feet wide and combine well with almost everything. Other than their roaming ways, they are fine plants, but those tendencies have resulted in them being more shunned than a decade ago. Full sun, hardy in zones 4 to 9. Variety *latiloba*, whose entire leaf margins are lobed near the ends, is a far better garden plant. Plants grow about 2

feet tall and equally wide and are relatively well behaved. 'Valerie Finnis', named after one of England's grande dames of gardening, has silvery gray foliage. It is absolutely wonderful in the spring, but can melt out in the summer, particularly in the South. She looks great again in the fall. In all these plants, ugly yellow flowers are produced, detracting from the foliage. Full sun to partial shade, hardy in zones 4 to 8.

'Powis Castle' was used in every garden ten years ago, but it, like most of the genus, does not enjoy the same level of popularity today. That is not to say it suddenly became a bad plant, only that there is less interest in it than before. The evergreen, deeply cut gray leaves provide airiness to the garden and a focal point for the eye.

Artemisia 'Powis Castle' as a standard

Artemisia lactiflora Guizhou Group

Artemisia lactiflora

Artemisia schmidtiana 'Nana'

In fact, when properly sited, it is probably one of the first plants one's eye goes to—a garden designer's blue ribbon plant. Plants may be used to define a wall, introduce a garden bed or may even be trained as a small upright Powis tree. In general, plants grow 2 to 3 feet tall and equally wide. As they mature, the stems become woody (like a shrub) and may get lanky and untidy. If necessary, cut back in spring as new growth becomes active. Don't cut back in the fall. Full sun, hardy in zones 6 to 8.

I have always enjoyed white mugwort, *Artemisia lactiflora*. It grows 5 to 7 feet tall and is quite unartemisia-like. The leaves are green rather than gray, plants are tall rather than short, and the flowers are white rather than yellow. The foliage consists of many leaflets, somewhat like an astilbe, and while it is a big plant, it is fairly airy. Plants often need staking so if low maintenance is an issue, the species may not be for you.

The best cultivar is 'Guizhou', or more correctly, plants in the Guizhou Group. With this selection, you will have a plant that matures about 4 feet tall, with dark green, almost bronze, foliage made up of coarsely-toothed segments. The branched flower stems have the same white flowers as the species and can be quite handsome.

This is a far better selection for the garden, requiring less maintenance and providing foliage which combines well with lighter hues of flowers or leaves.

Artemisia schmidtiana has been a mainstay in northern gardens for years, however the only form available is the dwarf selection ('Nana'), sold as 'Silver Mound' and known as the silver mound artemisia. It is a gardener's dream because of the 1-foot-tall compact mounds produced in spring and early summer. Plants are beautiful in rock gardens and in containers, although for ground covers, I think there are better choices. In too many gardens, South as

Artemisia stelleriana 'Silver Cascade'

Artemisia vulgaris 'Limelight'

Artemisia vulgaris 'Limelight'

well as North, plants often melt out in the centers as temperature and humidity rise. This can be a rather ugly scene after summer rains. I recommend this beautiful plant in the northern tier of states and Canada but not in the South. Full sun, hardy in zones 3 to 7.

There are a number of other gray-leaved artemisias, my favorite being 'Silver Cascade', a cultivar of *Artemisia stelleriana*.

Plants are only about a foot tall but the wonderful intense gray foliage makes it one of the easiest plants to use in combinations. In the wonderful Niagara School of Horticulture in Niagara Falls, Ontario, plants

Aruncus dioicus male flowers (left), female flowers (right)

Aruncus dioicus

Aruncus aethusifolius

Aruncus dioicus 'Kneiffii'

were handsomely combined with Begonia 'Dragon Wing'. Loved it.

I must also mention one of the worse thugs I have met. *Artemisia vulgaris*, common mugwort, has few ornamental characteristics going for it; but it does have some exceptional medicinal properties credited to it, so occasionally it is worthwhile trying in the herb garden. However this cannot be said about the beautiful cultivar called 'Limelight'. When you see a photo, you will want to rush out and purchase it. Do not! 'Limelight' is beautiful, showing off sparkling yellow and green leaves and is

almost impossible not to love in the container touted by retail stores. However, the plants quickly become invasive, taking over large areas of the garden within a couple of years. Love it, but love it from a distance.

Aruncus
GOATSBEARD

Goatsbeard is well known, even though there are only two species and a few cultivars. Both species are highly ornamental and useful garden plants, and once established, live to ripe old ages. Male and

female flowers occur on separate plants (dioecious), but garden performance is not affected by the gender of plant.

Common goatsbeard, *Aruncus dioicus*, provides a grand explosion of upright flower stems consisting of hundreds of small white flowers in late spring, on plants growing up to 7 feet in height. The flowers are the main reasons for growing the plant, but the massive habit is most impressive. Diminutive fruit may be formed on female plants, but due to their slight size and show, they are not missed if male plants are used. The alternate leaves are bipinnately

Aruncus 'Misty Lace'

compound and doubly serrated. I have always enjoyed the vigor and sheer size of the plant, and I admire plants in the Northeast, Midwest, and Northwest. Unfortunately it languishes in the South, so the Armitage garden is beardless. Full sun, zones 3 to 6.

'Kneiffii' is a smaller cut-leaf form with deeply cut dark green leaves resulting in a far more delicate-looking plant. Flowers are less showy and, while horticulturally interesting, the plant is not nearly as eye-catching as the species. It is not quite as coarse and a little easier to use.

As grand and (some say) overbearing as the former species is, Korean goatsbeard, *Aruncus aethusifolius,* is the antithesis. Similarities include the same dark green compound leaves and small white flowers held above

the plant. However, Korean goatsbeard is only about a foot tall and is far more useful for small areas and rock gardens. Three to four flower stems are produced in late summer, and although the flowers are reasonably handsome, they don't provide a long-lasting show. Actually, the foliage is the best part of the plant, handsome throughout the season regardless of the presence or absence of flowers. Full sun to partial shade, well-drained soils, zones 3 to 7.

'Misty Lace' is an exceptional hybrid between the two species. Plants are intermediate in height and demonstrate remarkable hybrid vigor. In bud, in flower, and in leaf, this plant has proven to be a great addition to the goatsbeard cupboard. The foliage remains handsome all season,

and the white flowers occur early in the spring. This is allowing the genus to be grown in the South as well as the North. Full sun in the North, partial shade in the South, zones 3 to 7.

Asarum
GINGER

The best thing about this group of plants is that they are fun. I know that sounds somewhat childish, but really, why else would you grow green blobs whose flowers you cannot see without serious acrobatics? Sure, they are handsome, some far more than others, but to me, they are playthings. First things first: these wild gingers are not the culinary ginger—that is, they are not

Asarum arifolium

Asarum canadense with golden ragwort

Asarum canadense

Asarum arifolium little brown jugs

the same as the spice you use for ginger-glazed chicken or ginger snaps (that is the root of *Zingiber*). Wild gingers occur throughout the world, but most of the garden forms are found in Asia and North America.

The fun part of the plants are the "little brown jugs" (and some not so little) of flowers borne beneath the foliage. It is great fun to crawl around on hands and knees, and pry under the leaves to find those elusive flowers. This belly crawl is a great equalizer of young and old and rich and poor plant explorers. The handsome leaves are also wonderfully ornamental and may be gray-green to deep green and often mottled. All the gingers grow well with woodland species like Virginia bluebells and mayapples. Gardeners keep demanding gingers, resulting in new species and selections being introduced every year. A few are available at good retail outlets, many more by mail order and on the Internet.

Arrowleaf ginger, *Asarum arifolium* (*Hexastylis arifolia*), is a North American native and is a hard plant not to enjoy. Plants bear dark green leaves in the shape of an arrow, and foliage may be mottled or entirely green. They are evergreen, although the winter foliage looks dull and somewhat beaten up. As with many "evergreen" plants (which, if truth be told in catalogs, would be described as "everbrown" in the winter), I cut off the tired leaves in early spring before the new growth occurs. This allows the fresh, light green spring leaves to really show off. Silver mottling, if present, shows up as the leaves mature. You will also see the tan flower buds that form well before the new leaves emerge, followed by lots of darker "jugs." Shade and moisture are necessary, hardy in zones 4 to 8.

In the introduction, I irreverently described gingers as green blobs, hardly a fair moniker for the Canadian ginger, *Asarum canadense*, a wonderful ground cover whose light green kidney-shaped leaves cover ground with great enthusiasm. Unlike most of

Asarum canadense flower

Asarum splendens

the ornamental gingers, they are totally deciduous, disappearing in the winter and reappearing in early spring. The 3- to 5-inch-wide leaves unfurl at the same time the small brownish red flowers occur at the base of the leaf stems. The three sepals on the flowers are almost red and curled back on the "jug." Arguably the best ground cover of the available gingers. Plants combine well with other shade-lovers like golden ragwort (*Packera aurea*), and while they can become a bit of a nuisance, they are easy enough to divide and pass along to neighbors. Leaves are larger and plants more aggressive in the North than in the South but are excellent wherever they are grown. Shade and moisture, hardy in zones 3 to 7.

Many excellent gingers have been introduced from Asia and although they can be quite—okay, very—expensive, crazy gardeners (like me) have to have them. One of my favorites is Chinese wild ginger, *Asarum splendens*, with its big dark green evergreen leaves obviously marked with silver throughout. The leaf variegation is "cleaner" than on some of our native forms and immediately draws the eye. The large purple jugs are buried under the foliage but, once unburied, are quite eye-catching. Plants are slow to grow compared to the arrowleaf or Canadian gingers but eventually make a wonderful, exuberant colony. Hardy in zones 6 to 9.

The other member of this wacky genus I can't do without is *Asarum maximum*, often lovingly referred to as the panda face ginger, also native to China. A few selections are out there, including 'Green Panda' and 'Ling Ling'. The former has shiny lustrous green leaves, while the latter has silvery green blotches on either side of the midrib. Both are evergreen, both are beautiful in leaf, and both sport some of the largest, most wonderful flowers in the genus: the flowers are where the panda face part comes in. These are definitely "get down on your knees" plants. Unfortunately, plants are not particularly cold hardy, only to about zone 7.

Asarum maximum

Asarum maximum 'Ling Ling'

Aster carolinianus

Aster divaricatus

Aster carolinianus

Aster novae-angliae 'Andenken an Alma Pötschke'

Aster

I love the fall, but I must admit, both my garden and I are a little tired by mid September. I mean, gardening is great and all that, but people who tell me how lucky I am that I can garden almost the entire year must be from Connecticut. The coolness of fall rejuvenates me after enduring the heat and humidity of the summer: the annuals are pooping out, the hostas are starting to turn yellow, and I just want to go hike the Appalachian Trail. Oh, wait . . . Then, just when I'm ready to plow up the whole place, the asters explode.

The genus *Aster* was immense, bearing species from China, Japan, and Europe, but it is best known for those from the eastern United States. Unfortunately, the taxonomists have taken a liking to our plants species but a definite dislike to the old names. Based on characteristics such as chromosome number, inflorescence shape, the presence of rhizomes, and characteristic basal leaves, the genus has been split into new and gruesomely unspellable genera. The names have all been coolly embraced by botanists and totally ignored by gardeners (perhaps because we can't pronounce them). As for me, I am at a crossroads; I want to give the new names some love, but I also realize that no one will have a clue what I am talking about if I toss out the old ones. So I provide both names as the various species are discussed. Regardless of the name changes, some of the best of our native species are the New England (*Aster novae-angliae*) and

Aster novi-belgii 'Winston Churchill'

Aster novae-angliae 'Hella Lacy'

Aster novae-angliae 'Purple Dome'

Aster 'Wood's Purple'

the New York (*A. novi-belgii*) asters, but a couple of other natives are also well worth trying, such as the white wood aster (*A. divaricatus*) and the climbing aster (*A. carolinianus*). Some people still look upon asters as weeds. What are they thinking?

Most asters grow like other perennials: some are big, others small, some make tidy clumps, some sprawl. But what about one that climbs all over everything? *Aster carolinianus* (*Ampelaster carolinianus*) doesn't actually climb over anything, but it has so many stems, going in so many different directions, that it can be trained to scale the highest wall or, with its own kudzu-like cunning, can totally obliterate your marigolds, which is probably a good thing. Get

a strong trellis, a reinforced wall, or a circle of 4-foot-tall galvanized steel fencing to support this wonder, which can grow 9 to 15 feet tall and 6 feet wide. The pink to lavender flowers open in mid October and can be cut down to the ground in the spring if it gets too rollicky for its own good. Hardy in zones 6 to 9.

Our native wood aster, *Aster divaricatus* (*Eurybia divaricata*), with its small white flowers and 1- to 2-foot-long dark stems is a great plant for almost all of North America. This is one of the few asters for which partial shade is desirable, so tuck it in with astilbes, hostas, or bergenias, or under baptisias. It does not want to stand up tall; in fact, it looks much better sticking out from

under these other plants, where its September flowers can be shown off but its lanky stems are hidden. Even though the plants can look rather weedy in the summer, they are well worth the wait. Plants may be cut back in midsummer, but no later than 15 July. Full sun to partial shade, zones 4 to 8.

Aster novae-angliae (*Symphyotrichum novae-angliae*) and *A. novi-belgii* (*S. novi-belgii* var. *novi-belgii*; also known as Michaelmas daisy) started out as ditch weeds and pasture plants and may still be enjoyed as such, but they are also valued for their persistent flowering, tough garden demeanor, and outstanding performance in a flower arrangement. Horticulturally speaking, little separates the two species:

Aster 'Wood's Light Blue'

Aster 'English Countryside' unpinched

Aster oblongifolius 'Raydon's Favorite'

the New England asters do have rougher, hairier leaves than the New York asters, but extensive breeding has made these slight differences even more subtle. Both these native plants had to go to finishing school in England and Germany in the early 1900s before they were acceptable to American gardeners. They came back with names like 'Andenken an Alma Pötschke' (3 to 4 feet) and 'Winston Churchill' (2 to 3 feet). However the wonderful 'Hella Lacy' (3 to 4 feet), 'Purple Dome' (18 to 24 inches), and many others were developed by American gardeners. All these are relatively tall, and many gardeners don't want to mess with staking or pruning or anything for that matter. That is why I enjoy Ed Wood's series, all of which are less than 2 feet tall. They are colorful and perform well throughout the country. Those with purple and light blue flowers are particularly good. Full sun or afternoon shade; if plants are shaded, even medium forms will need support. Hardy in zones 4 to 8.

Aster oblongifolius (*Symphyotrichum oblongifolium*; aromatic aster) is loaded with blue-purple daisylike flowers that

Aster tataricus

Aster 'Blue Lake'

Aster tataricus 'Jin-Dai'

Aster oblongifolius 'October Skies'

persist into late October, one of the last wildflowers in bloom. Plants are native to dry prairies and rocky bluffs from Pennsylvania to Wisconsin and south to North Carolina and Texas. The base of the flowers contains glandular hairs, which when brushed lightly release a subtle but pleasant fragrance. Plants attain a height of 2 to 4 feet in the wild and bear dozens of violet to blue flowers, each about an inch wide. The plants are spectacular without

any selection at all, and they earned a Plant of Merit designation from the Missouri Botanical Garden in 2003. Enough said.

'English Countryside' is likely a natural hybrid between aromatic aster and New England aster. Plants bear beautiful lavender-blue flowers that absolutely smother the plant in late fall. The plants are big and without a pruning, they flower on 4-foot-tall plants. Plants definitely need a hard prune by early June in the South,

late June in the North, or they will be far too vigorous. However, it may too late for northern gardeners, or as Judy Laushman of Oberlin, Ohio, so aptly states, "It flowers so late in northeast Ohio it's in danger of being snowed on." Found in Athens, Georgia, by the great garden designer Anne English.

'October Skies' is a low-growing version of 'Raydon's Favorite', introduced by the Primrose Path. They have excellent

Aster 'English Countryside' pinched

Astilbe ×*arendsii* 'Bressingham Beauty'

lavender flower power but grow only about 2 feet tall, even without pruning.

'Raydon's Favorite' is even better, with purple flowers with yellow centers in the fall on stiff, hairy, 2- to 3-foot-tall plants. The foliage also has a nice hint of mint. Plants originally came from south Texas, and are especially beautiful at the San Antonio Botanical Garden, a treasure of a place that should be on every plantsperson's map. Plants need full sun and well-drained soils.

Many asters, like the wood asters, are sprawly wonderful things, but if you are not into sprawl, you might want to try the Tatarian aster, *Aster tataricus*, a tall, late-flowering aster from Siberia. Flowering at the same time as the fall sunflowers and toad lilies (*Tricyrtis*), they can be the dominant element in the late September and early October garden. The leaves look like big bunches of green chard in the spring and remain so until late in the summer, when the 7-foot-tall stems begin to erupt with hundreds of pale lavender flowers with yellow centers. They can get top-heavy and fall over without support. The good thing about the plants is that they multiply rapidly; the bad thing is that they multiply rapidly. If you feel kind, give a gift that keeps on giving.

Astilbe ×*arendsii* 'Venus' with sedges

A smaller offspring of this big mama, called 'Jin-Dai', needs no support and is only about 4 feet tall. Full sun is best; plants in partial shade will be taller and sprawl more. 'Blue Lake' is much better branched and makes a large clump, a far better habit than others. It is likely a hybrid because it flowers in late spring and early summer, very unusual for Tatarian asters. A wonderful selection, I highly recommend it. Hardy in zones 4 to 8.

Astilbe

How useful does a group of plants have to be to make the group a must-have for all gardeners? Some would argue that the moist, partially shady conditions and cool night temperatures needed for best performance eliminate astilbe from such a list. However, I would argue that the impressive diversity of cultivars puts this genus on the "must-try" list, at least for those in zone 7 and north.

Astilbe ×arendsii 'Irrlicht'

Astilbe ×arendsii 'Fanal'

Astilbe ×arendsii 'Radius'

As landscapes and gardens mature, shade becomes more of an issue, and plants that offer colorful flowers in shady conditions will continue to be in high demand.

Most of the choices of astilbe are the hybrids of *Astilbe ×arendsii*, and the number is almost endless. Choosing one of the hybrids is only slightly less confusing than choosing a hosta, iris, daylily, or peony. They are popular, to be sure, but they can't be planted just anywhere. Regardless of where you live, plants prefer partially

Astilbe ×*arendsii* 'Venus'

Astilbe ×*arendsii* 'Gladstone'

Astilbe ×*arendsii* 'Elizabeth Bloom'

Astilbe ×*arendsii* 'Mainze'

Astilbe ×*arendsii* 'Ostrich Plume'

Astilbe ×*arendsii* 'Color Flash'

Astilbe chinensis 'Pumila'

Astilbe chinensis 'Veronica Klose'

Astilbe chinensis var. *taquetii* 'Superba'

Astilbe simplicifolia 'Sprite'

Astilbe chinensis 'Visions'

shaded conditions, soils rich in organic matter, and consistent soil moisture. People who live in zones 3 and 4 can put astilbes in full sun, but afternoon shade is still preferred. They are particularly at home on creek banks but not in standing water. I see fine astilbes throughout this country and Canada, but it is hard to beat the elegance at Longstock Park Water Garden in England where sedges (*Carex*) and 'Venus' astilbe share the edge of ponds. However, since most of us are not blessed with ponds or creeks, to say nothing of English weather, the next best thing is irrigation. Find a spot under high shade, provide organic matter if necessary, and water as needed. There is no answer to the question of what cultivars are best, try whatever you can find.

In my travels, I have always been impressed with 'Bressingham Beauty', a 3-foot-tall pink-rose form that brings the Armitage shade alive. Great red color comes from the old-fashioned but difficult-to-

Astilbe chinensis var. *taquetii* 'Purple Lance'

Astilbe simplicifolia 'Sprite'

Astilbe simplicifolia 'Dunkellanchs'

beat 'Fanal' and the new and extraordinary strawberry-red 'Radius'. The latter is one of the few astilbes that provides consistently good color and performance in the South. For whites, 'Irrlicht' and 'Gladstone' are excellent, while I can't get enough of 'Venus' and 'Elizabeth Bloom' for soft pinks and 'Mainze' for a deeper pink. Every now and then, I like to get away from the spires of flowers that characterize the genus and will try 'Ostrich Plume', unique in habit. Recently introduced, 'Color Flash' is an interesting selection with multicolored foliage. It is just that—interesting—but I can handle that.

It must be obvious from the few cultivars I have selected that I cannot recommend one over the other—I am enamored with them

all when they grow well. However, I have also seen many sickly and ragged astilbes where conditions are too warm, sun is too strong, winters are too mild, and water is too scarce. Either site them properly or save your money. Astilbes grow well in zones 3 to 7

The Chinese astilbe, *Astilbe chinensis*, has always been a rather staid cousin of the more flashy hybrids in the family. The deep purple compact flowers of the common form, 'Pumila', are only about 18 inches tall and don't contrast particularly well with the dark green leaves. However, they have many fans, including this fellow. I have seen these running all over the shade as ground covers, and I especially love that it can be tucked into nooks and crannies

Astilbe chinensis 'Pumila' tucked into a corner

Astilbe simplicifolia 'Willy Buchanan'

Astrantia major

to enhance a locale. In general, given sufficient moisture, plants perform much more like ground covers than the Arendsii hybrids and are great low-maintenance plants. They are tough and are more drought tolerant than the hybrids but will not move around nearly as much if conditions are dry. The stodgy image of 'Pumila' has been chipped away with the appearance of a number of good cultivars. 'Veronica Klose' bears wonderful light pink flowers, while 'Visions' is a must-have plant. The common color is rosy red but other colors are also available.

The other main member of the species is the variety *taquetti*, grown in North American gardens for years. The common selection is 'Superba', whose hairy plants rise to 5 feet in height and produce long columns of purple flowers. This is a great plant for early summer flowering, sure to catch the eye. 'Purple Lance' with purple-red flowers is even more impressive and grows 4 to 4$^{1}/_{2}$ feet tall. All prefer moisture with a little shade, lots of shade in the South. Hardy in zones 3 to 7.

Perhaps the most ornamental foliage occurs in the star astilbe, *Astilbe simplicifolia*. The flowers are handsome, but the dark glossy green leaves forming compact clumps really complete the plant. Seldom growing more than 2 feet in height, plants are perfect for the front of the garden or around a small garden pond. The flowers are much more open than other astilbes, providing a light, airy look. Even the final stage of seed production is ornamental, providing another few weeks of pleasant viewing. The best known and probably still the best selection is 'Sprite', whose shell-pink flowers have proven outstanding for many years. 'Dunkellanchs' is similar to 'Sprite' but has more compact flower heads. 'Willy Buchanan' is another dwarf member, whose dwarf habit (less than a foot tall) and light pink to almost white flowers set it apart from others. As with other astilbes, moisture and partial shade are conducive to good performance, hardy in zones 4 to 8.

Astrantia
MASTERWORT

A few plants like masterwort have such nonsensical names that I want to see what they are. Sneezewort is such a name, having to do with snuff. If sneezewort had to with sneezing, then what about masterwort? The suffix "wort" often signals that something is used medicinally, but the master part eludes me. Maybe they are masters of something or somebody. It is neither a name to enchant gardeners nor is it a name they will find at their local garden center. However, common name aside, it is a plant that can do great things for partially shaded areas, particularly if water can be provided regularly. Two species occur, neither grown as much as they should be in North American gardens.

The most common is great masterwort, *Astrantia major*. American gardeners have not embraced this plant, perhaps because

Astrantia major

Astrantia major subsp. *involucrata* 'Shaggy'

Astrantia major 'Lars'

Astrantia major 'Ruby Wedding'

Astrantia maxima

they seldom see it at the local retail outlet and if they do, there is not much to admire in a 6-inch pot in the spring. However, given moist conditions and partial shade, there is much to recommend it. Sure, the white to pink flowers that occur in early to mid spring are rather weird, about 2 to 3 inches wide and consisting of short papery bracts, which stick out beneath the flowers like rounded collars on a shirt. The 2- to 3-foot-tall plants spread by seed and stolons and, where comfortable, form an impressive display. They are much more comfortable in cooler summer climates than in hot, humid summers.

A number of outstanding cultivars have been collected. My favorite for sure is subspecies *involucrata* 'Shaggy', so called because the collar of bracts is greatly elongated, providing a truly shaggy mane. While the muted colors of the species are fine, the pink to scarlet flowers of recent introductions are particularly eye-catching. 'Hadspen Blood' provides rosy red flowers, but the bloodiest flowers are found in 'Ruby Wedding' and 'Lars', the latter being the darkest of all. For those who enjoy weird flowers on variegated leaves, try 'Sunningdale Variegated'. The variegation disappears with summer temperatures, which

may be just as well. Best for the West Coast or in zones 5 to 7a.

Astrantia maxima, large masterwort, may be the most handsome of all the masterworts; unfortunately, very few nurseries offer it for sale. I have seen this species here and there on my travels, but one of the finest specimens was in the garden of Terri Leblanc outside Quebec City, attesting to its cold hardiness and persistence. Plants are more difficult to propagate, which may be one of the reasons why it is so little known. However, find a few (they are out there), plant them, and let's get it in more gardens. Plants perform best in partial shade,

Astrantia major 'Sunningdale Variegated'

Astrantia major 'Hadspen Blood'

Astrantia maxima

Athyrium filix-femina 'Vernoniae Cristatum'

probably hardy in zones 4 to 7a as well as on the West Coast.

Athyrium
LADY FERN

Having grown up in a garden-challenged family in Montreal, I thought that everyone used ferns simply to cover the dirt. Outside our little semi-detached, Dad stuck a few ferns in the ground and immediately forgot about them. Boring, never-changing green things that blackened at the first touch of frost. However, they were great for us boys, whose interest in hockey and baseball was far greater than in garden maintenance. Since then, my eyes have seen the glory of the coming of the ferns, and my mind has expanded. Eureka, I like ferns. Age does have some value.

I suppose the lady fern, *Athyrium filix-femina*, may be considered a boring, never-changing green thing, but it is a boring, never-changing green thing with style and class, and better than that, this lady is tough as nails. She is deciduous, blackening at the second touch of frost, but her early fiddleheads give rise to beautiful feathery fronds. The stem and midrib of the fronds are often pink or red, providing wonderful contrast to the green leaflets. Plants stand upright and make handsome airy clumps. While such plants are common, there are also a few variants in this lady's closet. This is probably the most variable of all the ferns. I rather like the dwarf form, 'Minutissimum', but I have to work on liking the rather contorted 'Vernoniae Cristatum', with its plume-like crested fronds. There

Athyrium filix-femina

Athyrium filix-femina 'Minutissimum'

Athyrium niponicum var. *pictum*

Athyrium 'Ghost'

Athyrium niponicum var. *pictum*

are many others, but most do nothing more than provide curiosity, like a car wreck; they don't hold a candle to the species. But these aberrations do reduce the sameness factor a little. Provide shade and moisture, hardy in zones 4 to 8.

Japanese painted fern, *Athyrium niponicum* var. *pictum*, is an absolute no-brainer for almost any gardener. Plants provide toughness, style, and technicolor fronds, making fern growing a lot more exciting. The colors on this popular plant are indescribable; that is, I don't know how to describe them. Someone wrote that it is "a metallic gray suffused with reddish or bluish hues"; suffice it to say, the fronds are a pastel blend of many lovely colors.

Athyrium 'Pewter Lace'

Athyrium otophorum var. *okanum*

Athyrium 'Wildwood Twist'

Baptisia sphaerocarpa 'Screamin' Yellow'

Where conditions are to their liking, plants routinely spread themselves around. They tolerate heavy shade but are at their best in morning sun. Plants tolerate wet soils but prefer moist, and do just fine in "normal" soils. Truly an easy fern to grow.

If that were not enough, breeders have hybridized these two species and come up with handsome colors on vigorous plants. 'Ghost' is still one of the favorites, and with its silvery gray foliage, appropriately named. 'Pewter Lace' and 'Wildwood Twist' are well worth trying. In the Trial Gardens at UGA, both stop traffic. Hardy in zones 3 to 8.

Finally, let's meet the eared lady fern, *Athyrium otophorum*, seldom seen but well known among fern aficionados. She grows about 18 inches tall and is a true specimen plant, easily visible from a long distance. Variety *okanum* is often offered—cream-colored fronds with red to maroon stems and midribs. This is way underused.

Baptisia
FALSE INDIGO

I always enjoy a good story, and the history of the blue false indigo, *Baptisia australis*, makes for good reading. This blue-flowered species was the first plant to be subsidized by the English government: in the 1700s, the farmers in the colonies of Georgia and South Carolina grew it as a row crop for the British Empire to supplement true indigo (*Indigofera*). It was a good substitute, but not of the quality of true indigo, and thus came to be known as false indigo, or wild indigo. The false indigos come in three main colors—blue, white, and yellow—but new hybrids and selections are bringing this fine plant into mainstream gardening. Great plants, great stories, great fun.

Baptisia australis is an excellent "last forever" plant, easily persisting for ten years, yet much to the chagrin of retailers, it looks like a stick in a pot when first purchased. Don't fret: plant that stick and soon enough, your friends will no longer be laughing. Plants take time to establish, but after a couple of years in the garden, they

Baptisia australis bud stage

Baptisia minor

Baptisia australis

Baptisia alba emerging in early spring

flower profusely and take on their classic form and substance. Even in the bud stage when only a few flowers have opened, it is stately. Plants, 3 to 4 feet tall and equally wide, look terrific by themselves or towering over other plants in the garden. Flowers make excellent, albeit rather ephemeral, cut flowers for local occasions. After flowering, fat brown pods are formed. As the seeds within them mature, they come loose from

the pod walls, and the whole pod becomes a miniature maraca. Few insects and diseases bother the plant; however, they do collapse in the late fall, and the first frost turns everything about them black and mushy. The dwarf species *B. minor* is outstanding and resembles its big brother in every way except size (2 feet tall). Full sun is necessary for best performance; keep them out of poorly drained soils. Hardy in zones 3 to 8.

Many gardeners, including this one, believe that the white forms of baptisias are easier to establish than the blues. White wild indigo, *Baptisia alba*, is ornamental from early spring, when the black stems emerge (looking like black asparagus), through the spring and summer, with the many clean white flowers and light green foliage. In late summer and fall, the upward-facing "pea pods" are the legacy of

Baptisia alba

Baptisia alba fruit

Baptisia 'Carolina Moonlight'

Baptisia 'Purple Smoke'

the flower fling, although in 'Pendula', the pods are (you guessed it) pendulous. One reason they may be easier to grow is that they are a little more shade tolerant than the blues or yellows. I don't recommend shade; however, as the canopy gets older and provides more shade, these will hang in there longer than most. Well-drained soils are necessary; hardy in zones 5 (perhaps 4) to 8.

Blues and whites are wonderful, but the yellow indigos should not be ignored. Brightening up the sunny garden, forming interesting fruit, and offering good foliage, they are beginning to find their way

Baptisia bracteata var. *leucophaea*

into North American gardens. The bright yellow-flowered form is *Baptisia sphaerocarpa* (yellow wild indigo); its selection 'Screamin' Yellow' is indeed a screamer, but nobody is going to walk past it without taking a second look. A beautiful creamy yellow is found in *B. bracteata* var. *leucophaea* (longbract wild indigo). They are early to emerge and bloom with the white-flowering baptisias. Full sun, hardy in zones 4 to 8.

The breeding in baptisias has heated up, and a number of hybrids can be found. 'Carolina Moonlight' has large, soft yellow flowers and effortlessly complements nearly everything else in the garden. A hybrid between *Baptisia australis* and *B. alba* is 'Purple Smoke', whose smoky-colored stems and flowers make it unique; others are emerging rapidly, but this is

still one of the consistent performers and I recommend it highly.

Bergenia
PIGSQUEAK

I have never been a fan of pigsqueak, but what does that matter when so many others seem to enjoy it so? In general, plants are terrific in cool climates with moderate winters but, except for one species, do poorly in the South. However, the name pigsqueak is reason alone to have one and if you learn to make the pig squeak, then you really have something useful. If you want to impress your garden friends, place a leaf between your thumb and index finger. Then move them back and forth, squeezing the leaf while you do so. With a

little practice, everyone will soon hear the pig squeak. Really, I'm not smart enough to make this stuff up. Be sure to practice on your own before you make a fool of yourself in public.

Bergenia ciliata, fringed bergenia, is a wonderful, little-grown plant that can make even a nonbeliever like me want to take home a pigsqueak. Like other bergenias, the light green leaves are the best part of the plant, but with this species, they are densely pubescent (hairy) with small hairs (cilia) surrounding the leaves. Plants look best in rock gardens or where the leaves can be admired close up. Consider the white flowers, flushed with rose, a bonus; the plants don't flower as well or grow as vigorously as common bergenias. Plant in partial (preferably afternoon) shade and

Bergenia ciliata

Bergenia ciliata

Bergenia cordifolia

Bergenia cordifolia growing across path

Bergenia cordifolia in winter

Bergenia purpurascens

Bergenia 'Bressingham Ruby'

Bergenia 'Baby Doll'

protect from drying winds. Hardy in zones 5 to 7.

In my opinion, making the pig squeak is the best reason to purchase *Bergenia cordifolia* (heartleaf pigsqueak) and its hybrids, but thankfully for the breeders and sellers of bergenia, my opinion doesn't count for much. The 12-inch-tall plants have glossy

lustrous green leaves that can act as ground covers where shade and slightly moist conditions occur. Occasionally plants can be allowed to flow across garden paths, making both the path and the plant better. The early spring flowers rise 8 to 12 inches above the leaves in early spring and persist for weeks if temperatures remain cool. Flowers are

generally red or pink, but white is also available. The early flowers are often damaged if late freezes occur. In warmer areas of the country, plants are evergreen (actually "everbronze") and if the weather is not too harsh, the winter colors are quite striking. However, plants can get badly battered in subfreezing temperatures. In the North, snow mercifully

Bergenia 'Distinction'

Bergenia 'Evening Glow'

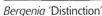
Bergenia 'Morning Blush'

Brunnera macrophylla

Brunnera macrophylla
SIBERIAN BUGLOSS

puts them out of view. On the West Coast, they are as perfect as most plants are. The bronze foliage in the fall and spring is one of the main selling points for gardeners. Partial shade, hardy in zones 4 to 8.

The many cultivars and hybrids amply demonstrate the diversity of bergenias. They are hybrids of this species and purple pigsqueak, *Bergenia purpurascens*, with outstanding deep purple foliage, especially when emerging in the spring, and others. I have admired handsome clumps of purple foliage in March on 'Bressingham Ruby' but even darker foliage in the same month on

'Baby Doll'. Rosy red flowers of 'Distinction' or deeper red flowers of 'Morning Blush' may appear a few weeks later. As temperatures warm up, the lustrous growth of bergenias is best exemplified by plants like 'Evening Glow' with its handsome green foliage. There are dozens more with similar characteristics, which makes me believe there are far more cultivars of bergenia than needed—but I guess the same can be said for ice cream. Lots of people love these plants; that I am not one of them does not diminish my appreciation when I see pigsqueak growing well.

Here is a plant that just keeps getting better as new selections become available. The green-leaved species is quite lovely and in moderate climates spreads quite aggressively, especially in moist, shady conditions. They are at their best in the mild climates of the West Coast and British Isles, but a trip to Old Westbury Gardens on Long Island or Gardenview Horticultural Park in Strongsville, Ohio, will show the remarkable vigor of these plants.

"Look at the forget-me-nots" is probably the first thing you'll think when you see the plants in flower. The wonderful little blue flowers with small yellow centers look for all the world like forget-me-nots, but the large, deep green heart-shaped leaves

Brunnera macrophylla with hostas and other shade lovers

Brunnera macrophylla 'Variegata'

Brunnera macrophylla 'Langtrees'

Brunnera macrophylla 'Hadspen Cream'

Brunnera macrophylla 'Jack Frost'

Brunnera macrophylla 'Jack Frost'

Brunnera macrophylla 'Looking Glass' beneath alocasias

Brunnera macrophylla 'Looking Glass'

give away the plant's true identity. Where summer temperatures are cool, leaves can be 3 inches long or more, and plants make a beautiful ground cover in moist, shady soils, holding their own against hostas and other shade-tolerant plants in the same site. *Brunnera macrophylla* is not for everybody—consistent moisture is essential, otherwise the margins of the leaves turn brown. In the South, the species and some of the older cultivars really struggle. Plants do well in zones 3 to 7a.

Brunnera macrophylla 'King's Ransom'

Campanula carpatica 'Blue Clips'

Campanula carpatica var. *turbinata*

Campanula 'Birch Hybrid'

I am so impressed with the cultivars now available to the gardener. While the beauty of older selections like 'Variegata', 'Langtrees', and 'Hadspen Cream' cannot be denied, they are far more persnickety in their demands for cool temperatures, moisture, and soils. Recently, however, 'Jack Frost', with its silver venation, the silvery elegant 'Looking Glass', and the tough 'King's Ransom' have invigorated the genus. Not only are they handsome, they have been shown to be more heat tolerant and can be grown successfully in the South, where older selections perished. They may not look wonderful in August and September in warm climes, but they will provide lots of pleasure until then.

Campanula
BELLFLOWER

The genus *Campanula* offers so many species, cultivars, and varieties that any gardener, north or south, will never run out of plants to try. The species generally bear blue, lavender, or purple flowers, but many other hues, such as white, rosy red, and pink, have been selected. As to habit, the bellflowers offer something for almost every gardener, from upright 4-foot plants with large flowers to 6-inch rock garden subjects. The only drawback to the genus is that it is more appropriate for northern climates; southern gardeners have to struggle to find taxa that perform south of zone 6.

Campanula carpatica 'White Clips'

Campanula 'Samantha'

Campanula portenschlagiana

Campanula portenschlagiana 'Bavarica'

Among the low growers is *Campanula carpatica*, the Carpathian bellflower. Standing only 9 to 12 inches tall, this bellflower has some of the biggest, most colorful flowers, relative to the size of the plant, of any campanula. The bell-shaped flowers can be up to 2 inches across and are copiously produced in early to mid summer. Provide full sun and good drainage, and place them around some rocks or near the front of the garden. This species is native to eastern Europe, and plants are not tolerant of high temperatures and high humidity. I have had little success with them south of zone 6 in the eastern United States, but they can

Campanula poscharskyana

Campanula poscharskyana 'Blue Gown'

Campanula lactiflora

Campanula lactiflora 'Pritchard's Variety'

be produced in zones 7 and 8 on the West Coast. They are terrific in the northern Plains states, the Midwest, and Canada.

The Clips series provides excellent small-statured plants with large flowers. *Campanula carpatica* var. *turbinata* is lower growing and produces large (relative to plant height) blue flowers. Two low-growing hybrids using Carpathian bellflower as one of the parents are excellent performers as well: 'Birch Hybrid' has deep purple flowers, and 'Samantha' has light blue flowers. The hybrid vigor of 'Samantha' allows her to grow well even in warmer climates, normally death sentences for Carpathian bellflowers. All these plants are exceptional for rock gardens in full sun.

Campanula punctata 'Plum Wine'

Campanula garganica 'Dickson's Gold'

Campanula punctata 'Pantaloons'

Both *Campanula portenschlagiana* (Dalmatian bellflower) and *C. poscharskyana* (Serbian bellflower) offer similar low-growing habits (6 to 9 inches tall), handsome blue to purple flowers and unpronounceable names. Both are best for rock gardens or for tumbling over hillsides and out of pots. The differences between them are few; the bell-shaped flowers of the Dalmatian form separate it from the star-shaped flowers of the Serbian form, but otherwise they are similar in habit, color, and use. We North American gardeners normally take whatever can be found at the nursery or in the mail-order catalog. The color ranges from lavender to purple, depending on location, and flowers open in late spring. When not in flower, the plants make good-looking clumps of dark green foliage, or they can be hidden by bigger plants as summer progresses. *Campanula portenschlagiana* performs well in zones 4 to 8, *C. poscharskyana* in zones 3 to 7. I find both species more heat tolerant than most

others in the genus, having been successful in the Armitage garden.

The species are just fine in and of themselves; however, *Campanula portenschlagiana* 'Bavarica' offers lavender-purple flowers, while *C. poscharskyana* 'Blue Gown' has wonderful blue-and-white blooms. Another interesting low grower is the Adriatic bellflower, *C. garganica*, particularly the golden 'Dickson's Gold'. The foliar color is vivid only in the spring, but the contrast between the leaves and the flowers at that time is quite striking.

Campanula lactiflora (milky bellflower) is the antithesis of the low growers just mentioned, often reaching 4 feet in height; it produces hundreds of small lavender or white flowers on many-branched plants in midsummer. Among the best selections are 'Pritchard's Variety', with flowers in the lavender to purple range, 'Alba' with clean white flowers, and my favorite, 'Loddon Anna', with soft pale pink flowers on sturdy 4-foot-tall stems. But beware: all can reseed

prolifically, and the resulting offspring may be any color. For best results, provide full sun or some afternoon shade and reasonably well-drained soils. Plants are most successful on the West Coast but may also be found growing in gardens in zones 5 to 7. They don't do well in areas of hot summers and are seldom grown successfully in the southern half of the country. The low growers are more forgiving of heat and humidity than the upright forms.

Many gardeners consider *Campanula punctata*, spotted bellflower, a thug, moving swiftly through the garden with no respect for its neighbors. I don't disagree, as I must yank it up every other year before it eats its brethren. However, in the South I am so pleased to have a good bellflower that doesn't tire during hot summers, I keep it in. My student workers are not as enamored as I. So beware.

Two selections that I think are quite wonderful are 'Plum Wine' and 'Pantaloons'. 'Plum Wine' has tubular light pink

Campanula lactiflora 'Loddon Anna'

Campanula medium 'Champion White'

flowers. Plants are a bit more mound-forming than others, but they also break the mound with time. The rosy pink flowers of 'Pantaloons' are "hose in hose," that is, one flower is seemingly inserted in the other; they are conspicuously gorgeous, prolifically produced, and are even more fun when viewed close up. 'Sarastro' is a hybrid and fast becoming a favorite for its better behavior and handsome deep blue flowers. Plants seem to flower all the time, taking only a short breather every now and then. However, it can get quite big and can overwhelm smaller plants near it.

Canterbury bells, *Campanula medium*, is enjoyed by all who see it, whether in the garden, the greenhouse, or in a vase of cut flowers. Plants are biennials, meaning they take two years to flower and then gener-ally disappear. These are far better for the conservatory than the garden; nevertheless,

Campanula 'Sarastro'

Campanula medium 'Champion Pink'

Campanula lactiflora 'Alba'

Canna 'Princess Di'

Canna 'Tropicanna'

they are so beautiful that if you are conservatorily challenged, planting them outside is worth a try. The best selections are the Champion series, in a couple of wonderful colors. They are usually available from seed; start the seed in the winter for spring planting. All the tall campanulas make excellent cut flowers, but this is the best for longevity of bloom in the vase.

Canna
CANNA LILY

Some readers may be scratching their heads, wondering why canna lilies are included in a book on perennials. While they must be dug and stored north of zone 6 (some north of zone 7), they are planted every year, like dahlias, and just seem perennial. Even though they may be winter wimps, they are summer tough. In some communities, cannas are an important landscape plant for road medians or public parks, attesting to their toughness. Many years

Canna 'Northstar Red'

Canna 'Bengal Tiger'

Canna 'Picasso'

ago, plants were boring, green-leaved, red-flowered things that did little for a garden design. Today, there are many outstanding cultivars from which to choose, and while they are no more cold hardy or disease- or insect-resistant than their predecessors, new colors and the need for large, bold plants in the garden have made them more prominent in the landscape.

Flower color is one of the more important buying considerations for green-leaved cannas. Bright red ('Northstar Red'), spotted yellow ('Picasso'), salmon ('Princess Di'), and apricot ('Apricot Ice') are only some of the choices out there. For the largest, perhaps most overwhelming foliage, 'Musifolia' (banana canna) may be just the ticket.

Green banana-like leaves, red stems, and handsome flowers quickly fill the garden.

If I were buying cannas for my daughters, I would likely choose those with eye-catching foliage; the flowers in these cases are simply less important. 'Bengal Tiger' has been around for some time and is still used a good deal. For the darkest foliage, it is hard to beat 'Australia', whose almost black leaves contrast wonderfully with the red flowers. However, as much as I love 'Australia', my favorite is still 'Tropicanna', aka 'Phaison'. The boldly multicolored leaves are handsome all season; they go well with other flowers, and the orange blooms top them off in perfect style. 'Tropicanna Gold', with muted striped foliage,

Canna 'Apricot Ice'

Canna 'Australia'

Canna 'Australia'

Canna 'Tropical White'

Canna 'Tropicanna' with cape daisies

Canna 'Musifolia'

Canna 'Tropicanna'

Canna 'Tropicanna Gold'

Cerastium tomentosum

is also big but not nearly as exciting as its namesake. However, the golden flowers are attractive. All the above cultivars are 3 to 5 feet tall.

Cannas for the most part are propagated vegetatively, and the incidence of plant viruses in cannas is now a valid concern. One symptom may be the browning of the edge of the leaves, and although this is not a serious problem for the cannas themselves, producers don't want them in their greenhouses or fields for fear of spreading the virus to other plants. This situation has resulted in fewer new cannas for the gardener; however, it has also spurred the production of cannas from seed, essentially eliminating the viruses. We have trialed a number, and 'Tropical White' has been a winner and is only 2 to 2½ feet tall.

I'm not sure the love affair with cannas will continue for much longer. Other problems, such as leaf rollers and Japanese beetles, make them more of a challenge than some gardeners want, but as long as clean cultivars are introduced, they will be

around for a while longer. Full sun, winter hardy in zones 7 to 10; the addition of winter mulching may allow overwintering into the southern end of zone 6 as well. Further north, treat them like dahlias: lift in the fall and replant in the spring.

Cerastium
SNOW-IN-SUMMER

This is one of my favorite plants, particularly when I see it planted here and there in alpine gardens, or spotted among rocks or occasionally on hillsides. The main species found in gardens is *Cerastium tomentosum*, whose combination of leaves, flowers, and habit have made it a popular plant. As temperatures warm up in the spring, the handsome silvery gray leaves flow over rocks, and like artemisias and lamb's ears, they make marvelous softeners for more colorful plants at the front of the garden. The plants, covered with half-inch-wide white flowers, are not like snowflakes, but snowbanks. We can learn a few things

Cerastium tomentosum

Cerastium gibraltaricum

Cerastium tomentosum as edging

about our garden cousins in eastern Australia, where plants are used as snowy borders around the entire garden or where they are placed in tall containers as a greeting by the garden gate. Flowers occur as temperatures warm up and daylengths lengthen, persisting for four to six weeks, depending on temperature. Drainage becomes more important the further south one gardens. With poor drainage, plants melt out south of zone 7a but are still useful in that area in raised beds or containers. Full sun in the North, afternoon shade in the South, excellent drainage required. Hardy in zones 3 to 7.

Cerastium tomentosum as a container "spiller"

Ceratostigma plumbaginoides

Ceratostigma willmottianum 'My Love'

A couple of other species, such as *Cerastium gibraltaricum* (also known as snow-in-summer), may be found, but they offer little obvious differences. Plants are less vigorous, which may be a plus for gardeners in places where *C. tomentosum* becomes too aggressive. Hardy in zones 3 to 6.

Ceratostigma
LEADWORT

I always enjoy telling stories when I do walkabouts in the garden, and I love sharing that the suffix "wort" was often connected with the idea of healing some part of the body (liverwort, lungwort, spleenwort)

Ceratostigma willmottianum 'Forest Blue'

or easing some problem (spiderwort), but obviously something went wrong here. However, the leadworts, healers or not, are versatile and are excellent both for foliage and flowers, particularly for the late summer and fall garden.

The most common species by far is trailing leadwort, *Ceratostigma plumbaginoides*. I see this plant everywhere from

Washington State to Ontario to Georgia, used as a ground cover or simply as a handsome clump of blue flowers in late summer and fall. The ½- to 1-inch-wide blue flowers are normally produced in late summer and fall, but flowers or not, it is one of the toughest little ground covers available. If planted en masse, like at the Niagara School of Horticulture in Niagara Falls, Ontario,

Ceratostigma plumbaginoides

Clematis heracleifolia 'Côte d'Azur'

Ceratostigma willmottianum 'Forest Blue'

the foliage provides a short boxwood-like quality and a handsome edging. The leaves are small (less than an inch long) and are dark green most of the time but turn reddish as plants get older. You may hardly notice the plants until the flowers start in late summer, when they perk up and put on their finest blue dresses. Plants flower all fall and even until frost. They perform best in full sun and with good drainage, and are almost indestructible. Performs well in zones 5 (4 with protection) to 8.

Hardly seen in North American gardens, Chinese leadwort, *Ceratostigma willmottianum* bears similar late summer and fall flowers, but the habit, the foliage, and the hardiness are markedly different from the previous species. Its hardiness is the largest

impediment to popularity; it's winter hardy only to about zone 7. Plants are about 2 feet in height, with handsome blue flowers for about six weeks in late summer. Although not as tough and adaptable as the trailing leadwort, its foliage is more handsome, and I believe it to be far more ornamental in the areas where it is comfortable. All leadworts are woody at the base; this one is essentially a small shrub. 'Forest Blue' is the most common cultivar, and I recommend it for southern and West Coast gardeners. 'My Love' provides beautiful chartreuse foliage in the spring and looks fabulous in the retail outlet but has not proven very effective when planted outdoors, at least for me. Full sun to partial shade, hardy in zones 7 to 9.

Clematis

I have been writing about clematis forever, and the story never changes. The characters do, but the story of marvelous vines, bearing flowers in all sorts of sizes, shapes, and colors, does not. More cultivars are available than you will ever have space to grow, and that is just the common ones. Recently, native clematis such as *Clematis viorna* have joined well-established native species like Texas clematis, *C. texensis*, while cultivars relatively unknown a few years ago, like *C.* 'Rooguchi', have almost become household names in the clematis lexicon. They can be grown up pillar and post, tree and pergola, and many a postal carrier has cursed the vine while trying to deliver mail to a mailbox surrounded by the cursed things. Still relatively ignored are the nonvining forms, which, though not the eye candy of some of the vines, are quite

Clematis heracleifolia 'Wyevale'

Clematis heracleifolia 'Mrs. Robert Brydon'

Clematis integrifolia

Clematis integrifolia

Clematis integrifolia 'Rosea'

Clematis texensis 'Duchess of Albany'

Clematis texensis 'Princess Diana'

spectacular and far more useful as garden companions.

Big and sprawling, *Clematis heracleifolia* (tube clematis) is nonvining and shrublike in its habit. The ends of the stems produce dozens of tubular flowers, making for showy inflorescences in late spring and summer. The large compound leaves are up to 12 inches long, and if the plant is over-fertilized, the leaves will almost obscure the flowers. Flowers range from light to dark blue. The plant's main drawbacks are rangi-ness and leafiness; support tends to make the plant less rangy. Plants may be cut back in late summer if the foliage declines.

Clematis viorna

Clematis cirrhosa

Clematis terniflora

Clematis texensis

Clematis terniflora

Clematis heracleifolia can be more weedy than useful—but when in its prime, it is a showstopper. 'Côte d'Azur' and 'Wyevale' are the most common offerings and differ only slightly from the species. 'Mrs. Robert Brydon' has a touch of blue on the mostly creamy white flowers. Full sun, zones 3 to 7.

Clematis integrifolia (solitary clematis) has been around for eons but is still one of the big-time underused plants in herbaceous perennials. I often rank it as an Armitage top ten plant; just goes to show how many people listen to me. This nonvining member produces dozens of solitary flowers of deep blue and bears opposite entire leaves. It has been obscured in the marketplace by the omnipresent vines but is well worth a place in the sunny garden. The numerous thin, 3-foot-tall stems should be supported as they grow; otherwise, they flop on the ground. The flowers begin in late spring and continue for six weeks, then off and on throughout the season. If that is not enough, the fluffy seed heads that form in late summer and fall are almost as ornamental as the flowers. Rose-colored ('Rosea') flowers are occasionally seen— they provide a nice splash of color, but I'll take the wonderful deep blue of the species any day. Full sun, zones 3 to 7.

Vining *Clematis* species and hybrids are everywhere—and with good reason. Where their roots are cool and their foliage is in sunshine, they can be as vigorous and colorful as any plant in the garden. The best support for many of the vines is through shrubs and trees, where they can climb to their heart's content and, in general, make any woody plant look better. In the

Clematis montana

Clematis montana 'Broughton Star'

Clematis armandii

Clematis montana 'Grandiflora'

Armitage garden, nary a shrub escapes the twining embrace of a clematis.

I love the tubular flowers of *Clematis texensis*, the Texas clematis, one of the best species for southern gardeners, replete with rose-red blossoms in the spring and summer and stunning fruit later on. 'Duchess of Albany' and 'Princess Diana' are two excellent selections of Texas clematis. They are both more vigorous and bear larger and more flowers than the species. A little-known native clematis is our native vase vine, *C. viorna*. Nothing to really knock your socks off, but a subtle beauty all her own.

How can you not love Armand's clematis, *Clematis armandii*, whose wonderful white flowers cover southern gardens, and even announce the entryway into the house in early spring? 'Apple Blossom' has pink appleblossom-colored flower buds. I also enjoy the winter clematis, *C. cirrhosa* for its combination of glossy evergreen leaves, small flowering chalices, and cottony fruit, but it is a little more difficult to find. I have learned my lesson about planting sweet autumn clematis, *C. terniflora*, a beautiful but self-seeding thug. One needs to experiment with such explosive plants, although after a few springs of removing seedlings from all over the garden, I practice the creed of "rip and replace" with this species. Many people have complained about the aggressive vigor of the mountain clematis, *C. montana*, but when properly trained and sited, what a sight. I love all the montanas, but 'Broughton Star' has to be almost perfect. As perfection goes, 'Grandiflora' is not half bad either.

Clematis armandii 'Apple Blossom'

Clematis viticella 'Purpurea Plena'

Clematis tangutica

Clematis tangutica

Clematis ×*jackmanii*

Clematis ×*durandii*

Clematis 'Huldine'

"Clematis mailboxensis"

Clematis 'Cezanne'

Clematis 'Silver Moon'

Clematis 'Guernsey Cream'

Clematis 'Bees Jubilee'

Outstanding as well is the Italian clematis, *Clematis viticella*, but some of her selections, like the purple 'Étoile Violette' or the double-flowered 'Purpurea Plena', can really stop people in their tracks. The orange peel clematis, *C. tangutica*, has thick yellow flowers (like an orange peel) and is another vigorous beast. However, the yellow flowers also produce some of the most outstanding displays of fluffy fruit of any clematis. Interspecific hybridization has resulted in a number of well-known hybrids, which many gardeners prefer to the large-flowered hybrids.

Old-fashioned hybrids like Jackman's clematis, *Clematis ×jackmanii*, and Durand's clematis, *C. ×durandii*, are still excellent plants and should not be ignored, but it is the large-flowered and fancy forms most gardeners seem to salivate over. The choice depends on the desired color, and the number of structures, including woody plants, one can find to grow them over. They are tough and grow almost everywhere. In Quebec City (zone 3), 'Bees Jubilee' (red) and 'Huldine' (white) had no trouble with their frosty winter, while in the Armitage garden (zone 7), the flowers of 'Guernsey Cream' softened the shrubs they rested on, showing that arctic chills are not needed for good flowering either. The large-flowered 'Silver

Colchicum leaves in spring

Colchicum autumnale

Colchicums naturalized

Moon' (silvery lilac) and 'Cezanne' (light lavender) are also special. The list goes on and on, as do the uses, from growing up a mailbox to enjoying in a container on the patio.

Enjoy them all. If you must, go out to buy a few more trellises, but now it may be a better time to purchase a few more hollies and spireas and slap a few vines over them. Full sun, zones 3 to 8.

Colchicum
AUTUMN CROCUS

I am not sure why I still write about this corm (*Colchicum autumnale*, *C. speciosum*, *C. byzantinum* and hybrids); there are so many other plants that perform better. They are expensive relative to many other bulbous plants but, if they can be established, provide exotic entertainment.

Colchicums with leadwort

Colchicum 'Waterlily' with coneflowers

The straplike leaves emerge in the spring and, a few weeks later, simply disappear; however, like the resurrection lily (*Lycoris*), the flowers magically appear much later in the season. The single or double flowers, in late summer and fall, are lavender to rose in color. As colorful as they are, they are large, unkempt, and uncooperative. Few of the flowers stand upright for any length of time, and a single rainfall can make them look like wet mangy cats. Pink cats, of all things. However, people buy them, so someone must think they are pretty neat. I enjoy them best in a rock garden setting where they can be somewhat protected; however, I have marveled when I see them naturalized. They are known as autumn crocus but differ from crocuses by having six stamens, rather than the three in *Crocus*.

Although colchicums often disappoint gardeners by having too rapid a flowering

time in the fall and too short a life span, they can be better integrated into the garden by combining them with other plants like coneflowers and leadworts. Plant in shady areas and in well-drained soils. Hardy in zones 4 to 7 (8 on the West Coast).

Coreopsis
TICKSEED

No matter how hard we try to abuse this group of native plants, they seem to come back for more in every box store, catalog, and garden center each spring. Along with Shasta daisies and columbines, this genus continues to be among the top ten perennials sold every year. The bright yellow flowers of most of its members, combined with its willingness to put up with most any garden soil, have made it a favorite. That

Coreopsis grandiflora 'Santa Fe Yellow'

it is easy for producers to grow, looks good in a container, and appears outside every gas station from coast to coast also tends to keep it around. In the last few years, plant breeders have rediscovered the diversity of the genus, and there are even more selections, and not just yellow, from which to choose.

Coreopsis auriculata 'Nana'

Coreopsis auriculata 'Zamphir'

Coreopsis grandiflora 'Sunfire'

Coreopsis verticillata 'Golden Showers'

One of my favorites is *Coreopsis auriculata* 'Nana', particularly when it keeps my concrete frog company. The 12- to 15-inch-tall form is tough and well-behaved, and explodes with bright yellow flowers in early spring. Its small size is balanced by the intense color of the 2-inch-wide blooms. The leaves are spoon-shaped, somewhat like a mouse's ear, I am told. Another more recent selection is 'Zamphir', with fluted "petals" and bright yellow flowers. Perhaps a little taller, but the foliage and habit are similar. Neither selection is long lasting, perhaps three years if drainage is good, but most coreopsis are similarly disposed. Good drainage a must, full sun, zones 4 to 9.

One of the mainstays of the beginning gardener and landscaper looking for something bright and easy to grow is *Coreopsis grandiflora*, common coreopsis. In full sun, plants can be spectacular for the first year or two, but by the third year they will usually need dividing, or they crash on all sides. This is not a problem unless a person doesn't look forward to such chores. Which is most of us. The trick to keeping these plants happy is to remove the dead flowers as soon as possible. The more seed produced, the shorter the useful life of the plant.

'Early Sunrise' was the mainstay in the industry due to its ease of production and propensity to stay in flower; plants are about 2 feet tall. However, numerous cultivars such as 'Santa Fe Yellow' and my favorite, 'Sunfire', have performed far better, bearing brighter yellow flowers and more compact habits. They all still require deadheading. Full sun, good drainage, zones 4 to 9.

Coreopsis verticillata, threadleaf coreopsis, is the tough guy of the group, providing classic yellow flowers, reasonably strong stems, and persistence of flower and plant in the sunny garden. The leaves are cut into thread-like leaflets, and plants are almost as good-looking in leaf as in flower. One of the brightest of the available cultivars is the large-flowered 'Golden Showers', but the best-performing selection is 'Zagreb', a 15- to 18-inch trouper with golden yellow flowers. 'Moonbeam' was for many years the number one seller in many areas of the country, because its soft light yellow flower

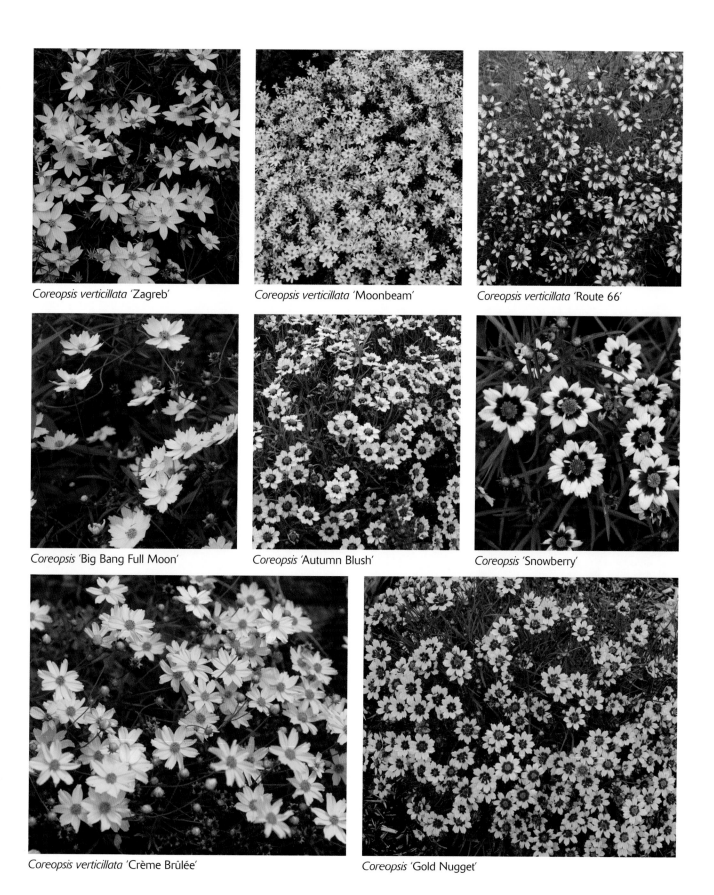

Coreopsis verticillata 'Zagreb'

Coreopsis verticillata 'Moonbeam'

Coreopsis verticillata 'Route 66'

Coreopsis 'Big Bang Full Moon'

Coreopsis 'Autumn Blush'

Coreopsis 'Snowberry'

Coreopsis verticillata 'Crème Brûlée'

Coreopsis 'Gold Nugget'

Coreopsis 'Pinwheels'

Coreopsis 'Jethro Tull'

Coreopsis 'Sweet Dreams'

Coreopsis 'Heaven's Gate'

Coreopsis 'Rum Punch'

color goes well with most other flowers in the garden. Still available, still a great color. A new selection that I am particularly taken with is 'Route 66', with its two-tone flowers and exceptionally long bloom time. Full sun, zones 5 to 9.

All the aforementioned species and selections are still excellent, but the breeding of coreopsis has been most impressive in the last ten years. Today there are so many hybrids (new and old), it is hard to trial them all. Here a few of my favorites.

Two-tone flowers on low-growing plants have been all the rage recently. 'Autumn Blush' can be outstanding in its mounding habit, and 'Gold Nugget' really brightens up the garden. 'Pinwheels' is somewhat similar in color, but the flowers are like, well, pinwheels. 'Snowberry' has more white in the flowers, and I still love the old-fashioned 'Sweet Dreams'. It is exceptional in a container.

For yellow tones, a little yellow hue is available in the low-growing selection

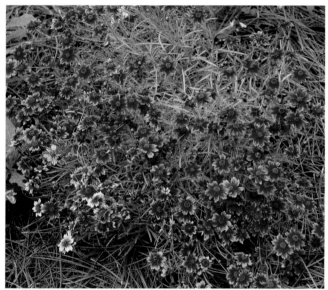

Coreopsis 'Strawberry Lemon'

Corydalis nobilis

Coreopsis 'Mango Punch'

Corydalis cheilanthifolia

'Crème Brûlée' and the taller, far more vigorous hybrid 'Big Bang Full Moon'. Quite a mouthful! And what a terrific plant! I am not sure, but I think if I was asked for one name to recommend, it might be 'Jethro Tull', who as we know was an eighteenth-century agriculturist, oh yes, and a small English rock band. This star-studded coreopsis has bright fluted "petals" and is a good performer to boot. Not a name you will likely forget.

Non-yellow coreopsis are becoming the rage, incorporating species like *Coreopsis rosea*, perhaps *C. tinctoria*, and others.

Most are low growers, rising to no more than a foot in height. 'Heaven's Gate' and 'Strawberry Lemon' produce light and dark rosy red flowers, respectively, while 'Rum Punch', only 8 to 10 inches tall, is the first of many "Punches" yet to come. These don't appear to possess the hardiness found in the yellow forms. All are likely not cold hardy north of zone 7, but time will tell.

Corydalis

As with many of the genera in this book, the exciting news is that plant breeders are not only paying attention to mainstream plants like *Heuchera* and *Echinacea* but also trying to introduce lesser-known groups to gardeners. This is true for this genus, and although some of the species, like yellow corydalis, have been around for years and are often viewed as weeds, others that are appearing are well worth trying in the garden. *Corydalis* is diverse, and includes plants with white, yellow, and blue flowers. They are mostly thought of as rock garden subjects, but some can be quite wonderful in gardens, rock or otherwise. The ferny leaves, one of their more enchanting

Corydalis cheilanthifolia

Corydalis flexuosa 'China Blue'

Corydalis lutea

Corydalis nobilis

characteristics, are charming even when no flowers are present. A number of species are available but have not enjoyed great success, either due to lack of visibility at retail, or perhaps being insufficiently cold hardy. All require excellent drainage (as in rock gardens) and prefer partial shade or morning sun.

I have always enjoyed ferny corydalis, *Corydalis cheilanthifolia*, but I seem to be in the minority as it is seldom seen in North American gardens. Plants are large, relative to other species in the genus, growing up to 15 inches tall. The pinnately cut leaves resemble the lip fern (*Cheilanthes*—thus its specific name) with many yellow flowers arising from the blue-gray rosette. I have had no success with this plant in my own garden, but what else is new? Gardeners in the Midwest have been luckier than I. Partial shade, excellent drainage, and cool summers are recommended. Hardy in zones 3 to 6.

Another yellow-flowered form, *Corydalis nobilis*, is even less known than the above. Plants are large, with blue-green foliage, and bear large yellow flowers, usually with a touch of purple at the ends. That it is so unknown is not because it has not been in the country. As the great Louise Beebe Wilder wrote in the July 1919 issue of *The Garden Magazine*, this "truly noble" corydalis forms "a great tuft of leaves not unlike those of the Bleeding-heart (*Dicentra spectabilis*), from which arise leafy stems closely hung at the ends with pale yellow snap-dragony flowers gaily ornamented with orange and black." It may go summer dormant but should return. Probably cold hardy to zone 6.

Bluish flowers are found in blue corydalis, *Corydalis flexuosa*, and related species. They arrived on the American gardening

Corydalis lutea 'Alba'

Corydalis 'Canary Feathers'

Corydalis 'Manchu'

Corydalis 'Berry Exciting'

scene about ten years ago with a roar. The fernlike foliage is often smoky gray, and the flowers are blue to purple. They look particularly handsome in containers, where soil conditions can be more easily controlled, but regardless of where they are placed in the garden, they perform best in cool climates. I saw happy plants all over the place in Calgary, Alberta (zone 3), and in Portland, Seattle, Vancouver, and Columbus, Ohio. In such places, plants do fine and are indeed worthy of the inevitable oohs and aahs. However, the further south one gardens, the less chance of success. Unfortunately, the Armitage garden is like hell on earth for this plant, and the oohs

and aahs are replaced by "Where did it go?" I suggest you might want to plant them with other more stable plants, since it is not uncommon for plants to go dormant in the summer. This happens faster in warm summers than cool, but they will reemerge the next spring (except in the Armitage garden). A number of similar cultivars are offered; 'Blue Panda' is the most common, and 'China Blue' has smoky blue flowers. Partial shade, excellent drainage, zones 5 to 7.

The easiest, brightest, and most vigorous of the corydalis for most gardeners—*Corydalis lutea*, yellow corydalis—can be found rocking and rolling in nooks and crannies in Northeast, Midwest, and

Northwest gardens. Small, plentiful yellow flowers cover the green ferny foliage on the 9- to 15-inch-tall plants. These happy musical plants form a billion or so viable seeds resulting in more plants, all happy little critters. Such exuberance is most visible on the West Coast and in the Midwest, but the music is quite faint in the South. 'Alba', a white variant of the species, is worth a try if you get tired of yellow. Partial shade, good drainage, zones 5 to 7.

A few hybrids and one or two other species have quietly found their way to North American gardens, and although I have not tried them all, I have seen enough to know I want to try more. I believe I enjoy the

Crocosmia 'Lucifer'

foliage as much as the flowers. The leaves of 'Manchu' are soft and fernlike and soften the plants around it. Similarly, leaves of 'Berry Exciting' are equally easy to love and complement the purple flowers. One of the best I have seen is 'Canary Feathers', whose blue-green leaves and large yellow flowers are indeed eye-catching. Find these and try them out; you may be pleasantly surprised.

Crocosmia

When a well-grown crocosmia is in full flower, it is like a magnet. Plants produce entirely unexciting 8- to 15-inch-long strap-like leaves, but when the flowers appear, get out of the way! Up to a hundred flowers occur on stems held well above the foliage. Cultivars may be found in bulb catalogs as

Crocosmia 'Walberton Red'

Crocosmia 'Lucifer'

Crocosmia 'Emberglow'

well as general plant catalogs, which speaks highly of the widespread performance and popularity of this group of plants.

The most popular is 'Lucifer', whose scarlet-red flowers blaze through the summer, combining so well with everything that it makes it difficult to take your eyes off that devil. 'Lucifer' has been fashionable for years, and his intense color combined with his vigor and ease of cultivation will keep him near the top of the crocosmia list for years to come. However, there are certainly other choices. In the reds, I think 'Walberton Red' is almost as good, and in fact, its smaller stature is quite useful where 'Lucifer' can get out of hand. 'Emberglow' is also a good choice, also a little less vigorous than 'Lucifer'. Yellow- and orange-flowered forms can also be found. 'Rowallane' has been

Crocosmia 'Rowallane'

Crocosmia 'Walberton Yellow'

Crocosmia 'Star of the East'

around for some time and is a handsome addition to the garden, but in the yellows, I would choose 'Walberton Yellow' if I could find it for sale. Vigorous, full of flowers, and outstanding color. Another crocosmia that's caught my eye is 'Star of the East', producing compact plants with many handsome orange-yellow flowers. All crocosmias are terrific for cut flowers as well.

Full sun for all cultivars. Wet soils result in rotting roots; container planting is useful to improve drainage. Spider mites are a common problem, especially if plants are stressed. Hardy in zones 5 to 8.

Dahlia

Dahlias are plants that people seem to love or dislike with equal passion. In some areas of the country, they are true no-brainers, the mainstays of the summer and fall garden; in others, they require the weekly maintenance chores of stalking, spraying, deadheading, and Japanese beetle--plucking. Yet their beauty is undeniable, and the diversity within the hybrids equals that of chrysanthemums or peonies. The hybrids are roughly divided into two camps: the taller, more traditional display types, and the low growers, often raised from seed and thought of almost as a bedding plant. Some of the latter forms include the Amazon series, such as 'Amazon Pink and Rose' and 'Amazon Salmon Yellow'. Other beautiful forms are 'Bicolor Scarlet with Yellow' and the fabulous 'Goldalia'. I have always enjoyed the purple-leaved forms because of the interest the foliage provides even when not in flower. Two good choices are 'Mystic Illusion' and 'Moonfire', but many others are available. These shorter forms are meant to flower most of the season and provide persistent flowering and good color for a long period of time.

Dahlia 'Amazon Pink and Rose'

Dahlia 'Amazon Salmon Yellow'

Dahlia 'Bicolor Scarlet with Yellow'

Dahlia 'Goldalia'

Dahlia 'Mystic Illusion'

Dahlia 'Moonfire'

Dahlia 'Murdoch'

Dahlia 'Dare Devil'

Dahlia 'Lindy'

Dahlia 'Prince Charming'

Dahlia 'Worton Blue Streak'

Dahlia 'Vassio Meggos'

However, in the medium to tall display forms, there are hundreds from which to choose. In reds, 'Murdoch', 'Dare Devil', and 'Lindy' are excellent, while you won't be disappointed with 'Worton Blue Streak' or the crazy-looking 'Vassio Meggos' when looking for pink to lavender shades. 'Prince Charming' offers a nice white, an essential color when trying to combine dahlias in the garden. The taller forms are at their best in late summer and fall, and with their amazing colors and huge flowers, they simply blow people away. Tubers must be dug after the first frost in zones 6 and colder. In areas of hot, humid summers, diseases and insect pests can make gardeners question their belief in their purchase. Full sun.

Delphinium

How can anyone not appreciate a well-grown delphinium? I knew that plants in many colors, sizes, and flower types were offered, but I never had the opportunity to see their forces aligned until I wandered into a cultivar trial at Wisley Gardens, Surrey, England. It was almost enough to make me renew my vows to the Commonwealth and Queen. Although we see fewer than ten percent of the available taxa in our

Delphinium elatum hybrids on trial at RHS Wisley

Delphinium at Quatre Vents with Vinnie

Delphinium 'Sonata'

Delphinium 'Molly Buchanan'

Delphinium 'Alice Artindale'

gardens, it was nice to know that interest in this Old World plant has not diminished. I was not disappointed when I wandered up to Quatre Vents Garden near Quebec City in Canada and reveled in a delphinium fog. They were spectacular. My good friend Vinnie Simeone, a dyed-in-the-wool tree man, almost hugged them. Not quite, he has his standards, but he too was in awe.

Delphiniums will never be as beautiful in Atlanta as they are in Montreal, but people will try nevertheless. They can be grown in the South, but the term "perennial" must be discarded. It is simply necessary to accept that delphiniums are annuals there (plant in October, enjoy in early spring, and pull out in June), and two- or three-year perennials elsewhere. In the South, plant

at least a full one-gallon plant in October, otherwise insufficient rooting will occur by spring. In the North, plant either in the spring or in September.

A wide range of *Delphinium* species has been used in breeding; some of the more common hybrids, most often involving *Delphinium elatum*, are mixtures sold under the names of Round Table series, Mid-Century

Delphinium 'Sungleam'

Delphinium 'Candle Lavender Shades'

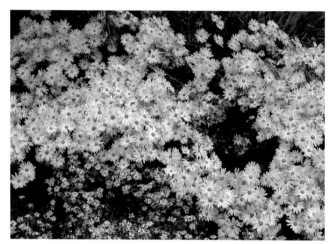

Dendranthema 'Ryan's Daisy'

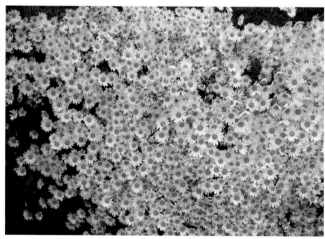

Dendranthema 'Apricot Single'

hybrids, and Connecticut Yankee series. It is worth spending the time, however, trying to locate named cultivars in shades of deep blue ('Sonata', 'Molly Buchanan'), light blue ('Alice Artindale'), lavender ('Candle Lavender Shades'), or yellow ('Sungleam') for next spring's garden. All delphiniums, from dwarfs to six-footers, love cool summers and cold, snow-covered winters for best perenniality.

The older cultivars are grown from seed and are tall and vigorous. With the many newer selections, there seems to be no end to the colors and sizes of this fine plant. Full sun, good drainage, zones 3 to 6 in the East, zone 8 on the West Coast.

Dendranthema ×*koreana*
KOREAN MUM

Plants in the genus used to be included in the genus *Chrysanthemum*, but taxonomists split up the large genus into different groups, including this one. *Dendranthema* includes cut mums, pot mums, and fall mums, but in my opinion, the very best

Dendranthema 'Apricot Single'

Dendranthema 'Ryan's Daisy'

Dianthus barbatus 'Sooty'

Dianthus barbatus 'Indian Carpet' in bud

Dianthus barbatus 'Indian Carpet'

Dianthus barbatus 'Sweet Coral Magic'

garden plants are the Korean mums. My favorite is 'Apricot Single', simply one of the very best fall-flowering plants I have ever trialed. The plants grow about 2 feet tall and bear hundreds of flowers; it is almost impossible to see the foliage when plants are in flower. The flowers are white, tinged with apricot. A no-brainer! 'Ryan's Daisy' produces hundreds of beautiful pink and white flowers. Both selections flower late in the fall and may be too late for Northern gardeners. Full sun, zone 3.

Dianthus
PINKS

The garden pinks just keep getting better. I bet I have trialed hundreds of these things if I have trialed one, and yes, there are dogs, but in the main, the pinks are simply great garden plants. You have to love the fact that the common name does not come from the fact that many dianthus flowers are pink, but rather from the fact the petals are cut, as if by pinking shears. Even though most people younger than thirty will not have

a clue what pinking shears are, it is still fun to tell their mothers. With about three hundred species of *Dianthus*, it should not come as any surprise that many people find a few of them better-than-average garden plants. By far the best-known member of this large genus is the carnation, *Dianthus caryophyllus*; millions of stems a year are cut from farms in South America and shipped to your downtown florist. (They travel a long way to get to your table, so don't be too surprised if they are not as fresh as you would like.)

Dianthus gratianopolitanus 'Bath's Pink'

Dianthus gratianopolitanus 'Firewitch'

Dianthus 'Garden Spice Pink Imp'

Dianthus 'Garden Spice Pink Bicolor'

Dianthus 'Garden Spice Coral'

Dianthus 'ItSaul White'

If you ask a hundred gardeners what their very favorite dianthus is, more than eighty of them would respond, without hesitation, "Sweet William," *Dianthus barbatus*. It's hard to understand how such a beautiful plant could be named after William, duke of Cumberland, best known for brutally crushing a handful of revolts against the English in the mid 1700s. "Sweet" is not exactly the name William would have chosen for himself. But these biennials have been around for a long time and will surely be popular for years to come. They are easy to identify by their unique flower buds and clusters of flowers in an array of colors. 'Indian Carpet' is an older selection and still quite available, but look for 'Sooty', another old timer and one of my sentimental favorites, or 'Sweet Coral Magic', another preferred cultivar. Messenger Mix makes a fine cutting mixture; flowers persist for about five to seven days in a vase of water. Sweet Williams persist for only two years but occasionally reseed to provide some long-term guests. Provide full sun and well-drained soils. Hardy in zones 3 to 8.

Most pinks being sold today are cultivars of cheddar pinks (*D. gratianopolitanus*) or hybrids with them. They originated in an area around the town of Cheddar, in southern England, where the famous cheese is made. The plant that made these pinks explode was 'Bath's Pink', a wonderful pink-flowered plant with blue-green foliage named for Jane Bath of Stone Mountain, Georgia. In areas of mild winters, the leaves are evergreen and bring useful color to the winter scene. In the spring, they cover ground, hang over walls, and are almost indestructible. 'Firewitch' was developed in Germany, and with her rosy flowers and rounded habit, she has proven to be one of the best plants developed in recent years. She tends to flower on and off in the season, being one of the best return-

Dianthus 'Miss Pinky'

Dianthus 'Neon Star'

Dianthus 'Pixie Star'

Dianthus 'Cranberry Ice'

Dianthus 'Raspberry Swirl'

Dianthus barbatus Messenger Mix

Dicentra canadensis

Dicentra 'Bountiful'

flowerers in the genus. These plants have a pleasant fragrance, some subtle, some not so, but I can think of nothing better than eating cheese, drinking wine, and watching the cheddar pinks flower. Full sun, zones 3 to 8.

In recent years, a number of extraordinary hybrids have appeared. I can't say enough good things about the Garden Spice series, in many colors. Plants include a fabulous 'Garden Spice Pink' and 'Garden Spice Pink Bicolor'. The best performer is probably 'Garden Spice Coral', with plants that flower for months at a time. They are tolerant of heat, cold, wet, and drought. Garden Spice members are short, no more than a foot tall, but if you are looking for something with a bit more oomph and double flowers, try 'Miss Pinky'. It is part of the Devon Cottage series, and others in that group are almost as good. The Star series is another front-of-the-garden short selection, in many colors. 'Pixie Star', 'Neon Star', and 'Shooting Star' are examples of this fine group of pinks. They must have excellent

drainage as they will suffer with wet feet. Additional hybrids keep coming out of the woodwork, like 'Cranberry Ice', with its pink and raspberry flavors, and 'Raspberry Swirl', part of the Dessert series of pinks. Fragrance is usually present in all the pinks, but it is hard to beat the fabulous fragrance of 'ItSaul White', aka 'Vanilla'. Absolutely one of the favorites in the garden when in flower. For all pinks, full sun is necessary.

Dicentra
BLEEDING HEART

The genus *Dicentra* is a popular old-fashioned group of plants that appeals to almost all gardeners. It contains woodland, garden, and vining members, all shade tolerant, with flowers in shades of white, pink, red, or yellow. Plants vary from the quite spectacular Japanese bleeding heart to handsome

Dicentra 'Luxuriant'

Dicentra 'Snowflakes'

Dicentra scandens 'Athens Yellow'

Dicentra spectabilis 'Alba'

natives like fringed bleeding heart—and we certainly can't forget about the most beautiful but fleeting woodlander, squirrel corn, *Dicentra canadensis*. The forms are quite different, but as with other well-established plants, additional cultivars and hybrids have appeared on the garden scene.

Perhaps because our native fringed bleeding heart (*Dicentra eximia* in the East, *D. formosa* in the West) is a homeboy rather than a guest, people tend to consider it a little too common. Many novice gardeners look at it and don't see as brilliant a plant as the common bleeding heart, *D. spectabilis*, from Japan, but in fact, it offers the gardener a great deal more. First, our native species don't go dormant, and second, they offer much

more diversity than the imports. If one visits the open spaces of an eastern or western forest, fringed bleeding heart is likely much in evidence.

Green leaves with pink flowers are the norm, but breeders continue to provide us with leaves of green to bronze and flowers of white, purple, pink, and red; some may be selections of *Dicentra eximia* or *D. formosa*, or hybrids between the two species. 'Bountiful' and 'Luxuriant' offer deep red and rose-red flowers, respectively, while 'Snowflakes' brings white to the garden. The Heart series consists of large-flowered selections on relatively small plants; my favorite is 'King of Hearts'. If you can find the old-fashioned 'Percy Piper', you will discover a plant with handsome blue-

green leaves. Many other cultivars, equally handsome, are also available. Partial shade (morning sun) is recommended, but too much shade results in few flowers. Hardy in zones 3 to 8.

A climbing bleeding heart . . . with yellow flowers? Who knew? If you are looking for a plant that stops people in their tracks, try *Dicentra scandens*, a climber with hundreds of yellow lockets of flowers. They meander through shrubs or up a trellis, growing from dozens of twining stems. These vigorous plants grow about 10 feet tall, and starting in late spring or early summer, bright yellow flowers cover the vine. The leaves and flowers of this yellow climbing bleeding heart are much smaller than those of vines like *Clematis*, but its

Dicentra 'King of Hearts'

Dicentra scandens 'Athens Yellow'

Dicentra 'Percy Piper'

June and August, depending on summer temperatures and rainfall. This is a normal part of the growth cycle for this Japanese species. Annuals and late perennials can be used to cover the soil left bare by plants that have died back. In early spring, plants push through the ground, their compound leaves and flowers already formed. They can make substantial specimens, growing 4 feet tall and equally wide on well-established plantings. The pink and white lockets of flowers, whose hearts are no doubt bleeding, hang down from the flower stems in spring and persist for four to six weeks, depending on temperature. It is the most impressive of the bleeding hearts, especially in containers in the retail stores—and that helps to explain its wild popularity.

The pink-flowered species itself is by far the most common. 'Alba', with its white hearts and slightly smaller plants, is no less beautiful. However, as if people did not find them spectacular enough, they will flock to 'Gold Heart'. The chartreuse foliage lights up the garden in early spring and still maintains a handsome glow as temperatures warm up. Flowers are similar to the

uniqueness will more than make up for the effort needed to find it. Plants require more sun than other species of bleeding heart; full afternoon sun should still be avoided. Hardy in zones 7 to 9.

'Athens Yellow' came from seedlings of a plant brought to Athens, Georgia, from Ireland; it has brighter yellow flowers and

is more vigorous than the type. Most plants sold are likely this cultivar.

Dicentra spectabilis, common bleeding heart, undergoes a major metamorphosis each year, emerging early in the spring and going dormant in late summer. Gardeners sometimes wonder what they did wrong as they watch plants disappear between

Dicentra spectabilis 'Gold Heart' in early spring

species. Place plants in friable, loose soil. Plants tolerate full sun in the North but prefer afternoon shade in most other areas. The more sun, the more the soil dries out and the faster plants go dormant; on the other hand, too much shade results in few flowers. Hardy in zones 3 to 7.

Digitalis
FOXGLOVE

Best known for that wonderful English weed, *Digitalis purpurea* (common foxglove), the genus includes some other outstanding, but little-known, members as well. All are characterized by many flowers held on long spike-like rods in spring or early summer, and slowly but surely, the other lesser-

Dicentra spectabilis 'Gold Heart' later in spring

Digitalis grandiflora

Digitalis ×mertonensis

Digitalis ×mertonensis

Digitalis grandiflora

Digitalis lutea

Digitalis lutea

known members of the genus are strutting their stuff. All the same, at least ten times more *D. purpurea* is sold than all other foxgloves together, the result not only of its availability but also of its functionality, large flowers, and many colors.

The "grandiflora" of *Digitalis grandiflora* (yellow foxglove) means "large-flowered"—a bit of a misnomer. Large they are compared to some foxgloves (such as *D. lutea*, another yellow-flowered species), but they are smaller than those

of common foxglove and others. They do, however, have a couple of good characteristics going for them. First, the yellow flowers, with their brown spots within, are rather handsome, and second, the plants are much more persistent than *D. purpurea* in the landscape. These true perennials should return for at least five years; eight-to ten-year stints are not uncommon. They grow 2 to 3 feet tall and tolerate partial shade and moist conditions. Hardy in zones 3 to 8.

The diversity of the genus *Digitalis* never ceases to amaze me, and when I first discovered strawberry foxglove, *Digitalis ×mertonensis*, I was charmed. The rosette of large leaves is darker green than common foxglove and far more ornamental. The large pink to rose-red flowers—like a ripening strawberry, not yet edible—are borne on one side of the flower stem only. Put about three plants together so that sufficient flowers are massed to catch the eye. These 3- to 4-foot-tall hybrids persist

Digitalis purpurea 'Giant Shirley'

Digitalis purpurea 'Emerson'

Digitalis purpurea with tulips

for about two to three years, longer than *D. purpurea* but shorter lived than *D. grandiflora*. Place in partial shade and moist soils. Hardy in zones 3 to 8.

Most of the foxgloves we use in our gardens are native to the European continent and the United Kingdom. A native stand of *Digitalis purpurea*, common foxglove, in Ireland or Scotland is as breathtaking to the American traveler as our stands of asters are to the visiting European. As long as one remembers that *D. purpurea* is a biennial and needs to be purchased either as a one-year-old plant in the spring or planted in the fall to receive sufficient cold, then this species is a no-brainer. The need for a cold treatment is absolute, but since it is so popular, nobody seems to give it much thought. Plants may produce 4-foot-long flower spikes in the spring in any number of colors. In flower, they are awesome and look beautiful with late tulips. The leaves decline soon after, as plants start to die back. Plant removal might as well be done sooner than later. All plants are raised from seed.

Separate colors of white, like 'Emerson', as well as apricot or yellow flowers can sometimes be found, but most cultivars are available as a mixed bag of colors. Some of the best loved are the tall Excelsior Group, the shorter but equally brilliant Foxy Group, and 'Giant Shirley'. The admiration of these noble plants is shared by hundreds of gardeners and millions of bees, both of whom are ever present when the flowers open. While the pharmacological properties of common foxglove are well known, nobody but my hypochondriac friends tucks it in the garden for that reason. Place in partial shade; provide morning sun and moist organic soils. Hardy in zones 4 to 8.

Disporum flavens

Disporum flavens

Disporum sessile 'Variegatum'

Disporum sessile 'Variegatum' filling in

Disporum sessile 'Variegatum' filled in

Disporum
FAIRY BELLS

The fairy bells are one of those woodland flora that separate a lover of plants from a lover of garden design. As one of my garden colleagues stated, "I can't design a garden to save my life, but I love fairy bells." *Disporum* consists of about fifteen species of shade-tolerant plants, native to North America, China, and Japan. While I want to be a native kind of guy, I must admit that I most enjoy yellow fairy bells, *Disporum flavens*, from Japan. This plant ranks right up there in my great shade plant list, alongside some of the jacks (*Arisaema*) and gingers (*Asarum*). In the spring, the plants emerge from their leafy winter quarters with a mighty stretch, first unfurling their light green foliage then showing off their butter-yellow flowers. Sounds pretty impressive, especially when you realize the plant is 2 to 3 feet tall and 12 inches wide. Place in threes and you will be rewarded with a stunning sight. The flowers persist for many weeks, followed by round black fruit. Plant in partial shade; dense shade is tolerated but not appreciated. Avoid heavy clay soils. Hardy in zones 4 to 8.

'Variegatum', a selection of *Disporum sessile*, is not as tall or as vigorous, but its white-and-green variegated foliage is pleasing to the eye. Plants are more stoloniferous and thus spread around more easily than *D. flavens*, but they are only about 12 inches tall. I plant mine at the edge of my woodland garden, so it gets a few hours of light. However, even in reasonably deep shade, plants will grow. In fact, this is best thought of as a ground cover, moving through the ground with stolons. Plants are 9 to 12 inches tall and will form a carpet after two to three years. The flowers tend to blend into the foliage because they too are variegated; the black fruit which follows continues to be ornamental. A fun plant—get down on your hands and knees to admire it fully. Partial to full shade, zones 5 to 8.

Chinese fairy bells, *Disporum cantoniensis*, comes out of the ground like gray shoots of bamboo and can grow to

Disporum cantoniensis

Disporum cantoniensis

Disporopsis fuscopicta

Disporopsis pernyi

Dryopteris erythrosora with Solomon's seal

considerable size, especially if tied to a support. Most people don't go to such trouble, and the plants will stand up until a good wind or rain knocks it over. The nodding flowers are the lightest yellow, fading to white. Zones 5 to 8.

A similar genus is *Disporopsis*, which means "looks like *Disporum*" (and they do). While they don't compete with *Disporum flavens* for color, they are even better plants for the shaded garden; the leathery bright green leaves persist all year, and the white flowers, similar to Solomon's seal, are handsome in the spring. The easiest is the evergreen Solomon's seal, *Disporopsis pernyi*, native to China. It is a slow grower, produces small nodding white flowers in

the spring, and generally stays less than a foot tall. Plants require absolutely no maintenance. Chinese Solomon's seal, *D. fuscopicta*, is more vigorous than the previous species but with equally wonderful shiny leaves. Small white flowers occur in the spring. Disporopsis are likely cold hardy to zone 5.

Dryopteris
WOOD FERN

So much of the Armitage garden was in deep shade that at first I despaired of ever finding good tough plants for the area. It took me no time at all to realize that shade was not at all bad. Soon I found all sorts of goodies,

and in the process, reacquainted myself with the world of ferns. I found a half-dozen easy, no-maintenance ferns that made life much easier in the shade, one group being the wood ferns. They are among the toughest, adaptable, and versatile ferns available to the North American gardener.

Dryopteris erythrosora, autumn fern, tolerates deep shade (where it can be united with other shade lovers like Solomon's seal) but is also adaptable to areas of full morning sun. Plants can grow 2 to 3 feet tall and equally wide, making a significant impact in the shaded garden. The large fronds, up to 2 feet long and 10 to 12 inches wide, are the best part of the fern by far, emerging bronze in the spring and tending to stay

Dryopteris erythrosora new growth

Dryopteris erythrosora 'Brilliance'

Dryopteris filix-mas

Dryopteris filix-mas 'Barnesii'

Dryopteris filix-mas 'Linearis Polydactyla'

Dryopteris marginalis

that way throughout the summer, resulting in a subtle colorful look, and not just a filler for shade. Plants are evergreen the rest of the year. This is a no-brainer fern and will not disappoint. 'Brilliance' is a selection with the bronze color evenly distributed over the foliage. I can't say it is a great deal better than the species, but it is nice to see a cultivar of this fine fern now available. Plant in rich organic soils, zones 5 to 9.

Another outstanding tough fern is *Dryopteris filix-mas*, male fern. For years I have used male fern in the deepest shade and worst soil in the Armitage dungeon, and it is the one fern I can count on to return year after year, better than ever. For all its vigor, the planting remains in one

Dryopteris celsa

Dryopteris cycadina

Dryopteris sieboldii

Dryopteris marginalis underside

spot and does not run all over the place. Nothing colorful, nothing flashy, just a good blue-collar plant. Several selections are popular with male fern--ites, such as 'Barnesii' and 'Linearis Polydactyla'. They generally differ in the shape of the pinnae (leaflets) and tips of the fronds. Shade, moisture, and reasonable soil help in the performance of the plant, but they are tolerant of drying out and poor soils. Hardy in zones 4 to 8.

Dryopteris marginalis, the marginal wood fern, is a better fern for the North than the South, preferring moist, cool climes for best performance. The "marginal" part of its name comes from the arrangement of the spore cases on the margins of the undersides of the fronds. The fiddleheads (the unfolding fronds) are covered with a golden brown "fur," and the leathery fronds remain evergreen. Plants are about 2 feet tall and equally wide. Place in drifts of six to twelve plants in organically rich, moisture-retentive soils. Hardy in zones 4 to 7.

Dryopteris celsa, log fern, is a natural hybrid between southern shield fern, *D. ludoviciana*, and Goldie's wood fern, *D. goldiana*. Both parents are tough, and the 3-foot-tall clumps of evergreen leaves make a wonderful full show. *Dryopteris cycadina*, shaggy wood fern, should be better known. There is nothing flashy about it, but plants grow well and are trouble-free.

Many of these temperate ferns are difficult for those without a reasonable winter, so I think Siebold's wood fern, *Dryopteris sieboldii*, is well worth a try for gardeners in the Deep South. Plants are slow-growing but produce interesting compound leathery fronds. They may overwinter in zone 7, but they will never form a decent clump. Better for zones 8 to 11.

Echinacea
PURPLE CONEFLOWER

"Take your echinacea pill, dear" says my health-conscious wife as she presents me a tidy concoction of *Echinacea purpurea* (purple coneflower), ginkgo, and

Echinacea pallida lining driveway

Echinacea pallida

goldenseal to swallow. I no longer think of my stomach as a functioning organ of digestion but rather as my private botanical garden. On the other hand, after downing onion blossoms and ribs at the local restaurant, who am I to complain about healthy additives?

Few genera go through such a transformation in a decade that the genus is almost unrecognizable from what came before. This genus was always known as purple coneflower because, except for a few white selections, the flowers were purple. Today there are flowers in white, yellow, pink, and orange, in a "normal" daisy shape and even some that have been doubled, looking like a chrysanthemum whose belt is too tight.

Although the hybrids dominate the demand and the pocketbooks of gardeners, there are still a few species that are great fun. One that gets attention and a guaranteed second look is *Echinacea pallida*, the pale coneflower. The thin pale pink to purple ray flowers take a little getting used to; however, the combination of those flowers and the raised central disk is quite lovely. In a marvelous garden in Niagara-on-the-Lake, Ontario, created by garden designer Tom Laviolette, they were lining the driveway. Most creative. Plants grow to about 3 feet in height and tend to fall over in a good summer rain. They return for three to five years, asking little in the way of care. Plant in full sun, in almost any soil—include at least three plants, spaced a foot apart, to create a fuller-looking group of flowers. Blooms occur in summer. Hardy in zones 4 to 8.

When I first saw the purple coneflower with yellow flowers (*Echinacea paradoxa*), I was not at all sure what it was. "This is a paradox," my guide said, and I nodded sagely—then quickly went to my dictionary to look up the meaning of the word. Plants look like common purple coneflower, although not as vigorous, but they have

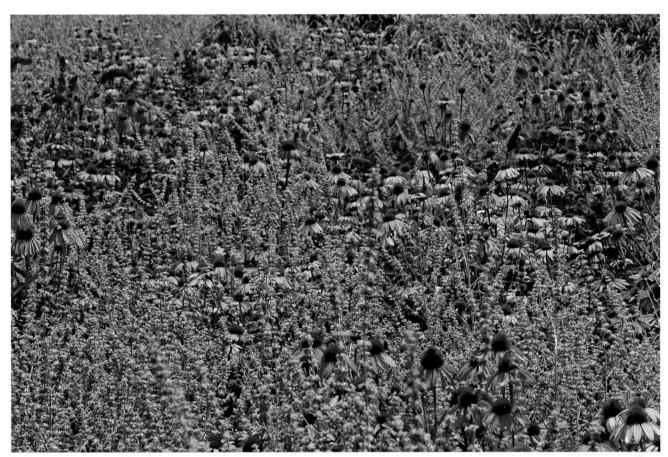

Echinacea purpurea and Russian sage

yellowish ray flowers and are surprisingly fragrant. They are not long lasting but may be worth trying just for the paradox of it. Hardy in zones 4 to 7.

Echinacea purpurea was and is one of the great prairie flowers of all times. Can you imagine Lewis and Clark first setting their eyes upon the majestic vistas of grasses and wildflowers and enormous populations of animal life in their journey across the American prairie? A trip to the great prairie gardens at the Chicago Botanic Garden or the Holden Arboretum outside Cleveland fills me with joy and sadness—joy at the incredible diversity of plants that graced the land, mixed with sadness that so few of these areas thrive any longer. Purple coneflower has made the transition from the prairie to the backyard as well as any native plant—and better than most.

Echinacea 'Kim's Knee High'

Echinacea paradoxa

Echinacea 'Magnus'

Echinacea 'Rubinstern'

Echinacea 'Vintage Wine'

Echinacea 'Crazy Pink'

Echinacea 'White Swan'

Echinacea 'Mars'

Echinacea 'Fragrant Angel'

The ray flowers often droop downward off the black central cone, and plants rise in height from 3 feet in full sun to 4 to 5 feet in partial shade. They are best if planted in full sun in almost any soil.

Some tinkering of this beautiful plant occurred when the breeders and selectors found plants with subtle differences in color and habit, making them neater and fuller in flower than the original. One of these is 'Kim's Knee High', a dwarf form that I recommend to my daughters, each beginning their garden journeys. Others that are purplish include 'Magnus', a very popular form, and 'Rubinstern'. Newer purple forms

Echinacea 'Kim's Mop Head'

Echinacea 'Orange Meadowbrite'

Echinacea 'Big Sky Summer Sky'

Echinacea 'Big Sky Sunrise'

Echinacea 'Tiki Torch'

Echinacea 'Flamethrower'

are 'Vintage Wine', with wine-colored blossoms, 'Crazy Pink', a floriferous plant with bright flowers over a compact plant body, and 'Mars'. There are dozens of purple forms and in truth, if all purple cultivars were lined up, I doubt seriously whether one person in a hundred could tell you which cultivar was which; I would be in the group of ninety-nine, that is for sure. Vigor is an important characteristic of purple coneflowers, and that is why I accept the white forms of purple coneflowers so readily. White always fits in with current garden styles. The oldest and in my opinion, still the best is 'White Swan'. 'Kim's Mop Head' and 'Fragrant Angel' have their moments—but not as many as 'White Swan'.

Breeders like Jim Ault, Dan Heims, and Richard Saul have made such extraordinary advances with the genus that all should get a medal of some kind. By hybridizing a number of species, including those mentioned above, these breeders have taken the gardening world by storm. The downside of these spectacular plants is that we have to learn how to grow them all over again. There are long discourses being written on why the new hybrids don't seem to be as vigorous or winter hardy as they "should be." The two most important things a gardener can do is first, look at the roots when buying, and second, plant them early. If the root system does not fill the container, the producer did not grow it long enough. Equally important, do not plant young plants after 1 July. We can abuse purple coneflowers and their purple and white selections, but not so with the fancy ones.

Echinacea 'Tangerine Dream'

I don't really know where to start with the fancy forms; perhaps we should begin with the beginning of the hybrid movement, 'Orange Meadowbrite' and 'Mango Meadowbrite'. They originated in the Chicago Botanic Garden, and they started it all. The Big Sky series has also made its

Echinacea 'Razzmatazz'

Echinacea 'Pink Double Delight'

Echinacea 'Pink Poodle'

Echinops ritro

Echinops ritro 'Taplow Blue'

mark and includes 'Big Sky Summer Sky' and 'Big Sky Sunrise' as well as many others. 'Tiki Torch', 'Flamethrower', and 'Tangerine Dream' can knock your socks off with their brilliant hues of orange, but I think the prize for the most bizarre must be the double forms. Starting with 'Razzmatazz', we then moved to the excellent 'Pink Double Delight'. They are reasonably good performers and possess a pleasant fragrance to boot. They still sort of looked like purple coneflowers, but oh my, how about 'Pink Poodle'? There is no end, and as I write this, there are another dozen cultivars hitting the trial garden. I am not sure where it will stop,

but if we spend our money carefully, it sure will be fun to try some of these. Full sun, zones 3 to 8.

Echinops ritro
GLOBE THISTLE

Blue flowers will always occupy an important place in gardens, and when a vigorous plant provides globe-like interesting blue flower heads, that plant becomes popular. The flower heads and leaves of this species are rather prickly to the touch, so I find it most enjoyable mixed in with other equally vigorous plants like the coneflowers and sea

hollies. They make excellent cut flowers, fresh or dried, but picking them is not a lot of fun. Plants grow to 5 feet in height and 3 to 4 feet across. They attract swarms of bees, so check the flowers before you put your nose too close. They also attract aphids, which can disfigure both leaves and flowers. Plants do better in the North than in the South.

A few selections are offered, but they are all similar to each other and if truth be told, similar to the species itself. 'Taplow Blue' is the main listing in catalogs and nurseries and grows 2 to 3 feet tall; 'Taplow Purple' is, well, a little more purple. Plant

Echinops ritro

Epimedium grandiflorum

Epimedium grandiflorum 'Rose Queen'

Epimedium grandiflorum 'Lilafee'

Epimedium ×*rubrum* 'Sweetheart'

in full sun, in any reasonable garden soil, zones 3 to 7.

Epimedium
BARRENWORT

If you have shade, you should have epimediums. Ten years ago, only a handful of species were available, but recent explorations in Japan and China and excellent breeding efforts have brought additional species and more interest to this fine group of plants.

Epimedium grandiflorum, longspur barrenwort, is easiest to find in nurseries and one of the finest species sold. The

deciduous plants have the typical oblique leaves of the genus; the tough good-looking foliage makes them excellent as ground covers under trees and in woodland environments. The flowers are among the largest in the available barrenworts, sporting long spurs on pale pink flowers in early spring. The flowers, which often emerge before or at the same time as the foliage, persist for four to six weeks. While tolerant of deep shade, they perform better in an area with morning sun and afternoon shade. Similarly, provide moisture when needed, especially if plants are competing

with tree roots. They are drought tolerant but not that tolerant.

'Rose Queen' is the most common cultivar of *Epimedium grandiflorum* offered, with outstanding rosy red flowers. The lilac flowers of 'Lilafee' are not quite as large, but they are outstanding when they stand above the foliage. Hardy in zones 5 to 8.

I love *Epimedium* ×*rubrum*, red barrenwort, for a couple of reasons. In the Armitage potpourri I call a garden, the plants remain evergreen and are even reasonably handsome in the winter, not just plants with leaves that refuse to fall off. The new leaves, which emerge in early

Epimedium ×rubrum 'Sweetheart'

Epimedium ×versicolor 'Sulphureum'

Epimedium ×versicolor 'Sulphureum'

Epimedium ×perralchicum 'Frohnleiten'

Epimedium ×perralchicum 'Frohnleiten' in winter

Epimedium ×rubrum

spring, are suffused with red, both around the margins and splotched on the bronzy leaf blades. The red flowers are not large, but they appear in numbers and persist as well as any other barrenwort. 'Sweetheart' is wonderful new cultivar with larger leaves and larger flowers. This is one cultivar well worth seeking out. *Epimedium ×rubrum* is easy, undemanding, and colorful. For tolerance to dry shade, it has few equals. Hardy in zones 5 to 8.

Let's face it. All barrenworts share many similarities: they are low-growing, work well in the shade, and are seldom noticed by those admiring some noble beech or elegant elm. The comments that accompany the other barrenworts mentioned can be dittoed here for *Epimedium ×versicolor*

Epimedium ×setosum

Epimedium brachyrrhizum

So many epimediums, so few known. Allow me to introduce a few more that have graced the dry shade of my garden. For small but delightful white flowers, *Epimedium ×setosum* is wonderful. Perhaps the antithesis for flower size is *E. brachyrrhizum*, with pale pink nodding flowers. The brilliant orange flowers of *E. ×warleyense* are small and can get lost among brown leaves in the spring, but it is still worth searching out. And lastly, *E. pubigerum* is among the tallest of the barrenworts and has lots of rosy pink flowers well above the foliage. And to the epimedium lovers out there, sit tight: we are trialing at least a dozen more as you read this.

Epimedium pubigerum

Eremurus
FOXTAIL LILY

'Sulphureum'. The flowers are the earliest to emerge, appearing before the foliage. The new foliage has the same red-bronze branding as those of the red barrenwort, but the leaves are much larger. The old leaves are also evergreen but should be removed as soon as you spy the first flower. They only detract from the wonderful yellow flowers, and additional foliage will appear, taking the place of what you remove. An exceptionally good plant, tough as nails and reliable.

Full to partial shade, moisture is appreciated. Hardy in zones 4 to 8.

While we are talking about yellow-flowered epimediums, I cannot in all conscience omit one of the most vigorous and reliable of the worts, *Epimedium ×perralchicum* 'Frohnleiten', with its dark green leathery leaves and wonderful bright flowers. Not only is it outstanding when it is supposed to be, it is the best epimedium for winter foliage. A winner in all respects!

Foxtail lilies are not for just anyone—their presence signifies an adventuresome person, willing to go places others fear to tread. It is not a plant to be found while roaming the plant bins at the local WalMart but is not at all difficult to find through mail-order catalogs and decent nurseries. However, once you see the stately colorful candles rising 3 to 8 feet in height in late spring and summer, you will have to procure some. Like a grand fireworks show, the foxtail lilies rocket with momentary greatness, then

Eremurus stenophyllus

Eremurus ×isabellinus Highdown hybrid

Eremurus himalaicus

Eryngium alpinum

totally disappear, nothing but an explosive memory. It is a stretch to portray pastels and whites as explosive colors, but the pastels of *Eremurus ×isabellinus* (encompassing several hybrid strains, including Highdown hybrids, Shelford hybrids, and Ruiter hybrids) or the glorious white of *E. himalaicus* cannot be described as subtle. When I was walking down the street in Waterloo, Ontario, I glimpsed the flaming flowers of *E. stenophyllus*, which are simply impossible to miss. I have seen plants as far north as Norway, in Canada and the upper Midwest, and on the northwest coast of the United States. They do not do particularly well in the South. In most gardens, plants seldom return for more than a year or two, but if they are protected and luck is with you, a few more years of fireworks may be

yours. Plant the tentacle-like rhizomes in a large hole, so that the tentacles are not cramped. They must not be allowed to dry out before planting, and moisture is necessary after planting. They will be the main show when in flower; however, place other plants around them so once they disappear, they will not be missed. Enjoy the show. Full sun, hardy in zones 5 to 7.

Eryngium
SEA HOLLY

Live near the sea, plant sea oats. Or sea kale, or sea thrift, or simply enjoy the seaside with sea urchins. If you need to be reminded of the sea, you can also try sea holly. A number of fine species can be found, and while many are not even

Eryngium planum

Eryngium alpinum 'Amethyst'

Eryngium alpinum 'Blue Star'

Eryngium ×zabelii 'Donard Variety'

remotely native to a coastline, they are all colorful (usually silver or bluish) and certainly interesting. Many make long-lasting cut flowers, but beware of the prickly

flowers—they are much better to look at than to handle.

Some of the largest flowers and intensely colorful plants in the genus belong

to *Eryngium alpinum*, the alpine sea holly. Certainly in northern climes, a blue tinge will appear on the stems and flowers of this species in early to mid summer, when the

Eryngium giganteum

Eryngium giganteum 'Silver Ghost'

Eryngium yuccifolium

Eryngium yuccifolium

flowers are at their peak. Even when not at their peak, the immature flowers can be as handsome as the finished product. 'Amethyst' has bright blue flowers and stems; 'Blue Star', with lavender-blue bracts, is probably the most common, while 'Donard Variety', a hybrid with *E. alpinum*, bears spectacular flowers. Plants grow 2 to $2\frac{1}{2}$ feet tall, and soft bracts extend from the flowers. Soft is relative, however, and even these bracts can provide some unwanted pain. The leaves are coarse and dull green. Place in well-drained soils and full sun. Their maritime upbringing makes alpine sea hollies more comfortable in sand than clay. Hardy in zones 4 to 7.

Eryngium giganteum, or Miss Willmott's ghost, may be the plant for people who have everything. The common name comes from an eccentric English gardeness who, like Johnny Appleseed, surreptitiously scattered seeds of this plant while visiting other gardens, so it popped up everywhere she had been. Plants provide history, surprise, and ornamental value, and large flowers of steely silver rather than blue.

These 3- to 4-foot-tall biennials tend to disappear after flowering, but in areas where the Lady is happy, she will return from seed—if not the next year, then the year after, sneaking up on you like the ghost she is. Unfortunately, Miss Willmott's ghost is not happy in warm summers and is not often seen in the East; but she haunts the Northwest with glee.

Eryngium giganteum 'Silver Ghost' is shorter (about 2 feet tall) and has large heads of gray-white flowers—not quite as ghostly but otherwise differing little from the species. Plant in well-drained soils, or sandy soils in full sun. Hardy in zones 4 to 8.

This genus seems to have an identity issue, and sometimes look like anything but a sea holly. The eastern native *Eryngium yuccifolium*, rattlesnake master, supposedly cures rattlesnake bites or even drives the snakes away. Right, I'll remember that next time I hear the hissing of a rattler. The leaves are narrow (like those of yucca), and the small flowers are creamy white and almost without bracts. Plants grow 3 to 4 feet tall.

Eryngium agavifolium

Eryngium variifolium

Eucomis comosa

Eucomis 'Sparkling Burgundy'

The foliage of *Eryngium agavifolium*, agave sea holly, looks like an agave and is similar to the previous plant, only much more spiny. Both *E. agavifolium* and *E. yuccifolium* are heat tolerant and amenable to poor soils. The best part about them is that they are fun to have in the garden: they keep people guessing as to just what those plants want to be when they grow up. Full sun, reasonable soils. Both hardy in zones 5 to 9.

Other species bring other ornamental properties to the garden. *Eryngium variifolium*, marbled sea holly, has silvery, spiny bracts atop a 1-foot plant. It is most unusual in having marbled evergreen leaves, looking good even before the flowers emerge. *Eryngium planum* bears dozens of small blue flowers and may be the best choice for small gardens; 'Jade Frost' is a variegated selection with green and yellow flowers.

Eucomis
PINEAPPLE LILY

Here is a small genus (approximately ten species) that has become more popular as more cultivars become available. The term "pineapple" comes from the pineapple-like bracts on the top of long beautiful flower spikes, which are also quite wonderful. The foliage too can be eye-catching, especially on those cultivars with purple leaves. *Eucomis comosa* bears large straplike green leaves and long spires of white flowers in late spring.

Eucomis 'Sparkling Burgundy'

Eucomis 'Sparkling Burgundy' in bud

Eucomis 'Tugela Ruby'

Eucomis 'Can Can'

Eucomis 'Tugela Ruby'

Eucomis 'Reuben'

Eucomis zambesiaca

This is not a small plant and can be quite spectacular when in flower.

The popularity of pineapple lily skyrocketed with the introduction of 'Sparkling Burgundy'. The emerging leaves are almost deep purple and stay that way for a month or two, depending on how rapidly summer temperatures arrive. The many white flowers are highlighted on purple flower stems. This is still the best selection—if pineapple lilies are in your future, find it and buy it. However, others are almost as good. 'Tugela Ruby' also emerges with dark leaves and is even more vigorous and larger

Eucomis 'Reuben'

Eupatorium purpureum 'Little Red'

Conoclinium coelestinum

than 'Sparkling Burgundy'. The flowers are creamy white but with an obvious purple eye. I believe 'Reuben' will be the next great pineapple lily, as numbers become available. The leaves have a hint of purple on the margins, but the dark purple flower buds give rise to rosy pink flowers. The green pineapple bracts top them off.

All the plants mentioned stand 2 to 3 feet and are significant garden plants. 'Can Can' is only 12 to 15 inches tall with cleaner white flowers and a pink eye. For those wanting even shorter plants, try the 9- to 12-inch *Eucomis zambesiaca*, with somewhat pleated leaves and white flowers.

Sometimes bulbs of lesser-known selections are hard to find. Leaves cut into sections will root if placed in well-drained soils and kept moist.

Eupatorium
JOE-PYE WEED

To see some of our native plants glowing on their own and complementing other ornamentals makes you proud to be an American; too bad you often have to go overseas to appreciate the glow. This was brought home most clearly when I took a fall trip to the British Isles and admired the Joe-pye weeds towering over our asters and black-eyed Susans. I knew I would see asters and Susans, but I

wasn't prepared for all the Joes. However, times are a-changing. We can now easily find half a dozen species in North American gardens, and as a group they are quickly attracting converts. Particularly good for the autumn, but some are impressive all season.

"Where did these fall-flowering ageratums come from? That is some bedding plant variety!" That was the first thing I thought when I came upon *Eupatorium coelestinum* (*Conoclinium coelestinum*; hardy ageratum) in a Midwest garden. Since I was supposed to be

Conoclinium coelestinum 'Album'

Eupatorium purpureum in a mixed bed

Eupatorium purpureum 'Bartered Bride'

Eupatorium purpureum with goldenrod

the expert, I kept quiet and listened as the real expert, the gardener, cursed this "darn weed." That is why experts are experts: they keep their mouths shut and learn from gardeners. The darn weed is pale blue to lavender and grows 2 to 3 feet tall. The lanky growth makes it a little weedy, and more people enjoy it at the edge of the woods rather than in the middle of the garden. It is essentially unnoticed until the flowers appear in late summer and fall, and then it is everywhere. A terrific weed, much more tolerant of heat than most other members of the genus. By the way, you might want to wear gloves when you pull out this weed, as it does not smell very good. A white selection, 'Album', is also available. Partial shade, good moisture. Hardy in zones 6 (perhaps 5) to 10.

Native in much of the eastern half of the country, *Eupatorium purpureum* (Joe-pye weed) is particularly impressive in the Smoky and Appalachian ranges. One certainly does not ever need to go to a "garden" to appreciate them; they are marvelous in their natural settings. However, in the garden, where a little fertilizer and water are provided, I have seen 10-foot-tall backdrops provided by just a few plants, each topped with large inflorescences of

claret-colored flowers in the fall. They are best in areas with cool summers and consistent rainfall, so unfortunately, the Armitage garden in north Georgia can only offer some puny 3-foot-tall excuses for the species. But when happy Joe-pyes are complementing the grasses, the goldenrods (*Solidago*), or the daylilies in the fall, the yard is magically transformed into a garden. 'Bartered Bride' is a washed-out white form that can grow to 8 feet tall. Butterflies,

Eupatorium purpureum 'Little Joe'

Eupatorium maculatum 'Atropurpureum'

Eupatorium maculatum 'Gateway'

Ageratina altissima 'Chocolate'

bees, and birds swarm about, and they look almost as good as they did when Joe Pye discovered them in the mountains. Shorter forms have been bred, none of which are exactly short. 'Little Red' has redder flowers on about 5-foot-tall stems; 'Little Joe' is compact with a height of 3 to 4 feet.

Nurseries and catalogs offer similar plants, such as *Eupatorium maculatum*, spotted Joe-pye weed. The main difference is that *E. maculatum* has purple-spotted stems; otherwise, the habit and flowers of the two species are nearly the same. 'Atropurpureum', a purple-leaved selection, provides stunning purple hues from soil level to flower top. If the thought of 8-foot-tall plants in the garden is a little overwhelming, *E. maculatum* 'Gateway', smaller

but still a robust 5 feet tall, is otherwise similar to the type. Provide full sun and well-drained soils for both species, hardy in zones 4 to 7.

White snakeroot, *Eupatorium rugosum* (*Ageratina altissima*), is beginning to attract a loyal following among adventurous gardeners. Plants grow to 5 feet in height and are topped by white flowers in summer and early fall. I have seen excellent specimens in European and North American gardens, but some of the best were in the outstanding display gardens at Blue Meadow Nursery in the Berkshires of western Massachusetts. Cold temperatures are no problem, but heat is not appreciated. A most useful cultivar, 'Chocolate', is admired more for its bronze to purple foliage than

Ageratina altissima 'Chocolate'

for its white flowers, which appear in late summer. Plants are only 2 feet tall and are more shade tolerant than the species. Full sun and reasonable soils are needed. Hardy in zones 3 to 7.

Euphorbia characias subsp. *wulfenii*

Euphorbia 'Blue Lagoon'

Euphorbia 'Rudolph'

Euphorbia 'Blackbird'

Euphorbia
SPURGE

In a complex genus of nearly two thousand species, where does one start? All spurges have colorful bracts and milky sap (keep it out of your eyes: it hurts!). The best known is the ubiquitous Christmas plant, the poinsettia, *Euphorbia pulcherrima*. Garden forms have multiplied recently, some far easier to grow than others. I certainly have tried a good number, with occasional success, but have killed my fair share as well.

The handsome 4- to 5-foot-tall upright plants of *Euphorbia characias*, Mediterranean spurge, have blue-green foliage and yellow bracts that are outstanding in early spring. That the species is native to the Mediterranean region should provide a hint as to its range of cold and moisture tolerance, but where winters are reasonably mild (zone 7 and south) and soils not waterlogged, plants thrive and reseed with abandon. Although they persist for only a few years, another population generally is starting up while others are dying down.

The most common variant, subspecies *wulfenii*, is shorter (3 to 4 feet tall) but otherwise quite similar. Many of the new hybrids have a good deal of this subspecies in their parentage. The 3-foot-tall 'Blue Lagoon' is a marvelous grower that tolerates warm climates better than most. 'Rudolph' has red stems and slightly red tips on the stems and yellow flowers, while 'Shorty' provides yellow bracts in early spring before the good blue-green foliage. Both are only about 2 feet tall. Breeders have recently paid more attention to the foliage. 'Blackbird', with its dark purple leaves is really quite beautiful, even without the purple bracts. 'Glacier Blue' and 'Tasmanian Tiger' are breakthroughs, although these plants struggle in areas where summer temperatures are hot. I have seen the latter very much at home in the Northwest, but save your money if you garden south of zone 6 in the East. One of the better selections is 'Helena's Blush'. Her multicolored foliage is handsome all summer and only gets better as temperatures get cooler in the late fall and winter (assuming they don't freeze). We use it in containers and have been very pleased

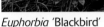

Euphorbia 'Blackbird'

Euphorbia 'Tasmanian Tiger'

Euphorbia 'Helena's Blush'

Euphorbia 'Glacier Blue'

Euphorbia dulcis 'Chameleon'

with its performance. Even if she doesn't overwinter, she makes an excellent annual. Most gardeners shouldn't expect more than three years of good performance with many of the hybrids— more in the northern limit of their hardiness, less as you move further south. Full sun to partial shade, and well-drained soils are essential. Hardy in zones 6 (occasionally zone 5) to 7 in the East, zone 8 in the West.

Some of the older choices are still available. The purple *Euphorbia dulcis* 'Chameleon' (chameleon spurge) grows in mounds rather than upright or spreading. It can be beautiful in combination with green or white plants around it, but its range has proven to be rather narrow: it looks poor where too warm and dies where too cold. However, it is certainly worth a try if loose change is rattling around in your pocket. Full sun, reasonable soils, hardy in zones 5 to 7.

Most garden spurges bear yellow bracts, but Griffith's spurge, *Euphorbia griffithii*, has red to orange ones. Vigorous growth with thick stems and fleshy leaves make this a winner where it can be

Euphorbia 'Shorty'

grown. Like *E. dulcis*, its range of happiness is limited in this country. In the Northwest, it thrives; in the Midwest, it also does well; in the South, it dies. 'Fireglow' (with bright orange-red bracts) is similar to the species. Full sun, well-drained soils. Hardy in zones 5 to 7.

Euphorbia griffithii 'Fireglow'

Euphorbia cyparissias 'Fen's Ruby'

Euphorbia myrsinites

Euphorbia myrsinites

Gaillardia 'Tizzy'

Euphorbia cyparissias, cypress spurge, is the antithesis of poor performance among spurges. This ground-hugging plant is aggressive and is listed as invasive in many states. Often called graveyard weed, it was widely planted in cemeteries. However, it grows well in shady areas, and its yellow flowers and delicate foliage can be hard to resist. If you absolutely cannot live without the plant, the best choice is 'Fen's Ruby', which provides colorful ruby ends to the stems. The color is lost in the summer but is quite eye-catching in the spring. Not quite as invasive, but no shrinking violet either. Wear gloves when ripping this out (which you will surely do in a few years) as there have been numerous reports of dermatitis from handling the plants. Zones 4 to 8.

The stems of *Euphorbia myrsinites*, the myrtle spurge, are covered in whorled blue-green leaves and terminate in sulfur-colored bracts. A great ground cover, but in areas of the Southeast and Southwest, where it reseeds with abandon, it may be considered a handsome 6- to 9-inch pernicious weed. On the other end of the height spectrum is *E. lathyris*, caper spurge, a fun-to-grow plant with an upright habit, wonderful green flowers, and bluish fruit that resembles capers. Plants may reseed but are not considered invasive. Its reputation of discouraging gophers and voles is suspect, but it certainly attracts attention. Great fun! Full sun to partial shade, moist soils. Myrtle spurge is hardy in zones 5 to 9, caper spurge in zones 6 to 9.

Gaillardia
BLANKETFLOWER

Blanketflower has been rediscovered by plant breeders and gardeners and is one of the most colorful and long-flowering plants in the garden. Most cultivars available today are hybrids (likely *Gaillardia* ×*grandiflora*) involving at least two species. One of the biggest issues is winter hardiness. Depending on parentage, they may return after Chicago winters; others may not return after an Atlanta winter. Blanketflowers are quite happy growing on a beach, that is, in sandy areas where water immediately drains away. Thus, poor drainage, especially if winter water is allowed to accumulate, is a sure ingredient for death.

Gaillardia 'Fanfare'

Gaillardia 'Goblin'

Gaillardia 'Oranges and Lemons'

Gaillardia 'Sunburst Halo'

Gaillardia 'Gallo Bicolor'

Regardless, plants are not particularly long-lived: four years is an excellent run, two years is frustratingly normal. Plants may grow up to 3 feet tall, but most available cultivars are shorter and more compact, usually extending only 12 to 18 inches. The daisy flowers are made up of many colors (thus the "blanket" in blanketflower) and may be up to $2\frac{1}{2}$ inches wide.

A number of relatively tall forms found their way to North American gardens, and they are terrific. The Commotion series brought vigorous plants with big multicolored crazy-looking flowers. The best was 'Tizzy'; the other 'Frenzy'. Wonderfully chaotic. 'Oranges and Lemons' was about 3 feet tall and showed off gorgeous flowers in those colors. The shorter, more compact

Gaillardia 'Mesa Yellow'

Gaillardia 'Sunburst Tangerine'

Gaillardia 'Georgia Yellow'

Gaillardia 'Georgia Yellow' with *Scaevola*

selections are by far more common; one of the earliest and best was 'Fanfare' a low grower with multicolored flowers, so named because the ray flowers ("petals") looked like small trumpets, thus the "fanfare." The excitement in gaillardia breeding has brought many more choices to the retail bench. All are compact and flower most of the summer. The choice in yellow and orange flowers are many; 'Goblin' is perhaps the oldest and best known. This is a fine performer, but newer ones like 'Sunburst Halo' and 'Georgia Sunset' flower longer and have fewer problems.

In yellow shades, no lack of options is evident. 'Gallo Bicolor' is the best of the Gallo series, while 'Mesa Yellow' is an excellent compact yellow form. 'Sunburst Tangerine' presents a beautiful color and is likely the best of that series. Lastly, for sheer flower power, it is difficult to beat 'Georgia Yellow': plants flower literally from the beginning of spring until the end of fall. Put it with a long-flowering blue like *Scaevola* 'Cajun Blue' and get out of the way. Full sun and well-drained soils are necessary. Good drainage is essential, otherwise plants rot overnight. Hardy in zones 4 to 9.

Gaura lindheimeri in containers

Gaura lindheimeri

The generic name comes from the Greek *gauros* ("superb"), a probable reference to the flowers of this genus, which consists of about twenty species; but only our Texas native, *Gaura lindheimeri*, has made its way into North American gardens. The plants have become popular because they are tough as nails, putting up with blistering sun, terrible soils, and parking lot abuse. They are excellent for containers, an important consideration in today's gardens. The foliage is handsome enough, although half a dozen plants are needed to make a full planting. It is, however, those superb flowers fluttering in the breeze like a swirl of butterflies that entrance gardeners.

Gaura lindheimeri 'Geyser White'

Gaura lindheimeri 'Pink Picotee' with needlegrass

Gaura lindheimeri 'Karalee White'

Gaura lindheimeri 'Summer Breeze'

Gaura lindheimeri 'Pink Picotee'

Gaura lindheimeri 'Karalee Petite Pink'

Gaura lindheimeri 'Geyser Pink'

Gaura lindheimeri 'Karalee Petite Pink'

Geranium macrorrhizum 'Ingwersen's Variety'

Geranium ×*cantabrigiense* 'Biokovo''

Flowers are available mainly in white, pink, or rose. The whites tend to be more vigorous. Some of the best are 'Geyser White', 'Karalee White', and my favorite, 'Summer Breeze'. All are about 3 feet tall, and all look terrific in containers or in the ground. The first good pink was 'Siskiyou Pink', introduced by Baldassare Mineo of Siskiyou Rare Plant Nursery in Medford, Oregon. That plant was the progenitor of many more excellent pink- to rose-flowered selections. 'Pink Picotee' is outstanding, especially when combined with soft grasses like needlegrass (*Nassella*). I also like 'Geyser Pink' with its softer shades of pink, but the best landscape plant, in my opinion, is 'Karalee Petite Pink'. Plants are short, never fall over, and bear outstanding deep pink leaves and flowers. It never fails to impress.

Deadheading spent flowers is necessary for best performance. When plants start to decline, take the flower stems like a hank of hair and cut them back to the foliage. New flowers will take their place, but only if old ones are removed. Full sun is necessary, good drainage. Hardy in zones 5 to 8.

Geranium
CRANESBILL

Geraniums are a collector's dream, so diverse that they can be collected like fine silver. From prostrate dwarfs to those that scramble through shrubs, from purple to rosy red flowers, geraniums provide something for everyone. As a gardener, I have gone through my "geranium stage of life" and no longer have to try every new (or old) geranium that finds its way into a catalog or the garden center. Now I can waste my

Geranium endressii 'Wargrave Pink'

Geranium 'Ann Folkard'

Geranium psilostemon 'Patricia'

Geranium ×cantabrigiense 'Karmina'

Geranium 'Ann Folkard'

money on other groups of plants, trying to find a single good one in a hundred tries. All geraniums have palmate (shaped like a hand) leaves, five-petaled flowers, and fruit reminiscent of a crane's bill, hence the common name.

Geraniums are not really known as a ground cover, but bigroot geranium, *Geranium macrorrhizum*, is used just that way in temperate climate gardens. Plants have large leaves and rose-colored flowers. 'Ingwersen's Variety' is one of the most common forms and bears lighter flowers than the species. Plants tolerate some shade and with a little moisture can soften the edge of a driveway or cover a hill. It's easy to identify this plant by smelling its leaves. I think

they smell somewhat medicinal, others think they smell worse, but nevertheless, it is smelly only if you roll in it. *Geranium ×cantabrigiense*, hardy geranium, is a hybrid using bigroot geranium as a parent. The flowers of 'Biokovo' are light pink, almost white from a distance, while those of 'Karmina' are far darker. They are mounding plants, not ground covers, and highly recommended by gardeners everywhere. Plants seldom grow taller than 12 inches, 8 to 10 inches being more common. Full sun to partial shade, hardy in zones 5 to 7.

Many hybrids have been produced, but a few species and their selections are still hanging in there. 'Wargrave Pink', a selection of Endress's geranium, *Geranium*

Geranium sanguineum 'Striatum'

endressii, is reasonably common in areas that do not get too hot or too cold, and enjoys consistently good reviews in many

Geranium phaeum 'Samobor'

Geranium sanguineum 'Tiny Monster'

Geranium sanguineum

Geranium phaeum 'Margaret Wilson' with tiarellas

Geranium sanguineum 'Alan Bloom'

Geranium 'Orion'

Geranium 'Midnight Reiter'

parts of the country. Plants can grow up to 18 inches tall and are covered in spring by 1-inch-wide, notch-petaled, salmon-pink flowers. This is one of my choices for the beginning geranium collector. Partial shade, good drainage, zones 4 to 7. *Geranium psilostemon*, the Armenian geranium, is a plant that can't figure out whether it should be a vine or a normal plant—and therefore has become a scrambler. Its long stems, if properly maintained, form shrub-like mounds of light green foliage, 3 feet tall and equally wide. Like a kid after a playground fight, each magenta flower sports a large black eye. This is a big lanky

plant, but if supported, it is a people stopper. 'Ann Folkard' is a hybrid involving *G. psilostemon* and is a true scrambler, growing through and over small shrubs. The leaves are almost chartreuse, and the flowers have similar rose-red to magenta flowers. Where happy, Ann takes the form of the plant it is growing through. It seems to be happiest on the West Coast, but gardeners in the Midwest and Northeast are claiming some success. The South has not been as friendly. On the other hand, 'Patricia' is far better in warm climates, and while not as exciting as Miss Ann, she is a far better plant for more stressful

environments. She has done well as far south as Athens, Georgia, and north to Columbus, Ohio. Full sun to partial shade, good drainage, zones 5 to 7.

Geranium phaeum, mourning widow, can get rather tall and kind of weedy-looking. The nodding purple flowers are handsome, although they don't show up terribly well against the leaves. 'Samobor' is a better plant, less lanky and with far more handsome foliage. Still big, and lousy in the heat. I can't wait to see more of 'Margaret Wilson', whose striking bright foliage is well worth a few nickels. I don't think she will do well in the heat, but there are plenty

Geranium 'Rozanne'

Geranium pratense 'Hocus Pocus'

Geranium 'Rozanne'

of other places in this country where she may look good.

Geranium sanguineum, bloody cranesbill, is the toughest species in the genus. Plants thrive in the North and the South, from the West Coast to the East. If other geraniums are letting you down, try the bloody cranesbill. The common name sounds like a medieval battle, and the name alone makes plants worthy of a little space. Growing about 12 inches tall, they are covered with magenta flowers beginning in the spring and continuing for six to eight weeks. The leaves are small, helping it to retain moisture in hot, dry times. This cranesbill is not nearly as sexy as many others

Geranium maculatum

Geranium maculatum 'Espresso'

but makes up for it by its reliability. 'Alan Bloom' is a wonderful mounding form and commemorates a great horticulturist. If magenta is a little hard to take, try my favorite, 'Striatum'. The pink flowers are easy to work in with other plants in the garden. We tried a plant called 'Tiny Monster', and we wondered if it would be tiny or monstrous. The biggest bloody cranesbill we have ever seen! But a lot of fun to grow. Full sun, reasonable drainage. Hardy in zones 3 to 8.

Dozens of other species and selections are available, and in recent years, some outstanding hybrids have been developed, making geranium growing a lot easier. 'Orion' is big but full of lavender-blue flowers. Tough as nails. I have seen beautiful stands of the dark-leaved 'Midnight Reiter', but they don't tolerate eastern conditions very well and have not been as persistent as hoped for. However, they are beautiful when they find the right place. 'Hocus Pocus' is also dark-leaved but appears to be far more resilient. I am looking forward to good feedback on this recent selection of *Geranium pratense*. There is no doubt, however, that 'Rozanne' is the most important geranium to come to the American garden in the last twenty years. The lavender flowers are handsome, the foliage is healthy and vigorous, but its claim

Hakonechloa macra 'Aureola'

to fame is the long blooming times. They flower from May until frost, and even then a little longer. If you have not tried 'Rozanne', do so—it will be money well spent.

I would be remiss if I concluded this great genus without mentioning our wonderful eastern native, the spotted geranium, *Geranium maculatum*. The leaves bear random white spots and the flowers are pink to lavender. Plants tolerate shade, very much unlike most of the others mentioned here. 'Espresso' has dark leaves and darker flowers and has grown well in the Armitage garden.

Hakonechloa macra
HAKONE GRASS

Where hakone grass is thriving, it is one of the most handsome and most eye-catching grasses of all. What a terrific sight! *Hakonechloa macra* (rolls off the tongue, doesn't it?) is a shiny 12- to 15-inch-tall green-and-yellow dwarf grass from Japan that sparkles in the late afternoon sun, bringing alive whatever corner of the garden it calls home. The foliage has a layered effect, sometimes layered too perfectly to be

Hakonechloa macra 'Albovariegata'

Hakonechloa macra 'All Gold'

Hakonechloa macra 'Aureola'

Helenium 'Riverton Beauty'

normal. This slow-growing grass's cascading habit, fresh look, and pinkish red fall color give it its season-long appeal. One of the few colorful grasses at home in partial shade, it consorts freely with the likes of astilbes and hellebores.

All the cultivars look similar from a distance, all sporting combinations of green and gold. The golden variegated *Hakonechloa macra* 'Aureola' is particularly handsome, ranging from plants with some gold to those that shimmer in the sunlight. 'All Gold', with golden foliage, was recently introduced, but I don't see a lot of differences between it and what is already out there. 'Alboaurea' and 'Albovariegata' are also listed—it really does

not matter. Get one for a partially shaded area, provide some moisture, and get out of the way. I like all the cultivars; I only wish they were a little quicker to grow and more tolerant of the abuse heaped upon them in southern gardens, where, truth be told, they struggle. Partial shade, consistent moisture, and compost-laden soils are best. Hardy in zones 6 and 7.

Helenium
SNEEZEWEED

I have been a hay fever sufferer forever, and many people have commented that I am allergic to my job, especially in the fall.

Obviously someone with hay fever coined the common name for this North American genus. I am not sure that sneezeweed competes with ragweed for sneezing honors, but I don't put my nose in the middle of a flower to test it either. Regardless of its name, *Helenium* offers some fine fall-flowering plants that are real color-makers at that time of year.

Although the genus consists of over thirty species, the hybrids associated with *Helenium autumnale*, common sneezeweed, provide the greatest color and diversity. Many of the available cultivars have been around for decades, but the yellow tones of 'Riverton Beauty' and 'Gartensonne' are

Helenium 'Moerheim Beauty' with *Solidago* 'Fireworks'

Helenium 'Gartensonne'

Helenium 'Moerheim Beauty'

Helenium 'Mardi Gras'

Helenium 'Mardi Gras'

still sought after. Tones of orange are common as well, and the very best of the older varieties is 'Moerheim Beauty'. The plants are 3 to 4 feet tall, but the large orange flowers really catch the eye. It is beautiful when paired with a goldenrod like 'Fireworks'. Most of the sneezeweeds are well over 3 feet in height and need support to keep them upright. That is why I choose the 2½- to 3-foot-tall 'Mardi Gras' as the best of the new introductions. It flowers profusely with handsome orange flowers and seldom needs support. Plants can be cut back once in early summer to make them shorter and stronger. Full sun, well-drained soils are best. Hardy in zones 3 to 8.

Helianthus angustifolius

Helianthus salicifolius

Helianthus angustifolius 'First Light'

Helianthus angustifolius 'First Light'

Helianthus
SUNFLOWER

The sunflowers offer annuals (*Helianthus annuus*) and many perennials for gardeners to enjoy, oil for cooks, seeds for baseball players, and even vegetables like Jerusalem artichoke (*H. tuberosus*). The perennial sunflowers bring sunshine and beauty to the garden and should be as well known as the annual types. All require full sun, and most are large.

Helianthus angustifolius, the swamp sunflower, is a big plant, growing 5 to 8 feet tall and lighting up the fall garden like a spotlight in the night. Plants produce dozens of 1- to 1½-inch-wide flowers in September and October and continue to do so until frost. The 5- to 7-inch-long leaves are opposite, entire, and seldom troubled by bugs; however, I have seen awful fungus-riddled plants after lots of rain—the leaves blacken and are not a pretty sight. Under such conditions, an application of some fungicide would be helpful. The other drawback to the species is its aggressive nature: it will spread and may soon become a nightmare, requiring fibbing to friends about why they should be thanking you for the basket of white roots you are a little too eagerly providing. Full sun is an absolute must, resulting in strong stems and many flowers. If grown in shade, plants will stretch to over 8 feet tall, and then fall over. Cutting back plants in early May and again in early July will help keep it down. If height is a problem, 'First Light' may be a solution. Plants are far shorter, only about 3 feet, and even better behaved if cut back once in late spring. A similar plant but with much more narrow leaves is *H. salicifolius*, willow sunflower. Plants are as tall as

Helianthus salicifolius

Helianthus giganteus 'Sheila's Sunshine'

Helianthus 'Marc's Apollo'

Helianthus 'Lemon Queen'

Helianthus mollis

Helianthus mollis

swamp sunflower, but the foliage is more handsome and the ray flowers (petals) are more widely spread. Swamp sunflowers are hardy in zones 6 (with protection) to 8, willow sunflowers to zone 5.

Large is the norm for sunflowers, but the giant sunflower, *Helianthus giganteus*, is not for the faint of heart. Plants are 7 to 12 feet tall and seem to grow a foot a day. It doesn't spread like *H. angustifolius*, but the clump gets bigger and bigger. The prettiest selection is 'Sheila's Sunshine', with primrose-yellow flowers. Great plant, but get the metal stakes out—it will topple like a pine tree in a storm if not supported. Hardy in zones 5 to 9. 'Marc's Apollo' a hybrid introduced by the late great Marc Richardson of Goodness Grows Nursery in Lexington, Georgia, is equally large and equally beautiful. All suffer from loss of bottom leaves; by fall they may look like Ichabod Crane wearing knickers. The 6- to 8-foot-tall 'Lemon Queen' is more persistently dressed and has wonderful lemony yellow flowers.

The last sunflower I want to mention is way underused in North American gardens. The hairy sunflower, *Helianthus mollis*, has wonderful felt-like gray leaves and grows in a nice rounded form in the spring and summer. The leaves are soft, like lamb's ears, and everyone wants to rub them. In late summer, the sunflowers appear with a vengeance. Unfortunately, when the plant flowers, it loses its discipline, stretches, and needs support. It is also an aggressive grower, not invasive but not staying in one place either. While it has its problems, I think it is one of our better natives for foliage and flower color.

Heliopsis helianthoides
SUNFLOWER HELIOPSIS

I like the sunny disposition of sunflower heliopsis; plants generally have bright flowers for six to eight weeks, and plants

Heliopsis helianthoides 'Bressingham Doubloon'

Heliopsis helianthoides 'Summer Sun'

Heliopsis helianthoides 'Goldgreenheart'

are reasonably easy to cultivate. They grow about 3 feet tall, and the dark green serrated leaves are pleasant to the eye even when not in flower. The yellow to golden daisy flowers, 2 to $2\frac{1}{2}$ inches wide, are produced at the end of every stem. Unfortunately, other critters enjoy them as well, particularly Japanese beetles, aphids, and other chewing things. However, since gardeners like to share so much, we might as well share with the bugs too.

Many of the selections of *Heliopsis helianthoides* are hybrids between the type and variety *scabra*, which provides the coarse feel to the leaves. 'Summer Sun', a 2- to 3-foot-tall plant, is an older selection that keeps proving its value throughout

the country. 'Goldgreenheart', with its green heart surrounded by golden petals, may be a little gaudy, but we all need a little kitsch every now and then. 'Bressingham Doubloon' has some of the largest blossoms. The centers are large and a lovely contrast with the golden flowers. 'Prairie Sunset' and 'Summer Nights' have bright reddish centers and reddish stems. They work very well among other plants as they want to sprawl. No sense supporting them, just plant them with other teammates.

One of the most innovative recent introductions is 'Loraine Sunshine', whose variegated leaves and yellow flower make quite a contrast. As much as I like her in

Heliopsis helianthoides 'Prairie Sunset'

Heliopsis helianthoides 'Loraine Sunshine'

Heliopsis helianthoides 'Summer Nights'

Heliopsis helianthoides 'Tuscan Sun'

Helleborus orientalis

Calgary and Vancouver, I seldom see her looking good in the Midwest, or south of zone 5 east of the Rockies. However, the dwarf 'Tuscan Sun' seems to do well in a far greater range, and its dwarf habit makes it easy to place in the garden or containers. Full sun, well-drained soils. Hardy in zones 3 to 8, but better in the North than the South.

Helleborus
HELLEBORE

I can't imagine a late winter garden without a hellebore or two. They are as much a part of the coming of spring as the melting of snow. Unless there is no shade or conditions are too cold or too hot to grow them,

why would you not? Flowering long before the calendar date of spring, they come in a mix of flower color, leaf size, and vigor. Plants are evergreen and produce dozens of flowers with white, purple, or green sepals.

The most popular hellebore is Lenten rose, *Helleborus orientalis*, and deservedly so. The diversity of flowers is such that a greeting bowl of various colors is easy to do, and what a greeting it makes. The flower buds appear in late winter, and flowers occur in quite early spring. White and mauve are the common flower colors, but numerous cultivars have been introduced. The Royal Heritage strain is one of the most vigorous and produces large flowers in shades of purple and rose. Even

double flowers have found their way to the gardener; the Party Dress series provides them in rose and mauve and occasionally white. One of the drawbacks of this plant is that flowers nod down and are difficult to see unless we bend and kneel. Planting on a wall above a path is a great way to enjoy the plants and the flowers. Another way to see the flowers easier is to cut off all the leaves in January, February, or March, before the flowers open. Then the flowers are not obscured by the foliage, and the new leaves that emerge later are beautifully fresh. They persist for years, reseed easily, welcome spring even in the snow, remain in flower and fruit for months, and blend into the rest of the landscape once their day

Helleborus orientalis flowers in a bowl

Helleborus orientalis Royal Heritage strain

Helleborus orientalis planted above a path

Helleborus orientalis 'Party Dress Rose'

Helleborus foetidus

Leaves of *Helleborus foetidus* and *H. orientalis*

Helleborus niger

Helleborus argutifolius

is complete. Partial shade and reasonably well-drained soils boost longevity and their ability to produce seedlings. Hardy in zones 4 to 9.

Bearsfoot hellebore, *Helleborus foetidus*, is also commonly grown. The compound leaves, which consist of narrow fingerlike leaflets, provide outstanding foliage, and the small greenish flowers provide a show from February to June. Even the fruit, which forms after flowers have lost their color, provides garden value into late spring or early summer. Planted with small-flowering daffodils, Virginia bluebells, and hepaticas, this hellebore is a no-brainer. Plants don't reseed as abundantly as *H. orientalis*. Provide afternoon shade and well-drained soils. Hardy in zones 5 to 9.

The white flowers of *Helleborus niger*, the Christmas rose, provide a beautiful sharp contrast to the dark green foliage, making it the "cleanest" looking of the hellebores. It is also one of the earliest hellebores to flower. Plants are more difficult to establish than the previous two species; it nevertheless thrives where conditions are to its liking. It certainly looks fabulous in the fabulous garden of my good friend Barbara Stratton, in Niagara-on-the-Lake, Ontario. Try them in different moist, shady locations and leave them alone. Once established, they will reseed, and the colony will be well on its way. Another wonderful species to consider is the Corsican hellebore, *H. argutifolius*. These are vigorous plants, far bigger than the other species mentioned. The leaves consist of three leathery, finely serrated leaflets, above which reside the creamy flowers. 'Janet Starnes' has mottled leaves that are interesting, although it takes a while to love a plant that looks to be riddled with spider mites.

In the last ten years, plant breeders have succeeded in breeding all sorts of new hellebores. So stand back—the hellebore train has loaded up and left the station. Crosses with *Helleborus argutifolius* yielded *H. ×sternii*, a wonderful mounding plant that thrives in

Helleborus ×sternii

Helleborus argutifolius 'Janet Starnes'

Helleborus Blackthorn Group

Helleborus 'Ivory Prince'

Helleborus 'Pink Beauty'

Helleborus 'Ruby Glow'

Helleborus 'Heronswood Yellow'

Helleborus 'Winter Moonbeam'

Hemerocallis 'Stella Supreme'

Hemerocallis 'Sears Tower'

Hemerocallis 'Stella Supreme' and *H.* 'Sears Tower', modeled by Ben

the Northwest and in cool climates; Blackthorn Group is but one introduction of that marvelous cross. 'Heronswood Yellow', from the great Dan Hinkley, is one of the few hellebores that has yellow flowers; they are not deep yellow, but they are exceptional. The greatest advance, however, came with the advent of 'Ivory Prince'. This complex hybrid provides leaves with three leaflets and dozens of ivory flowers tinged with pink in very early spring, even late winter if the weather cooperates. The flowers are truly upright, a true breakthrough in hellebore breeding, relieving sore knees and backs. Recent introductions from tissue culture like 'Ruby Glow' and 'Pink Beauty' are spectacular, and 'Winter Moonbeam' provides handsome foliage and more colorful, upright flowers. Partial shade and well-drained soil with plenty of organic matter. Hardy in zones 3 to 8.

Hemerocallis
DAYLILY

Wherever the sun shines, there resides another daylily. I cannot keep up with the number of daylilies, that is for sure. Just when I think I know a few, another ten muscle into the gardens of America, each one trying to outdo the others. That daylilies are so popular obviously points to the obvious: they are colorful, available, and essentially trouble-free. They have been bred to within an inch of their lives, providing gardeners with a vast panorama of options: singles, doubles, rebloomers, dwarfs, giants, diploid, tetraploid—the beat goes on and the beat is good. However, in the pursuit of the next great daylily, we need not leave all the old ones behind. Regardless of where I travel, I see the old-fashioned pass-along daylily, *Hemerocallis fulva*, in ditches, by old farm gates, and planted in landscapes that want that traditional look. They are

Hemerocallis fulva

Hemerocallis fulva with *Hydrangea* 'Annabelle'

Hemerocallis 'Happy Returns'

Hemerocallis 'Black Ruffles'

Hemerocallis 'Moon Traveler'

Hemerocallis 'Luminous Jewel'

Hemerocallis 'Black Magic'

Hemerocallis 'Frans Hals'

Hemerocallis 'Carrick Wildon'

tough as nails; they come back every year, adding gaudy splashes of orange wherever they are sited.

Hemerocallis hybrids are categorized into various heights (dwarf, low, medium, and tall) and a dizzying array of flower shapes and colors. The landscape trade loves the dwarf forms because of the compact height and long flowering time. The Stella series came on like gangbusters, and the greatly improved 'Stella Supreme' is the best of all. When I teach these dwarf types to my

Hemerocallis 'Benchmark'

Hemerocallis 'Atlanta Irish Heart'

Hemerocallis 'Kindly Light'

Hemerocallis 'Red Rain'

Hepatica americana

students, I try to show them that the history of daylilies was not always predicated on short, compact types. In fact, I try to include a few boisterous selections from the past. I particularly love 'Sears Tower', bred by Al Goldner of Goldner Walsh Nursery in Pontiac, Michigan, to commemorate the timeless tower. During one class I had my student Ben Watson hold up stems of 'Sears' and 'Stella' to show the old and the new. How times have changed.

But to have daylilies is to have diversity. 'Happy Returns' has been a great favorite with landscapers and gardeners for its calm colors and long flowering time. You might also want to try 'Black Magic' or 'Black Ruffles' for the rose-purple hue, and 'Frans Hals' or 'Carrick Wildon' for bright orange tangerine colors. For more subtle tones, I still enjoy 'Moon Traveler' as a soft yellow, and for whites, 'Luminous Jewel' fits the bill. 'Benchmark' and 'Atlanta Irish Heart' are still favorite colors, while 'Kindly Light' and 'Red Rain' are interestingly scary. The retail market for daylilies changes to the flavor of the day, and those may be just perfect. However, online sources can provide even more choice.

Abundant blooms are produced when daylilies are planted in soils amended with manure or leaf mold. When plants first emerge in the spring, provide a well-balanced fertilizer to give them a kick start. Plants are heavy feeders and require constant moisture to be at their best. Of course, they don't appreciate boggy soils, and good drainage is important. So is full sun; too little sun results in few buds, and in some cultivars, buds may not open at all. In essence, when planning a site for your daylilies, choose an area of full sun, provide some fertilizer and moisture in a well-drained area, and get out of the way. Aphids can be a problem, but in general, choosing the right daylily is simply a matter of taste. Hardy in zones 3 to 9.

Hepatica
LIVERLEAF

My excitement over diminutive hepaticas often causes eyes to glaze over. When I finally found a nursery that was propagating liverleaf, not just digging it out of the wild, I was ecstatic. I had studied up

Hepatica americana

Hepatica acutiloba

Hepatica nobilis 'Rubra'

Hepatica nobilis 'Light Blue'

Hepatica transsilvanica

on this wonderful wildflower and had long lusted after our two wonderful eastern natives, *Hepatica acutiloba* and *H. americana*. Never growing more than 6 inches tall and as wide (I have to get down on all fours just to admire them), plants nonetheless can carpet a woodland area once established. Both species have small white or light blue flowers that are among the earliest to flower in the spring. In the Armitage garden, they emerge in late February and flower through April. They differ mainly in the shape of the three-lobed leaves: the lobes of *H. americana* are rounded, whereas those of *H. acutiloba* are pointed. Foliage is usually bronze to purple in the spring and green by and throughout summer. Most available

plants are grown from seed, therefore leaves may be spotted or entirely green. Similarly, flower color ranges from deep blue to white.

Several nonnative species have also generated a good deal of interest but are even more difficult to locate. *Hepatica nobilis* is native to northern Europe and is similar to *H. americana*. The plants have larger, bluer flowers, and selections of it have been offered with red ('Rubra') or light blue flowers. There is something fascinating about hepaticas with atypical flower colors; unfortunately, the effort to stabilize the colors of our native species has not received the same attention. If you can find *H. nobilis* or its selections and live in the North, go for it: they may be expensive, but if they live, they

will have been worth every dollar. Similar wallet shedding should be done without a second thought if the blue-flowering *H. transsilvanica* comes up for sale; its numerous handsome large flowers occur in early spring. Outstanding and eye-popping.

Hepaticas are among the many ephemerals that grace our garden in early spring. They are best placed in deciduous shade (under oaks or beeches, for instance), where they can enjoy full sun while flowering then disappear in the vegetation of later-emerging shade plants once the canopy fills in. They enjoy the company of rue anemone (*Anemonella thalictroides*), Virginia bluebells, and trilliums. Hardy in zones 3 to 7.

Heuchera 'Obsidian'

Heuchera 'Blackberry Jam'

Heucheras in a basket

Heuchera 'Citronelle'

Heuchera
CORAL BELLS

"Every time I open a catalog, I see that someone has developed a new heuchera. They have been around for many years, favorites of our grandmothers. But how many of these things do we really need?" I wrote those sentences more than a decade ago, and the statement is even more valid today. I have trialed at least sixty different cultivars, and I have missed more than I have seen. However, my curiosity still gets the best of me and, undisciplined as I am, I must try a few more every year. There was a time not so long ago that gardeners, particularly native plant enthusiasts, embraced our eastern native, *Heuchera americana*. The dark green leaves and the totally unspectacular flowers filled in areas of the woodland floor and could be put with other shade-lovers like hostas.

However, breeders have aggressively combined various species of coral bells to form stunning plants in vibrant foliage colors. It is impossible to show even a small percentage of the coral bells available today, but I can show you some of my favorites. They all look good in containers, so when choosing a plant, find a reputable nursery or garden center and ask them what they would recommend.

Dark foliage colors were one of the first breakthroughs, and dozens are available. One of the consistently best dark-leaved forms has been 'Blackberry Jam'; every year, plants are voted by students as one of the best coral bells in the Trial Gardens at UGA. 'Brownies' too has done well in our trials.

Heuchera americana with hostas

Heuchera 'Brownies' in spring

Heuchera 'Lime Rickey'

Heuchera 'Brownies' in late summer

Large mocha-colored leaves are terrific in the spring and early summer, and although they fade in the heat of an eastern summer, they still maintain excellent shape and performance. I have been taken with the shiny dark foliage of 'Obsidian', but chartreuse foliage also catches the eye. 'Lime Rickey' and 'Citronelle' are the two best plants in that category. Both tend to fade a little in the heat, and both, but particularly the latter, need heavy shade. They will turn brown with too much direct sun.

Leaf color is not the only thing that breeders have messed with. Ruffled leaves are popular, and the two best are 'Chocolate Ruffles' and 'Crimson Curls'. The latter is really ruffled and remains so all season. Coral bells with variegated foliage

Heuchera 'Chocolate Ruffles'

Heuchera 'Crimson Curls'

are best used in moderate climates like the West Coast or southwestern Ontario. They do poorly with heat and do not have the vigor found in other plants to get through very cold winters. However, 'Monet' and 'Snow Fire' are truly beautiful when they are thriving. Silver-veined foliage can be seen in 'Paris', which also has handsome red flowers. Green foliage is found in the Spice series, some of the best performers in gardens across the country, and some of the best selections for excellent flowers.

I think some of the prettiest coral bells have lighter foliage in shades of peach, salmon, tan—I can't describe the foliage colors but boy, some of them are beautiful. My number one choice for leaf color and garden performance for all heucheras is 'Caramel'. It grows north, south, east, and west, and gets rave reviews from all. However, 'Marmalade' and 'Ginger Ale' are similar and have their share of fans. The list goes on and on! The names of 'Southern Comfort' and 'Georgia Peach' let gardeners know that these tolerate heat well, and oh my, their colors are truly outstanding.

Many readers may have noticed a dearth of information about the flowers. The fact is, many of the heucheras bred for fancy foliage color have underwhelming

Heuchera 'Monet'

Heuchera sanguinea 'Snow Fire'

Heuchera 'Paris'

Heuchera 'Green Spice'

Heuchera 'Caramel'

Heuchera 'Ginger Ale'

Heuchera 'Southern Comfort'

Heuchera 'Marmalade'

Heuchera 'Georgia Peach'

Heuchera 'Strawberry Swirl'

Heuchera 'Vesuvius'

Heuchera 'Pink Lipstick'

Heuchera 'Rave On'

flowers that do little, if anything, for the plant. However, whoa, Nellie, because there are a few that are quite overwhelming. 'Strawberry Swirl' and 'Vesuvius' can really make a show, but my two favorites (probably because I know they will look good regardless of heat or cold) are 'Pink Lipstick', with good green foliage, and 'Rave On', with foliage so fancy that it looks good no matter where it is planted.

In areas of high summer temperatures, some coral bells may poop out by August. Put compost against the crowns, and most will return good as new next spring. Plants do well in moist soils and partial shade.

Although they will grow in heavy shade, leaf colors are more vibrant with two to three hours of direct morning sun. Plants are generally 1 to 2 feet tall and 2 feet wide, hardy in zones 4 to 9.

Hibiscus
MALLOW

These excellent plants have had sufficient cold hardiness bred into them that hybrids are easily found from Chicago to Montreal. To be sure, some of the species such as swamp hibiscus, *Hibiscus coccineus* (zone 6) and the Confederate rose, *H. mutabilis*

(zone 7b), are not as cold hardy but where they can be grown, they are quite spectacular. The former grows 3 to 5 feet tall with deep red flowers, while in the latter, the flowers open white or pink, then change to deeper red by the evening (the specific epithet, *mutabilis*, means "changing"). The most common form is variety *flore-pleno*, with large, double, pink flowers. *Hibiscus grandiflorus* (zone 6) is another underused but beautiful species with velvety smooth leaves and handsome, although not particularly plentiful, light pink flowers.

Hibiscus moscheutos, rose mallow, also called crimsoneyed rose mallow, is the

Hibiscus coccineus

Hibiscus mutabilis var. flore-pleno

Hibiscus grandiflorus

Hibiscus 'Kopper King'

Hibiscus grandiflorus

Hibiscus 'Pinot Grigio'

Hibiscus 'Fireball'

hibiscus for the North, at least to zone 5, and brings the look of the tropics to Baltimore and Chicago. Patience is needed for the plants to emerge in the spring; they are often among the last to arise. Once they do, they produce many woody stems and grow 3 to 4 feet tall. Everyone loves the flowers,

including a squadron of flying pests. In particular, hordes of Japanese beetles flock to its yummy leaves.

Many cultivars (likely hybrids of this species and two or three others) are available, representing all sorts of colors. The Disco series bears large flowers in many

colors and has been popular because of ease of production and compact habit. There are a number of fine white choices, such as 'Pinot Grigio' and 'Old Yella', both of which have a rosy purple eye. The latter is said to be very light yellow, but I don't see it. Light pink flowers are shown off with

Hibiscus mutabilis var. *flore-pleno*

Hibiscus Disco series

Hibiscus 'Old Yella'

Hibiscus 'Luna Pink Swirl'

Hibiscus 'Bordeaux'

Hibiscus 'Moy Grande'

Hostas by the pond

'Luna Pink Swirl', but if you are looking for some arresting color in pink, try 'Kopper King'. The pink flowers range from light to pink but the dark bronze foliage is quite remarkable. Fire engine red is easy to find; I like 'Bordeaux', and 'Fireball', but if I had choose but one, it would be 'Moy Grande'. The flowers are up to 10 inches across and abundantly produced on tough and reliable plants. Garden hibiscus should be placed in full sun; shade results in lanky, tall plants. Most cultivars are hardy in zones 5 to 9.

Hosta

Shade—you can either curse your misfortune or celebrate your good luck. If shade is attributable to the presence of mature hardwoods or conifers, then feel blessed not to have your house in a clear-cut subdivision. If, however, the shade is cast

Hostas lining a walkway

Hostas by the pond, after deer

Hosta plantaginea

Hosta 'Francee'

Hosta 'Segae'

by an "I love Jesus" billboard or something equally unbearable, get rid of whatever stands between you and the sun. Simple Armitage rule of thumb: trees stay, tree products go.

Hostas have a similar dichotomy. People love them or hate them. They are the most perfect plant to invite you to follow a walkway. America's love affair with hostas is still ardent but perhaps not quite as passionate as it was ten years ago. On the one hand there is nothing that can fill in shaded areas with season-long color as hostas do, and few shade plants are as diverse or as colorful as hostas. The Armitage garden was a hosta depository, and I loved nothing more than to walk among

them, morning coffee in hand, admiring them. But oh what a depressing sight when on a given morning I would walk out to find that deer had come to dine overnight. What had been a gorgeous scene by the edge of the pond one afternoon was a disaster the next morning! And once eaten, hostas don't have another growth spurt. Deer have made a serious dent in the number of hostas sold in the last number of years, as people realize that deer and hostas cannot coexist peacefully.

However, there are products that can be sprayed on plants, and there are fences, and perhaps deer are simply not a problem where you live. If daylilies are the kings of sun, hostas are the kings, queens,

Hosta 'Abiqua Blue Edger'

princes, and princesses of shade. For some gardeners, they are a gift to brighten up the darkness; for others, they are obsessions, collected like baseball cards, resulting in a crop rather than a garden. I really like hostas, and every now and then I must stop

Hosta 'Frances Williams'

Hosta 'Frances Williams'

Hosta 'Blue Angel'

Hosta 'Elvis Lives'

Hosta sieboldiana 'Elegans'

myself from buying the next chartreuse or variegated one, lest my shade become a hosta nursery. In my garden, however, I have the unwelcome help of deer, voles, bugs—and for many years, my Hannah dog. Unfortunately Hannah has left me, but the rest of the critters are still around. I would put up with triple the deer if it meant Hannah was still in our life.

Hostas are noted for their beautiful foliage (visits from Bambi notwithstanding). The flowers, reminiscent of lilies, are handsome and quite useful as cut flowers. In fact, some of the most fragrant flowers belong to the fragrant hosta, *Hosta plantaginea*. There are too many hostas from which to choose, and as the new leaves push through the ground, plants of

Hosta 'Fragrant Bouquet'

Hosta 'Wide Brim'

Hosta 'Spritzer'

Hosta 'June'

Hosta sieboldiana 'Elegans'

Hosta 'Striptease'

Hosta 'Great Expectations'

Hosta 'Sun Power'

Hosta 'Gold Standard'

Hosta 'Zounds'

Hosta 'Hoosier Harmony'

greens, whites, yellows, and blues appear before one's eyes. They differ in habit, and their mature size helps decide their use. For example, plants may be used as ground covers (*H.* 'Francee'), edging (*H.* 'Abiqua Blue Edger'), background or fillers (*H.* 'Segae'), or specimens (*H.* 'Frances Williams').

Although height is certainly a consideration, most gardeners purchase hostas based on leaf color. And there is no lack of choice! Blue or blue-green foliage is a trendy choice—I enjoy the specimen 'Blue Angel' and if, for no other reason than the name, the subtle blues of 'Elvis Lives' are fun to have in the garden. *Hosta sieboldiana* 'Elegans' is one of the best blue choices and creates a blue veil even from across a spacious lawn.

Hostas with white variegated foliage are probably the most popular and are

Hosta 'Sum and Substance'

Hypericum calycinum

Hypericum calycinum 'Brigadoon'

Hypericum androsaemum

amazingly diverse. 'Fragrant Bouquet' has fragrant flowers, thus the name; the large and magnificent 'Frances Williams' has been one of the most popular choices for many years. Smaller ones like 'Striptease' and 'Wide Brim' provide clean white variegation and are also quite popular. Yellow variegated leaves are some of the most interesting and always eye-catching. 'Great Expectations' is quite beautiful but very slow; 'Spritzer' has always been one of my favorites and is particularly beautiful in the spring. Some of the variegation fades in the summer. 'June' has clean yellow and green foliage and shows off all the plants around it, and like many other hostas, can be placed in containers. 'Gold Standard' is the standard variegated choice and is essentially a no-brainer even for the hosta neophyte.

The hosta collector wants it all, and golden foliage is part of the scrapbook.

Golden leaves brighten up dark areas and can be seen from a good distance away. 'Sun Power' is among the brightest and with its small leaves can be placed almost anywhere. 'Zounds' is a soft yellow and a big plant, and I enjoy 'Hoosier Harmony' as it harmonizes with small ground covers around the pond. 'Sum and Substance' has large chartreuse leaves, and its bright color and vigorous growth has kept it as the most popular yellow hosta of all time.

Plant hostas in partial shade; they tolerate more sun than most people believe. The further north one gardens, the more sun hostas can tolerate. Few do not benefit from some afternoon shade. Keep plants consistently moist, or leaf margins become brown. Hostas are certainly not trouble-free, but they will remain popular with anyone who has shade. The challenge

offered by this plant is to choose one or two cultivars from the hundreds that bombard you each year. Hardy in zones 3 to 8.

Hypericum
SAINT JOHN'S WORT

Along with *Echinacea*, Saint John's wort is as often found in the medicine cabinet as in the garden. Its antidepressant properties have long been a part of herbal dosings in Europe, and our stressed-out society has also come to embrace *Hypericum* with a vengeance. The species that is helping to calm and placate is *Hypericum perforatum*, which is seldom grown as a garden plant; however, a number of others are widely planted for their large yellow flowers or ornamental fruit. All hypericums are actually shrubs, but they behave like perennials.

Hypericum androsaemum 'Albury Purple'

Hypericum ×inodorum

Hypericum ×moserianum 'Tricolor'

Hypericum androsaemum 'Variegatum'

Hypericum ×inodorum 'Elstead'

Hypericum calycinum

The long stamens in the 2- to 3-inch-wide flowers of *Hypericum calycinum* (Aaron's beard) look a lot like, well, long stamens, but perhaps Aaron's beard was unusually scraggly. In any case, the bright, beautiful flowers cover the plants in spring and early summer. They are best used as ground covers and can spread rapidly in areas of cool summers and mild winters. The glossy green leaves cover large berms and hillsides, making a splendid carpet or backdrop for a garden bench. 'Brigadoon' is a recent introduction with chartreuse leaves. Flowers are sparse and vigor is suspect. However, it does look good in cool climates. Plants do not withstand the difficult summer

Imperata cylindrica 'Red Baron'

heat and humidity in the South and often look ragged by August, but they do return fresh in the spring.

Hypericum androsaemum (tutsan) is a terrific plant in zones 5 to 7 for its upright habit, small flowers, and ornamental fruit. It grows to about 3 feet in height and bears small bright yellow flowers, which are somewhat hidden by the foliage. The flowers are far less noticeable than those of most of its cousins, but the colorful fruits, starting black then later turning red, are used as a filler in floral designs. The fruit-laden stems are also grown commercially by cut flower growers throughout the world. Plants do poorly in the heat of a hot summer, so they are a waste of money in the South; otherwise, they are a great addition to the garden. 'Albury Purple' provides good purple foliage and interesting fruit

on the same plant. 'Variegatum' is most interesting. The leaves are sometimes streaked in creamy white, other leaves are mostly white, but there is nothing crisp or clean about them. However I kind of enjoy it. Another fruit-laden form is *H. ×inodorum*, especially in the selection 'Elstead'. The flowers are small and bright yellow, but the fruit is a brilliant red. Great plant, also best for cooler climates. Plant in full sun to partial shade, zones 5 to 7.

'Tricolor' is a cultivar of *Hypericum ×moserianum*. Like many of the other hypericums, plants are really shrubs and have woody stems. The green, pink, and cream foliage is quite beautiful, and the plants produce small yellow flowers. We grow plants simply for the foliage, and they are handsome throughout the season. Cold hardy to zone 7.

Imperata cylindrica
JAPANESE BLOOD GRASS

I had never been a big fan of Japanese blood grass, having seen both poor plantings and invasive plantings, particularly of the green-leaved species. It is an unreliable plant south of zone 6, but further north the red-leaved forms such as 'Rubra' and 'Red Baron' make beautiful plantings. In early summer, the red color is obvious but not very exciting. As fall progresses, the plants become deep red, and even I cannot deny their beauty. At the marvelous Niagara School of Horticulture in Niagara Falls, Ontario, some of the beds of 'Rubra' in the parking lot are bloody beautiful, and I also really enjoyed the creative use of 'Red Baron' as a ribbon of red running through the gardens at The Ohio State University.

Imperata cylindrica 'Rubra'

Imperata cylindrica 'Rubra' in fall

Ipheion uniflorum

Ipheion uniflorum naturalized

This plant works, but the red forms are the only ones that can be recommended. The species is invasive. Plants require full sun and are hardy in zones 4 to 6.

Ipheion uniflorum
SPRING STARFLOWER

Blooming their heads off in early spring, a planting of a few dozen bulbs of *Ipheion uniflorum* produces hundreds of light blue star-shaped flowers in February and March in a couple of years. The flowers, sometimes so pale as to be almost white, are held on 4- to 6-inch stems. They are subtly fragrant; but the narrow, grasslike, pale green leaves

Ipheion uniflorum with light blue flowers

Ipheion uniflorum 'Wisley Blue'

Iris reticulata 'Cantab'

Ipheion uniflorum 'Rolf Fiedler'

Ipheion uniflorum (left), *I. u.* 'Wisley Blue' (middle), and *I. u.* 'Rolf Fiedler'

give off the scent of garlic when handled. It is this slightly unpleasant smell which perhaps limits more widespread use of this fine species. If you admire them with your eyes rather than your hands, I can think of no reason not to include a few of these inexpensive plants. Some areas, like Augusta, Georgia—somewhat known for being the home of the Augusta National Golf Club but far more famous for being the home of my daughter Heather and her family—have entire meadows where spring starflower has taken over. Her kids love them.

Most of what is offered through catalogs is *Ipheion uniflorum* itself, with light blue flowers; however, several selections of the species are available. The most common is the darker 'Wisley Blue', which is the best of the easy-to-find cultivars. 'Rolf Fiedler' has larger leaves, larger petals, and clear blue flowers on 4-inch stems, but Rolf does not produce nearly as many flowers as the others. They are quite similar, but the flowers, when placed side by side, can be told apart without too much difficulty. Plant in full sun, zones 5 to 9.

Iris

Iris is one of those genera in which so many species and cultivars reside that you could collect them over a lifetime and barely dent the surface. From America to Siberia, along with imports from Europe, Japan, and China, we have welcomed irises to our gardens with open arms. They are tolerant to all sorts of weather and can be found from Brainerd, Minnesota, to Lafayette, Louisiana.

Most are grown from rhizomes or regular fibrous roots, but a few arise from bulbs or corms. The bulbous irises tend to be early-flowering and short (4 to 9 inches), while the bearded irises and other more common forms flower later and are more robust and taller. The only drawback is that flowering time of a given plant is short; however, that's easily remedied by choosing many different types. That way, you can have iris in flower from early spring to late summer.

The bulbous species (*Iris danfordiae*, *I. reticulata*, *I. xiphium*, *I. bucharica*) and their cultivars tend to be early, short, and ephemeral. The Danford iris (*I. danfordiae*) is only about 4 inches tall, but its bright yellow blossoms stand out at a time when few other plants are in flower. I love to plant them as an annual (unfortunately, they seldom come back) by my rocks by the pond. Full sun to partial shade, hardy in zones 5 to 9.

The small bulbs of reticulated iris, *Iris reticulata*, belie the large flowers produced on the 4- to 6-inch plants. Occurring in various shades of purple and blue, the flared petals and small standards appear in February and

Iris danfordiae

Iris reticulata 'George'

Iris 'Eye of the Tiger'

Iris 'White Wedgwood'

Iris bucharica

Iris cristata

March, before the short leaves expand. After flowering, the leaves shoot up to about 12 inches long. Some excellent selections of reticulated iris include the soft blue of 'Cantab' and the deep purple of 'George'. Individual bulbs may not persist more than about three years, although once established, some may continue to flower for up to ten years. Full sun, hardy in zones 5 to 8.

The Dutch irises (hybrids involving *Iris xiphium*) send up their foliage early, but the 12- to 18-inch-tall flower stems open later than the other bulbous species. You may see this on most days in your local flower shop, as it is an excellent cut flower. The Dutch hybrids may be planted in the fall as far north as zone 6b and persist for two or three years. Foliage appears in late winter or early spring, and flowers of white, blue, purple, and yellow provide rainbows of bloom—beautiful or gaudy, depending on one's outlook. Cultivars include 'Eye of the Tiger', with dark purple and yellow flowers, and an outstanding white, 'White Wedgwood'. Full sun, hardy in zones 6b to 9.

Iris bucharica, corn leaf iris, is another bulbous member—little used but spectacular. Plants are only 6 to 12 inches tall and, like the other bulbous forms, can be used to great advantage in small spaces. The golden and white flowers are just wonderful. Plants are said to be hardy to zone 3; I have seen them in zone 5, so that could be so. They are easily found from a good bulb supplier, and if you haven't tried them, I recommend you do so.

Speaking of wonderful plants for small spaces, let us not forget our unassuming native crested iris, *Iris cristata*. Provided with shade and moisture, these spring-flowering 6- to 9-inch-tall plants aren't going to knock

Iris cristata

Iris 'All Aglow'

Iris 'Glittering Amber'

Iris 'Ecstatic Night'

your socks off, but their subtle beauty is enough. There are a number of cultivars out there, but I need to enjoy no more than the soft blue and white flowers of the species to be content. Plants make a substantial clump on their own but when placed near a fallen log or other accent are even better.

If an award were presented to "most popular perennial with too many choices," the bearded iris would undoubtedly be the winner. The "bearded" part refers to the band of hairs on the falls (the drooping petals). With all colors of the rainbow available in short to tall cultivars for sale, the gardener is hard-pressed to know which one to choose. The leaves are about 2 inches wide and often have a blue-green hue. Depending on cultivar, flowers are produced as early as very early spring to mid summer. Although leaf diseases and insects are creating more problems in the bearded irises than in the Siberians or Japanese, bearded iris will no doubt continue to be popular, if only by virtue of sheer numbers available.

The Royal Botanical Garden in Hamilton, Ontario, has some of the finest collections of many plants, bearded irises among them. It is impossible to elect one that is "better" than another when the beardeds are doing their thing, and what a thing it is! That garden is well worth a visit any time, but the panorama of color during iris time is outstanding. Some of my favorite hybrids are 'All Aglow', with salmon flowers, 'Glittering Amber', with peachy pink blossoms, and the almost black flowers of 'Ecstatic Night'. I could go on forever—suffice to say that it's hard to find a bad one. Simply choose a bearded iris based on the color and height you are partial to. Full sun, hardy in zones 3 to 9.

Some of the very best irises may not be the most common. I have a lot of trouble staying away from the large-flowering *Iris ensata* (Japanese iris) and its hybrids. Without doubt, the flowers are among the biggest in the genus and easy to tell from other irises because of their flat tabletop-

Japanese iris in a public park

Iris ensata 'Regal'

Iris ensata 'Summer Storm'

Iris ensata 'Rikki Pikki'

Iris fulva

Iris hexagona

Iris ensata 'Variegata' with heliopsis

Iris 'Llewellyn'

Iris 'Sinfonietta'

Iris 'King Creole'

Iris tectorum

like appearance. With so much breeding in the last century, more than sufficient color choice exists for any combination. Large leaves and immense fruit are also characteristic of this fine group of iris. They do well planted at the edge of ponds and water features, so wet feet is not a problem. However, normal garden soils are fine assuming they are irrigated in dry times.

There are hundreds of cultivars, but you might want to look for 'Regal', whose flowers are deep lavender with white streaks on its falls, or 'Rikki Pikki', one of the finest whites I have ever trialed. The plant was picked by Rick Berry at Goodness Grows Nursery in Lexington, Georgia. 'Summer Storm' is also quite beautiful and

performs well almost everywhere in the country. Perhaps the most interesting is 'Variegata', whose variegated foliage softens even bright yellow flowers. As much as I enjoy the variegation, they don't perform well south of zone 6. Plants are generally 3 to 4 feet tall. Full sun, hardy in zones 4 to 9.

The Louisiana iris has become more and more popular, no longer enjoyed only by gardeners in Louisiana and the Gulf Coast but much further north as well. The Louisiana irises are actually a complex made up of about five species, and because of increased demand and breeder interest, there are many hybrids from which to choose. Narrow leaves on 3- to 5-foot-tall plants and smooth (not bearded) flowers

with drooping standards (the upright petals) typify this group. Although they thrive in water and require it in serious amounts, swamps and bayous are not necessary as long as irrigation can be applied.

Two of the species making up the complex are fabulous garden plants in and of themselves. I grow my favorite, copper iris, *Iris fulva*, in a small whisky barrel water feature, so its feet are always wet. I am never disappointed. The Dixie iris, *I. hexagona*, with its blue and white flowers, has been perfectly at home in my "normal" soils and persists year after year. Hybrids are readily available and seem to require little special care. Someday, I will provide 'Sinfonietta' and 'King Creole' better,

Siberian iris at Longwood Gardens in Pennsylvania

Iris 'White Swirl'

Iris 'Sally Kerlin'

moister soils, but for the last half-dozen years, these plants have provided beautiful flowers during years of drought and plenty. To be sure, with all the Louisianas, irrigation is needed if rainfall takes a vacation. Probably zones 4 to 9. Full sun and consistent moisture are recommended.

Their dozens of colors—all with clean, narrow dark green foliage—make the Siberian iris (*Iris sibirica* and others in the series) a favorite among iris lovers. The leaves are among the cleanest in the iris family, seldom exhibiting disease or insect problems. But of course most gardeners don't purchase irises for their leaves,

Iris tectorum

Iris tectorum 'Album'

and choosing among flowers in hues of white, blue, lavender, and yellow should satisfy most of us. Plants grow 2 to 3 feet tall and quickly form significant colonies.

Find a good nursery with a comprehensive listing, and choose colors and heights that fit with your garden colors. 'Llewellyn' is a favorite because of its handsome blue flowers, but if a white is preferred, try 'White Swirl' with its ribbons of yellow on the falls. Any Currier McEwen introducvtion, such as 'Sally Kerlin', is a sure bet. Siberian irises do well by the side of streams where moisture is consistent, but they are one of the most tolerant of dry soils. Full sun translates into the most flowers per plant; plants grow well in areas of partial shade but produce few flowers. Plant different cultivars for a longer show, as Siberians are among the fastest to come in and out of flower. Hardy in zones 3 to 9.

Iris tectorum, the Japanese roof iris, offers large flowers of purple or white on short (12 to 15 inches tall) plants, making this easy-to-grow iris a favorite for the front of the garden. The short raised bristles borne along the midrib of the falls helps to identify this species as a member of the crested iris group. The light green leaves are wider than most of the other irises in the garden, but because they are shorter, individual plants don't take up as much room when flowering is complete. However, the good news is that plants move by above-ground rhizomes and can form a significant colony in two to three years. The deep lavender flowers with the white crest are formed prolifically in the spring.

The best cultivar of *Iris tectorum* is the white-flowering 'Album'. The yellow streak along the falls contrasts subtly yet effectively with the clean white of the rest of the flower. Partial shade and consistent moisture helps performance. Hardy in zones 4 to 8.

Kalimeris pinnatifida

Kalimeris
JAPANESE ASTER

With persistent single and double white flowers, cut leaves, and excellent weather tolerance, *Kalimeris pinnatifida*, the Japanese aster, is on the Armitage list of no-brainers for new gardeners. Other than its outstanding performance and how easily it consorts with all sorts of neighbors, I suppose there is nothing particularly remarkable about the plant. The 1- to 2-foot-tall plants start flowering in late spring or early summer and continue to do so until frost. They often start out as single flowers, and as the season progresses, double flowers are produced. A small piece obtained from a friend will fill out into a wide colony within a year or two. Full sun to partial shade, zones 4 to 8.

Kalimeris pinnatifida with *Hydrangea paniculata*

Kalimeris pinnatifida with verbena

Kalimeris yomena 'Shogun'

Kirengeshoma palmata

Kirengeshoma palmata

Kirengeshoma palmata

Kirengeshoma palmata fruit

Another species, *Kalimeris yomena*, is best known for its green-and-yellow selection, 'Shogun'. It is handsome, I suppose, but does not possess the outstanding performance of *K. pinnatifida*. A little afternoon shade is appreciated for this selection, zones 4 to 9.

Kirengeshoma palmata
YELLOW WAXBELLS

This unique species from Japan provides all sorts of subjects for lively conversation: leaves, flowers, fruit, and not least, debate over how to pronounce the generic name.

It is not a terribly well-known plant—last time I mentioned yellow waxbells, people referred to their bird books. The opposite palmately lobed leaves are light green, and the yellow drooping flowers are thick and waxy, thus the common name. The interest in the plant continues after flowering, with the appearance of fruit that might have been dreamed up by Stephen King: two to three pointed horns are borne on the inflated capsule. Plants are not the easiest to establish, needing protection from winds and an abundance of organic matter. Moist soils are recommended, but boggy conditions should be avoided. Place in partial shade, or at least

shaded from afternoon sun; not recommended for the hot, humid summers of the South. Hardy in zones 5 to 7.

Kniphofia
RED-HOT POKER

Learning all these crazy botanical names is tough enough, but learning to spell some of them is even harder. Who makes up names like *Kniphofia*? It is one genus (of many) I consistently misspell, never remembering if it is "ph" or "f," and in what order. However, I felt much better when I learned that the genus was named for German botanist J. H.

Kniphofia 'Atlanta'

Kniphofia 'Bressingham Comet'

Kniphofia 'Sunningdale Yellow'

Kniphofia northiae

Kniphofia 'Ice Queen'

Kniphofia 'Sulphur Gem'

Kniphofia northiae

Kniphof. (I'm just glad no plants are named for my friend Billy Goidehlpht.) And then we have the common name, red-hot poker, so called because the tall spires of flowers are often scarlet or fire-engine red. Hmm, sounds like something out of Elm Street.

The most common species is the old-fashioned *Kniphofia uvaria*, native to South Africa, whose many flowers still provide good value for the money. Red-hot they may be, but hybrids of yellow, green, and white are also part of this plant's palette. The sword-shaped leaves form a large tuft of foliage, giving rise to the upwardly mobile spires in late spring or early summer. Often the flowers at the top are scarlet; the older ones at the bottom of the spike are chartreuse-green, providing a bicolor effect.

The assortment of colors and heights is quite extraordinary. The classical look of *Kniphofia* is to produce lots of orange-yellow flower spikes above narrow foliage, as in 'Atlanta'. The spires of 'Bressingham

Comet' are more robust and equally colorful. However, that orange color can be a little too bright, so I find myself enjoying the white flowers of 'Ice Queen' a little more each year. Yellows can also be found; one of the best has been 'Sunningdale Yellow' but the more subtle shades of 'Sulphur Gem' are also pleasing to the eyes. Plants range from 2 to 3 feet to 5-foot spires. Full sun, zones 5 to 8. I am always impressed with the massive foliage of *Kniphofia northiae*, otherwise known as octopus poker, giant red-hot poker, or the aloe poker. The foliage looks like a giant aloe has parked in the garden, but the tall, broad flower spikes leave no discussion as to its identity. Its name honors famed botanical artist Marianne North (1830--1890). I have seen this only in West Coast gardens—not sure why it has not garnered more excitement, perhaps because it is cold hardy only to about zone 7.

Lamium
DEAD NETTLE

The lamiums are closely related to the stinging nettles (*Urtica* species, which are never forgotten by those who have meandered too close to them), but since lamiums lack the stinging hairs, they were dubbed dead nettles. The lamiums are embraced as shady ground covers, and they provide good-looking foliage and, in many cases, quite colorful flowers.

Lamium galeobdolon, yellow archangel, is one of the best plants for deep shade that I have come across. Its selection 'Variegatum' bears opposite, green and silver leaves on long square stems. Plants are only about 9 inches tall, but the long stems fall over themselves, resulting in the ground being quickly covered. The variegated leaves combined with deep yellow flowers brighten up even the darkest location. This is the kind of aggressive plant I like: it takes over

Lamium maculatum 'Chequers'

Lamium galeobdolon

Lamium galeobdolon

areas that no other plant wants to battle. I also recommend yellow archangel for containers, letting the plants spill over and root at the base, forming a crinoline of color around the base. Several cultivars have been selected, but for aggressive growth, nothing else comes close. 'Hermann's Pride' is far more compact and refined and forms

handsome clumps of intricately netted foliage. Partial to deep shade, consistent moisture. Hardy in zones 4 to 8.

Many selections of *Lamium maculatum*, spotted nettle, are offered for sale and while each claims to be better than the one before, they all do the same job: they slowly fill in with wonderful

Lamium galeobdolon 'Hermann's Pride'

Lamium maculatum 'Aureum'

Lamium maculatum 'Pink Chablis'

Lamium maculatum 'Golden Anniversary'

Lamium maculatum 'Pink Chablis'

variability of leaf and flower, though in the Armitage garden they don't seem to trip over themselves in their exuberance to do so. The 6- to 9-inch-tall plants have handsome multicolored leaves and flowers in shades of pink, mauve, and white. Better in the North than the South, where the humidity results in leaf-spotting problems.

Lots of foliar color is available. Some of the older selections are in golden shades, like 'Aureum', and the newer ones like 'Golden Anniversary' have green leaves with yellow margins. The flowers are rosy pink. One of the best performers I have tried, 'Pink Chablis', has silver foliage and pink flowers. This is a particularly good selection for containers. Another unusually good performer is 'Chequers', with large rosy red flowers and white and green leaves. Partial shade, zones 3 to 7.

Leucanthemum
SHASTA DAISY

This genus, too, was once a part of the large genus *Chrysanthemum*, which has undergone extensive taxonomic tinkering. Scientific study

Leucanthemum ×superbum with artemisia

Leucanthemum ×superbum 'Northern Lights'

Leucanthemum ×superbum 'Snow Lady'

Leucanthemum ×superbum 'Becky'

Leucanthemum ×superbum 'Broadway Lights'

Leucanthemum ×superbum 'Snow Cap'

of the plant structure and the date plants were originally named has resulted in the genus *Chrysanthemum* being split off to many genera, *Leucanthemum* being one of them.

Shasta daisy, *Leucanthemum ×superbum*, has been, is, and forever shall be one of the more popular perennials in the American landscape. They are in every outlet in every spring and are easy to grow and as comfortable as an old shoe. That many of them fall apart in a year or two seems not to make a fig of difference. Nearly all Shastas are clothed in white, whether in single, semi-double, or fully double attire, and look terrific with gray-leaved plants like artemisias.

'Northern Lights' is an example of the many semi-double and double-flowered forms out there and is a bit gruesome. Personally, I'll take single-flowered Shastas any day and strongly recommend the low-growing 'Snow Cap', an older introduction that never falls apart even in hot summers. 'Snow Lady' is an All-American Award winner that flowers the first year from seed and is a good performer throughout the country. If you are having problems with foliage falling apart after flowering, try 'Becky'. She bears single white flowers, and like the fine lady she was named for, she is one of the finest Shastas I have tried. In general, plants stand 18 to 30 inches tall and require full sun and well-drained soils. 'Broadway Lights' is reasonably new and stands about 2 feet tall, flowering for many weeks, at about the same time as the echinaceas.

Leucanthemum ×superbum 'Becky' in Montreal

Leucanthemum ×superbum 'Broadway Lights' with purple coneflower

Liatris spicata flowering from top down

Rainy, humid climates are not to the liking of any of the Shasta daisies. They do reasonably well in zones 4 to 9. Cut back after flowering in warmer areas of the country.

Liatris
GAYFEATHER

Gayfeathers—what a lovely name. A light-hearted feather is exactly what liatris conjures up as one looks at the purple or white flowers standing at attention. It is also an interesting plant when you note that its habit of flowering from the top down makes it unique among garden plants. The 3- to 5-foot-tall, mid to late summer spike of *Liatris spicata* consists of individual button-shaped, aster-like flowers, usually mauve in color but sometimes white or rosy red. It is an inhabitant of the Midwest, quite prevalent in undisturbed meadows or pastures. In such a setting, there does not appear to be a lot of "body" to liatris, as the plant grows much like a lily, with thin leaves surrounding the central stem. However, if placed in a garden and provided with a little love and care, plants make a wonderful colorful display. One of the best selections is the shorter 'Kobold', whose flowers tend to stay upright even in wind and rain. I also have noticed that the white-flowered forms like

Liatris spicata in meadow

Liatris spicata 'Kobold'

Liatris spicata in garden

Liatris scariosa 'White Spires'

Liatris graminifolia

'Floristan White' stand out particularly well in the garden.

The commercial cut flower industry long ago discovered that liatris makes an excellent cut flower. Cut the stems when the flower is about a third of the way open and place immediately in a solution of floral preservative for many days of enjoyment.

Several other species are also available. I enjoy the full flowers of *Liatris scariosa* and particularly its white selection, 'White Spires'. It is only about 18 inches tall; however the giant gayfeather, *L. pycnostachya*, at 6 feet, is large enough to be used as a weapon. And for something quite un-liatris like, try *L. graminifolia*, whose grasslike leaves demand a double take.

All have their moments in the sun, but it is the common gayfeather, *Liatris spicata*, that is the most available and the most

Liatris spicata 'Floristan White'

Ligularia dentata 'Britt Marie Crawford'

Liatris spicata after harvesting

widely grown. The gayfeathers are particularly prevalent in the Great Plains and the Midwest; gardeners in these regions are advised to plant them and get out of the way. Full sun, zones 3 to 9.

Ligularia

Ligularias work best in a large garden where the daring gardener has lots of room. They take front stage with their large leaves and impressive yellow and orange flowers. However, all ligularias are moisture lovers and do best, under all circumstances, where water is readily and consistently available. If water is lacking, the plant that looks so spectacular in the cool morning air looks like a limp rag doll in the warm afternoon

Ligularia dentata 'Othello'

sun. I would not plant a single ligularia if I didn't have a wet space for it.

The most popular plant in the group is probably bigleaf ligularia, *Ligularia dentata*. The large round leaves make it a favorite, particularly on the edge of water features such as streams and ponds. It is almost impossible not to have the leaves wilt on warm days, even though the wilting

does not seem to cause any permanent damage. Looks lousy, though. Slugs account for shot holes in the leaves, adding to the gardener's dismay. Several cultivars are sold, the newest and perhaps the best is 'Britt Marie Crawford'. She has the darkest purple leaves of all the available cultivars; 'Desdemona' and 'Othello', both very popular, are similar but less colorful.

Ligularia dentata 'Desdemona'

Ligularia dentata 'Britt Marie Crawford'

Ligularia stenocephala 'The Rocket'

The bright yellow flowers are secondary in appeal; it is the attractive foliage that is the charm.

Ligularia stenocephala, narrow-spiked ligularia, offers a much different look: its leaves are triangular to heart-shaped, above which the long slender flower stalks arise. Dozens of small yellow flowers open along the 1- to 2-foot-long flower stems in late spring. An excellent architectural plant where abundant, consistent moisture levels can be maintained. Without consistent moisture, leaves look wilted much of the time. 'The Rocket', the most popular selection, hoists lemon-yellow flowers on 18- to

Ligularia sibirica

Ligularia macrophylla

Ligularia wilsoniana

Ligularia ×hessei

24-inch-long stems. Absolutely outstanding plants where the environment consists of cool nights and warm days. Not recommended for the South. Full sun to partial shade, zones 5 to 8.

Other interesting species of *Ligularia* with yellow rocket-like flowers include *Ligularia macrophylla*, with large, wide sword-like leaves and an upright habit like no other, and *L. ×hessei*, both of which are cold hardy to zone 4 and a little less water-needy. I also love *L. sibirica* (cold hardy to zone 3), with silver backs to its large round green leaves, and *L. wilsoniana* has many yellow stems of flowers and looks particularly good in moist areas with cool nights. Unfortunately, neither of the latter two tolerates warm summers well.

Lilium auratum var. platyphyllum

Lilium canadense

Lilium martagon 'Album'

Lilium henryi

Lilium martagon

Lilium
LILY

Trying to choose a few lilies is like trying to choose a few salvias: with so many to choose from, where does one begin? That the choice is so difficult, however, is testament to the beauty and diversity of the genus *Lilium*. From little-known species to the dozens of hybrids, no gardener can complain about a lack of options. All prefer full sun and good soil drainage.

Most of the lilies sold today are rather complex hybrids, but many species are wonderfully handsome. If I could find them, I would likely start with the gold band lily, *Lilium auratum*, with its prominent gold bands down the length of each white petal. Variety *platyphyllum* has larger flowers than the species. Hardy in zones 4 to 9. How I wish I could grow the Canada lily, *L. canadense*—if I could, I would have an entire garden full of them. The pendent golden flowers stop everybody in their tracks with their classic beauty. Unfortunately, they are difficult to find and do poorly in warm climates. Hardy in zones 3 to 7. I also enjoy the orange, nodding flowers of *L. henryi*, Henry's lily. The bumps on the flower faces and the reflexed petals

Lilium with smoke bush

Lilium auratum

of the flowers make an impressive picture. They tower to about 6 feet in height and return year after year. Hardy in zones 4 to 7. There are far too many species to grow them all. However, I need fragrance in the garden, and it comes in spades with the exotic regal lily, *L. regale*. On a still evening, nothing can match the sweet smell emanating from the flowers in the garden. The buds are a soft wine color, and the flowers

Lilium regale

Lilium 'Butter Pixie'

Lilium 'Yellow Blaze'

Lilium 'Arena'

Lilium 'Campfire'

Lilium 'Leslie Woodruff'

retain that hue on the outside of the petals but are beautifully white when they open. The combination of buds and flowers is indeed a wonderful picture. Hardy in zones 3 to 7. Lastly, I would plant the Turk's-cap lily, *L. martagon*, or one of its cultivars. The "turban" look of the flower and the whorled leaves make it fairly distinctive in the garden. Flower color is usually purple-red, but the white 'Album' is especially handsome. Hardy in zones 3 to 7.

The number of hybrids now available to the gardener is mind-boggling. From large upright trumpet flowers to graceful nodding blooms, from ten-foot giants to two-foot pixies, the choices are seemingly endless. In general, the flowers and the leaves of the Oriental hybrids are larger

Lilium 'Black Beauty'

Lilium 'Pink Perfection'

Lilium 'Sunny Sulawesi'

Lilium 'After Eight'

and plants flower a little later than the Asiatics, but all are worth a try in the garden when the lily fever is upon you. Today, hybrids between them are also common. Lilies are like roses: they are best when incorporated into the garden, rather than in a "lily garden." I came across some vivid orange hybrids with a backdrop of smoke bush (*Cotinus*)—a great combination! However, if looking for named hybrids, I might try to find some sunshine yellows like the short 'Butter Pixie' or the tall 'Yellow Blaze'. Others like the white-flowered 'Arena' can

Lilium 'Mona Lisa'

Lilium 'Olivia'

Linum usitatissimum by the acre

take your breath away, while 'Campfire' has a clean orange-peach color. In the Oriental group, I enjoy the old-fashioned popular 'Mona Lisa', but the nodding rose flowers of 'Black Beauty' and 'Pink Perfection' on 4- to 6-foot-tall plants are really memorable. 'Leslie Woodruff' has large white flowers with a rosy red throat and stands 5 feet tall. They have provided immense enjoyment in the Armitage garden, but my all-time favorite has to be 'Olivia', who returns year after year to lighten up the garden. In the future, dwarf plants like 'Sunny Sulawesi' and 'After Eight' will be terrific for containers at the base of a patio.

Linum
FLAX

Entire oceans of blue can be seen in European farmfields, where annual blue flax, *Linum usitatissimum*, is still grown for the fiber and linseed oil the plants yield, but only a few species of flax are used for gardens. One of the most handsome but seldom seen is yellow flax, *L. flavum* (zones 5 to 7), with its 2-inch-wide butter-yellow flowers. *Linum perenne*, the perennial flax, is the most common species and with good reason. The tough stems terminate in nodding flower buds, which then turn

up to the viewer their beautiful blue hue. 'Caeruleum' is lighter blue, while 'Album' is a good white selection. A good plant for edges; prefers partial shade in the South, full sun in the North. Excellent drainage is necessary. Hardy in zones 4 to 8.

Lobelia

The most common lobelia is the dwarf annual, *Lobelia erinus*, mostly in blues and purples. They can be brilliant in the spring, particularly in the North. The perennial selections are upright and generally in shades of reds to handsome blues and

Linum flavum

Linum perenne

Linum perenne 'Caeruleum'

Linum perenne 'Album'

purples. Red is the classic color, found in the common *L. cardinalis* (cardinal flower) and some of the hybrids. A rather unusual but spectacular plant is devil's tobacco, *L. tupa*, with its large matte red flowers and handsome foliage. It is far more at home on the West Coast than in the East. But, boy, is it ever beautiful! Plants prefer full sun to partial shade, zones 7 and 8.

Cardinal flower can be a beautiful plant, often growing near water, with brilliant red flowers. To see dozens growing together in a colony is to have an out-of-body experience. The lipped flowers are held on a long flower stem, and the hummingbirds and butterflies will love them as much as you do. Provide full sun

Lobelia tupa

Lobelia ×speciosa 'Queen Victoria'

if sufficient moisture can be provided, partial shade if plants are growing in normal garden soils. Hardy in zones 2 to 9. The hybrids, collectively known as *Lobelia ×speciosa*, include 'Bee's Flame' and 'Compliment Scarlet'. For good-looking foliage, try the dark-leaved 'Queen Victoria'. All sport brilliant red to scarlet flowers on 3- to 4-foot-tall plants. Cultural recommendations are similar to *L. cardinalis*. Hardy in zones 5 to 8.

Lobelia cardinalis

Lunaria
MONEY PLANT, HONESTY

Lunaria annua has to be one of the best biennials (a plant that takes two years to flower, then dies) for the garden. The common flower color is lavender, but 'Alba' is even prettier and reseeds true. 'Variegata', with variegated leaves and lavender flowers, is outstanding. The silver-dollar-shaped fruit (hence one of its common names) turns translucent over time and may be dried for long-lasting indoor decorations. Although not easy to find, seeds of purple-fruited forms can result in even more interesting plants. Where the plants do well, they are lovely, but they also seed everywhere, so that your small plot, conceived as a place to grow a plant or two for dried fruit, soon resembles the Franklin Mint. Their propensity for self-sowing results in large

Lobelia ×speciosa 'Bee's Flame'

Lobelia ×speciosa 'Compliment Scarlet'

Lunaria annua 'Alba'

Lunaria annua

Lunaria annua 'Variegata'

colonies in the spring, but if most flowers are removed before the seed is released, the advance can be controlled. Partial shade is best. Hardy in zones 4 to 8.

Another species of *Lunaria* is the shrubby money plant, *Lunaria rediviva*. Much more perennial than its biennial

Lunaria rediviva

Lunaria annua 'Alba'

Lunaria annua fruit

Lunaria annua with purple fruit

Lupinus texensis

counterpart, *L. rediviva* has finely toothed leaves and fragrant flowers. Other than size, however, the most notable difference between the two species is the fruit. In *L. rediviva*, it is elliptical rather than round as in the more common *L. annua*. They are more difficult to grow but certainly worth a try if you are already a fan of this genus. Provide partial shade to full sun, well-drained soils. Hardy in zones 4 to 8.

Lupinus
LUPINE, BLUEBONNET

I am not sure there is a more perfect flower than the lupine. The perfection is somehow diminished when gardeners try to reproduce the wonderful Texas bluebonnets, *Lupinus texensis*, in their eastern yards or plant English lupines in their Midwest garden. However, even a few lupines are a

source of delight in the spring garden and can be enjoyed even though they don't look like the planting at Chatsworth in England.

Of course, sitting at the head of the table are the hybrids, a potpourri of species first popularized by Yorkshireman George Russell, who bred the famous Russell hybrids. Numerous crosses followed including the wonderful mixtures found in the Gallery hybrids. Additional cultivars are being

Lupinus Russell Hybrid mix at Chatsworth House, England

Lupinus 'Russell Hybrid Pink'

Lupinus Gallery mix

Lupinus perennis

offered more and more, but the Russells are still the most readily available and therefore continue to be the main game in town. Regardless of the lupine chosen, remember that they love cool weather, hate the combination of heat and humidity, and except for fortunate gardeners in the Northwest and perhaps the Northeast, the Russell hybrids and their cousins will not be as handsome the second or third year as they were the first.

The sundial lupine, *Lupinus perennis*, with its strong lavender-blue flowers, has been rediscovered as a plant that tolerates heat and some humidity much better than the English hybrids, although it still does not do well below zone 7a. All lupines are easily grown from seed, and nurseries often carry substantial containers of well-grown plants that may be planted out in the fall. If you can find them, go for it. Plant in full sun, well-drained soils. Hardy in zones 3 to 7.

Lychnis
CAMPION

I was scratching my head the other day, wondering what in the world a name like campion has to do with anything. Except for one of my students, whose last name was Campion and who saw no problem with the name, the rest of us couldn't figure out why anybody would hang that moniker on a plant. Turns out some of

Lychnis flos-cuculi 'Jenny'

Lychnis chalcedonica

Lychnis coronaria

Lychnis coronaria 'Abbotsford Rose'

Lychnis chalcedonica in salmon

Lychnis coronaria 'Angel's Blush'

Lychnis coronaria 'Alba'

Lychnis chalcedonica 'Flore Plena'

Lycoris aurea

dianthus or pinks family, and indeed the genera are closely related. The common form and color of the flowers are single and scarlet, but salmon-colored blooms are also available. Double flowers ('Flore Plena') are particularly colorful. Full sun, decent soils, zones 3 to 7.

The other reigning perennial is the short-lived but explosive *Lychnis coronaria*, rose campion, characterized by magenta to rosy red flowers and gray woolly leaves. It reseeds itself with abandon: individual plants may disappear, but in general, gardeners will find it returning year after year. The species has gaudy purple flowers, but several hybrids, in particular 'Abbotsford Rose', subdue the magenta and replace it with bright rose. For more conservative gardeners, a white selection ('Alba') and a bicolor ('Angel's Blush') help to make the garden even more beautiful. Full sun to afternoon shade, zones 4 to 7.

Lycoris
RESURRECTION LILY

Oh, that the fine genus *Lycoris* would have a little more tolerance to cold: its members may presently be enjoyed only by those who garden south of zone 6, although one species goes into zone 5. Resurrection lilies are similar to a small amaryllis

these plants grew wild outside Roman stadiums, used for athletic events, like Christians vs. Lions, and garlands of them were used to crown the champion (usually a lion), hence the common name. Several fine annual species are offered. One is ragged robin, *Lychnis flos-cuculi*, but it reseeds so prolifically it is almost a perennial. It is ragged, it is wild, it is pink, and it is a wonderful comeback plant. The double-flowered selection 'Jenny' is darker and even better than the species.

Two perennial species of *Lychnis* and their selections reign supreme in North American gardens. Maltese cross, *Lychnis chalcedonica*, a native of eastern Europe, has been a garden favorite for many years. Opposite leaves, swollen nodes, and the five-petaled flowers—with petals shaped like a cross—show its affiliation with the

Lycoris squamigera

Lycoris radiata

Lysimachia ciliata 'Purpurea'

(*Hippeastrum*). In late winter or early spring the foliage emerges, looks like thick grass on steroids, then goes dormant in the summer. Despondent gardeners look at the bare ground and are sure their plants have died. Like magic, in late summer and fall, naked stems emerge, as if resurrected, topped with brilliant flowers. The stems have given rise to another common name, naked ladies, and some gleeful gardeners like to plant them with *Ornithogalum umbellatum*, which also enjoys some interesting common names. Who says creativity is dead in North American gardens?

I love the brilliant yellow flowers of *Lycoris aurea*, but they remain expensive and not too easy to locate. However, most common in the lower Midwest and mid-Atlantic states are the large mauve flowers of *L. squamigera*. The most beautiful of them all, the fire-engine red *L. radiata* lights up the garden in the fall, appearing in places that you do not remember planting. The latter two can multiply rapidly, and passing bulbs across the fence is a common occurrence. *Lycoris squamigera* is hardy to zone 6, the others to zones 7 or 8. Full sun to partial shade. All are outstanding.

Lysimachia
LOOSESTRIFE

The genus *Lysimachia* ranges from plants that can be worst of thugs to the best of garden specimens; they all bring beauty, character, and the chance to shower your neighbors with plants they will have forever. The usual flower color is yellow, but white is not uncommon. When you plant lysimachias, you are planting the future. Line up your friends now.

Lysimachia ciliata (hairy loosestrife) is certainly aggressive and is distinguished by many yellow flowers and the many small cilia, or hairs, along its stem and beneath its leaves. The running root system of this green-leaved species provides a colony of plants in no time. 'Purpurea' is equally aggressive but much more handsome. I can put up with its traveling ways because its purple-leaved foliage provides terrific contrasts with other plants in the garden—it makes even my bishop's weed (*Aegopodium*) look good, and that's saying something! In hot, humid summers, the purple leaf fades somewhat but still remains a muted dark green. In the winter and early spring, it provides color in an otherwise barren landscape. Full sun to partial shade, zones 5 to 8.

Lysimachia clethroides (gooseneck loosestrife) is the reigning king of the roamers, but it is nevertheless a beautiful plant in the right place. The right place simply happens to be an island bed surrounded by concrete. While its traveling tendencies

Lysimachia clethroides

Lysimachia ephemerum

Lysimachia congestiflora 'Persian Chocolate'

Lysimachia congestiflora 'Persian Chocolate'

Lysimachia nummularia

Lysimachia punctata 'Alexander'

Lysimachia punctata

Lysimachia ciliata 'Purpurea' with bishop's weed

Lysimachia nummularia 'Aurea'

can be overwhelming, gooseneck loosestrife is a wonderful plant for filling in large areas and providing handsome white flowers for the garden and the vase. The many half-inch-wide flowers are arranged on a long, undulating (like a goose's neck) inflorescence. That it is a roamer is simply testament to its success. Grows in full sun to partial shade; moist soils are to its liking. Hardy in zones 3 to 8.

A closely related plant but without the roaming habit is another white flowerer, *Lysimachia ephemerum*, upright loosestrife. I thought this would be a wonderful introduction when I first saw it, that is, to have a plant with flowers similar to gooseneck loosestrife (without the neck) but without worrying that it would take over. It does well in areas of the Northwest, not too bad on Long Island, only fair in the Midwest

and Southeast. Still a plant worth trying if you're a frustrated gooseneck lover. Hardy in zones 5 to 7.

The common name of *Lysimachia nummularia*, creeping Jenny, includes a strong hint as to what the plant wants to do. Happily, this first-rate plant is a creeper that most gardeners enjoy and encourage. It's particularly good for filling in areas around steps, rocks, or places where people

Lysimachia punctata with *Achillea* 'Cerise Queen'

routinely traverse; stepping on it every now and then does no harm whatsoever. The yellow flowers add a little color, particularly to the green-leaved species, but the contrast is lost when one grows the gold-leaved 'Aurea'. The golden color brightens the spring, then fades a little in the heat of summer. Fewer flowers are produced, but they are lost in the foliage anyway. Rooting at the nodes between the leaves allows *L. nummularia* to be fairly aggressive, but it is easily pulled out if it gets too rambunctious. I love this plant but am still trying to figure out where Jenny was creeping. Partial shade, zones 3 to 9.

Another wonderful creeping member is not as cold hardy as most other species. *Lysimachia congestiflora* may be hardy only to zone 7 but occasionally returns if the winters are not too severe. 'Persian Chocolate' is my favorite, with small yellow flowers and chocolate-colored leaves. Full sun, zones 7 to 9.

In areas with moderate summers, yellow loosestrife, *Lysimachia punctata*, can be an incredible thug. They grow 1 to 2 feet tall with many bright yellow flowers that easily catch the eye. Plants grow together quickly and can almost make a small hedge, but they also look good with other plants like pink yarrow. They are sufficiently cold hardy to be a marvelous weed north of Quebec City, zone 3. A variegated form, 'Alexander', is really quite beautiful, even when not in flower. Yellow loosestrife does well in cold winters and with moist feet but does not tolerate hot summers. Full sun, zones 3 to 6.

Macleaya cordata
PLUME POPPY

The plume poppy is perfect for the courageous gardener for whom space is not a problem. They want to roam around, so I was particularly impressed when I saw them planted in large containers, on either side of an entrance, where their outstanding displays of plume poppies can be controlled. Their lobed leaves, light green above and gray-green beneath, have gained plume poppies quite a following. They are particularly handsome when plants are young, fluttering in the breeze. The small cream-colored flowers are held in long plumes at the top of the plants in early to mid summer, turning darker over time. After flowering, small tan fruits are formed.

Macleaya cordata

Macleaya cordata fruit

Macleaya cordata in youth

Macleaya cordata in September

Plants are 6 to 10 feet tall, spreading quickly by rhizomes to form large colonies. In fact, they are thugs and a nightmare to remove. When broken, they bleed a yellow sap, a characteristic common to the poppy family. No cultivars are available. Full sun to partial shade, hardy in zones 3 to 8.

Maianthemum racemosum
FALSE SOLOMON'S SEAL

False Solomon's seal is a common native in bicoastal woodlands, and although it is a fine companion to all sorts of other natives, *Maianthemum racemosum* (*Smilacina racemosa*) is lovely in its own right when seen in a large colony. While making your way through the woods, look for creamy white flowers, alternate leaves, and fruit changing from dull green to mature red. Such woodland walks are indeed good for the soul, and the soul will be further

Maianthemum racemosum

Maianthemum racemosum

Maianthemum racemosum fruit

enhanced if you buy some plants from the garden center and put them in the garden. Flowers open in early spring, and foliage remains handsome until late fall. Shade, cool nights, and well-drained soils are needed for best performance. Buy two or three nursery-grown plants, place them side by side, and bring a little woodland home.

Mertensia virginica
VIRGINIA BLUEBELL

Spring is the time of great promise in the garden, and I know that spring has sprung when the light green leaves and the blue flowers of *Mertensia virginica*, Virginia bluebell, show themselves in late winter and early spring. I love watching the pink

buds evolve from being coiled up like a scorpion's tail to opening to deep pink or blue flowers. They are big enough to be planted in front of small shrubs like *Pieris japonica*, and both plants look better. They are spectacular associated with the reds of azaleas and the yellow flowers of wood poppy, *Stylophorum diphyllum*. The primary colors complement each other, the flower combination a designer's dream. Lavender and blue are the normal flower colors, but some plants retain their rose-pink flower color until nearly the end of bloom time. The big floppy leaves look a little like donkey ears and get larger as spring progresses. Finally, in early summer, normal summer dormancy is reached and the plants decide to go to bed, leaving the area bare—but that usually presents no problem because by that time neighboring plants have grown over the area. *Mertensia virginica* is a woodland plant, best grown at the edge of

Mertensia virginica with azaleas and wood poppies

Mertensia virginica with pieris

Mertensia virginica 'Rosea' with spring starflower

Miscanthus sinensis

Miscanthus sinensis 'Cosmopolitan'

Miscanthus sinensis 'Nippon' at Cantigny in Illinois

Miscanthus sinensis 'Variegatus'

a woodland path or by a shaded pond. Few cultivars have been isolated; occasionally a rose-pink ('Rosea') occurs, which looks very nice with other small bulbs such as spring starflower (*Ipheion uniflorum*). Partial shade, zones 3 to 8.

Miscanthus
EULALIA GRASS

Of all the grasses used in ornamental horticulture, save those for turf, those of the genus *Miscanthus* remain far and away the most popular. As long as low maintenance is an important consideration in selection,

ornamental grasses like miscanthus will continue to be used. They have enjoyed steady increases in commercial and institutional landscapes, where low maintenance is even more important than in the urban or suburban garden.

All eulalia grasses should be grown in full sun, although plants will tolerate some shade. In partial shade, plants are taller and more floppy, requiring a cage to keep them from staggering over everything. They may be enjoyed all winter but should be cut back to the base in spring, as soon as new growth has commenced. Do so with heavy shears or a chain saw—these are not wimpy

plants, and have worn out many a robust tool and strong back.

Miscanthus sinensis itself provides a handsome planting in the summer and wonderful bronze foliage and flowers in the fall and winter, but so many cultivars have been selected for this grass, the species is not often available. Winter color and late flowering are the raison d'êtres of all *Miscanthus* cultivars and they look good in almost any setting, assuming sufficient space is available, as most of these are big plants. I love the fall flowers of 'Nippon', but flowers are not the only reason for including this grass. Summer

Miscanthus sinensis 'Gracillimus'

Miscanthus sinensis 'Malepartus' early fall

Miscanthus sinensis 'Strictus'

Miscanthus sinensis 'Malepartus' late fall

Miscanthus sinensis 'Gold Bar'

Miscanthus sinensis 'Purpurascens'

Miscanthus sinensis 'Gracillimus'

foliage is quite spectacular in selections like 'Cosmopolitan', whose variegated leaves are always handsome. 'Variegatus' is an old-fashioned form, but when well grown shines in the garden. Another older selection is zebra grass, 'Zebrinus', but 'Strictus' is much stronger and is far less prone to falling over in rain or wind. Recently, a dwarf form, 'Gold Bar' was introduced. It is a terrific, boldly patterned addition for smaller garden spaces. I think if I had the space and could choose but one cultivar, it would be 'Gracillimus'. With thin green leaves and spectacular bronze flowers in the fall, this is simply a "doer." It is almost bullet-proof. By itself or in combination with roses or other plants in the garden, it simply works.

However, if you don't like that choice, I recommend 'Malepartus' as a good plant in the summer and early fall, with a great show

Miscanthus sinensis 'Huron Sentinel'

Miscanthus sinensis 'Sarabande'

Monarda 'Beauty of Cobham'

of large flowers in late fall and winter. I don't know of any other selection with larger, more impressive flowers. However, for excellent fall color, 'Purpurascens' is another plant I would not hesitate to embrace. 'Huron Sentinel' stands up straight and is wonderfully weatherproof, while 'Sarabande' provides excellent performance and dozens and dozens of flowers in the fall. There are literally dozens of choices.

Some gardeners are concerned that their plants might reseed and cause a problem in the garden or the environment. This is becoming an issue with miscanthus grass! Be aware of cultivars that self-seed, particularly if you are near a natural ecosystem. If they do, best to remove them. Breeding for sterility is in full swing, but choosing late-flowering forms will help reduce seed set. Dealing with knowledgeable nursery people who can recommend sterile and nonseeding types for your climate is the best advice. Full sun, hardy in zones 5 to 9.

Monarda 'Raspberry Wine'

Monarda
BEEBALM

How much monarda have I given away in the last few years? Fragrant, handsome, and colorful beebalms may be, but well behaved they are not. Three plants will form a large colony the first year, surround their neighbors the next, and be pulled out the third. In areas where such multiplication is not a problem, however, and where powdery mildew does not make its host too unsightly, beebalm sports many beautiful colors and offers excellent performance. I am not sure where this place is or where these plants are, but I am assured they exist.

Several species may be found, but the main player, and the one that moves around the garden so well, is *Monarda didyma*, also known as Oswego tea because plants were first collected around

Monarda 'Petite Pink Supreme'

Monarda 'Croftway Pink', *M.* 'Raspberry Wine', and *M.* 'Petite Delight'

Monarda 'Raspberry Wine' with coneflowers and phlox

Oswego, New York, and used to brew a tea-like concoction. Many cultivars may be purchased, or more likely you will find a gardener who will welcome the opportunity to share some with you. Cultivars vary from each other in color and height, and in their susceptibility to powdery mildew. All breeders claim to have found the cleanest introduction, but until you actually try them in the garden, no one truly knows for sure.

I find that all *Monarda* hybrids grow well, in colors ranging from pink and red to blue and lilac. Many cultivars are available and even look good together, as the rose-pink 'Croftway Pink' does in the grouping of cultivars shown here. 'Beauty of Cobham' is an older cultivar but still popular

Monarda bartlettii

Muhlenbergia capillaris 'White Cloud'

Muhlenbergia capillaris

and has handsome lilac-violet flowers. One of the very best cultivars is 'Raspberry Wine'; it is reliably mildew resistant and looks terrific at The Ohio State University with white coneflowers and garden phlox. If plants are too tall, you might want to try 'Petite Pink Supreme', a 2-foot-tall selection with large pink flowers. I have grown many of them, including the breakthrough 'Petite Delight', and all have their moments, all are invasive, and none are absolutely resistant to mildew, no matter what is claimed. All prefer full sun, hardy in zones 3 to 7.

Monarda bartlettii, a little-known species native to Mexico, is not cold hardy north of zone 7. However, we have trialed it and have been very pleased with its garden performance and beautiful pink-rose flowers. Mildew is less of a problem than with other beebalms.

Muhlenbergia capillaris
MUHLY GRASS

When planted en masse and in flower, muhly is probably the most colorful grass I know. They remind me of orchids, in that when not in flower the 18-inch-tall plants are quite forgettable, consisting of light green thin leaves and not much else. In the fall, however, the transformation is

Muhlenbergia capillaris

Muhlenbergia capillaris backlit

Forget-me-nots in New York

anything but forgettable, and in fact the rosy pink flowers are traffic stoppers. They are best planted in groups of at least half dozen in a small area, dozens in larger areas. In North Carolina, they are used on highway dividers, and they beat the heck out of half-dead turf. Where they are used to landscape part of the road into the University of Georgia, the stone wall is bathed in pink. What a wonderful greeting for the

thousands of football fans streaming in to watch their beloved Bulldogs. And if that is not enough, an entire pasture of muhly grass lit up by morning light in October surely is. Recently, a white-flowered form, 'White Cloud', has become available and although it is not quite as exciting as the pink one, it is very handsome nevertheless. Full sun, zones 7 to 10.

Myosotis
FORGET-ME-NOT

I can't get enough of these old-fashioned cottage plants. Forget-me-nots are, by ones and twos, rather boring, with wispy foliage and small blue flowers. But oh my, plant them by the dozens and let them reseed by the hundreds, then stand back and let them make a beautiful sea of blue.

Forget-me-nots in Australia

Myosotis sylvatica

Forget-me-not meadow

At Old Westbury Gardens on Long Island, the walkway comes alive on either side; and across the world, at Red Cow Farm, in Australia, as another blue-edged path ended, it gave way to a stunning blue-clad meadow. The individual flowers, when they are seen up close and personal (as here on *Myosotis sylvatica*), may be small, but the blue petals with white centers are quite wonderful. A plant or two just doesn't do it—use lots. They get better as time goes on. Normal garden soils and consistent moisture help them perform well in zones 5 to 8.

Narcissus
DAFFODIL

I can't think of an easier way to obtain color in the spring garden than to plant bulbs in the fall, and narcissus are almost foolproof. Nature—and the Dutch—have

Narcissus 'Spellbinder' (trumpet group)

Narcissus 'Accent' (large-cupped group)

Narcissus bulbocodium 'Primrose' (bulbocodium group)

Narcissus cyclamineus

Narcissus 'Ice Follies' (large-cupped group)

Narcissus 'Double Smiles' (double group)

Narcissus 'Exception' (trumpet group)

Narcissus 'Baby Moon' (jonquilla group)

Narcissus 'Smiling Twin' (split corolla group)   *Narcissus* 'Raoul Wallenberg' (poeticus group)

Narcissus 'Lancaster' (tazetta group)   *Narcissus* 'Elka' (misc. group, miniatures)

Nepeta ×faassenii 'Blue Wonder'

already done the hard work, providing us with a self-contained flowering unit that allows us to expend a minimum of effort to reap the maximum benefit. The perenniality of daffodils is outstanding: from the Deep South to the frozen North, they come back year after year.

So much hybridization has been accomplished with daffodils that they have been classified into different groups. For hybrid daffodils, twelve divisions have been identified, based on the size of the perianth (petals) and the corona (cup), resulting in daffodil terms like trumpet, large-cupped, small-cupped, and double. The single-flowered trumpet and large-cupped daffodils are probably the most popular harbingers of spring, but let us not ignore the many colorful cultivars that produce flowers in clusters. *Narcissus bulbocodium*, the hoop petticoat daffodil, and *N. cyclamineus*, cyclamen

daffodil, are small but interesting species daffodils (a thirteenth division) useful for naturalizing and rock garden work. These species, less vigorous than the hybrids, are seen more on the West Coast than in the rest of the country. Full sun, zones 3 to 8.

Nepeta
CATNIP

Nepeta consists of more than 250 species, thus one would expect a good deal of diversity, but for most gardeners, it is difficult to get past the fact that it is some kind of catnip. *Nepeta* is in the mint family, whose members may be recognized by their square stems, opposite leaves, and whorled flowers. One helpful way to discriminate between *Nepeta*, *Salvia*, and other minty plants is by using your nose. *Nepeta*, in general, smells like—well, like nepeta! Pick

a leaf of nepeta, one of salvia, and one of mint, and let your nose do the walking. Of course, when I do this, my nose does more running than walking, as well as sneezing. All species of *Nepeta* are excellent for the edge of garden beds or even along a pathway, where their fragrance is released when one touches the leaves in passing.

The main species in the trade is Faassen's hybrid, *Nepeta ×faassenii*, with numerous short cultivars such as 'Blue Wonder'. The highly popular *N. ×faassenii* 'Six Hills Giant', sometimes referred to as *N. gigantea* because of its large leaves and 3-foot height, is a terrific plant for cooler climates but tends to be weedy-looking in warm summers.

A tall species, with only the faintest catnipy odor, is the very cold hardy (to zone 3) Siberian nepeta, *Nepeta sibirica*. This is a beautiful plant, not as floppy as *N.*

Nepeta ×faassenii

Nepeta sibirica

Nepeta racemosa 'Snowflake'

Nepeta racemosa 'Walker's Low'

Nepeta ×faassenii 'Six Hills Giant'

×faassenii and others and much more classic in habit. *Nepeta racemosa* has become popular in recent years; 'Walker's Low' is the best known and an excellent performer. Most catnips are blue or violet, but 'Snowflake' is white. All require full sun, although afternoon shade is useful in the South. Most are hardy in zones 4 to 7.

Oenothera
EVENING PRIMROSE, SUNDROPS

Many plants go under the name of evening primrose (those that open during the evening) or sundrops (those that show their colors during the day). With the introduction of new species and hybridization among species, the distinction has

Oenothera speciosa

become blurred, and the common names are used interchangeably. The flowers of *Oenothera* have four petals; the sepals are pink to purple, particularly in bud; and the distinctive pistil is in four parts. Most have yellow flowers. A good number of species are weeds, but half a dozen ornamental forms are offered. All enjoy full sun and require good drainage.

Easily discernible from most other species is the south-central native, *Oenothera speciosa* (showy evening primrose), which bears pink rather than yellow flowers. The flowers are about 2 inches across, and the linear leaves are 2 to 3 inches long. Plants can easily become weeds, taking over entire counties in a single growing season. A dream plant at first glance, a bit of a nightmare after a few years. The white-flowered

Oenothera speciosa 'Twilight'

Oenothera speciosa 'Alba'

Oenothera speciosa 'Golden Summer'

Oenothera speciosa 'Twilight'

Oenothera berlandieri 'Siskiyou'

Oenothera speciosa 'Twilight'

Oenothera berlandieri 'Woodside White'

Oenothera fruticosa 'Lady Brookeborough'

Oenothera macrocarpa 'Greencourt Lemon'

'Alba' is equally aggressive. A new selection is 'Golden Summer', and I was quite impressed with the golden foliage, but it still travels a good ways, although not as aggressively. Well worth a try, but the jury is still out on this one. I thought 'Twilight', with its gorgeous pink flowers and unusual purple variegated leaves, was going to be a winner until it too took over the world. However, their beauty is undeniable; it is their ravenous appetite for space that is a problem. Full sun, zones 5 to 8.

A very similar species is Mexican evening primrose, *Oenothera berlandieri*, native to the Southwest and the Pacific Coast. Differing only slightly in appearance from *O. speciosa*, it is a bit less aggressive. Available in several cultivars; 'Siskiyou', with 2-inch-wide pink flowers, and 'Woodside White', the white entry, are worth looking for. Full sun, zones 6 to 8.

Oenothera fruticosa 'Lady Brookeborough' has dozens of small bright yellow flowers open most of the day, even if the sun is not shining. Plants grow 15 to 18 inches tall. Full sun, hardy in zones 4 to 8. *Oenothera macrocarpa*, Ozark sundrops, has the largest flowers relative to the size of the plant in the genus. The yellow flowers are up to 5 inches across (although 3 inches is more common) and are held on 6- to 12-inch-tall plants. Sepals are also tinged pink, and leaves are long, narrow, and entire. They are excellent plants for the rock garden, enjoying the extra drainage found there, but do not cope particularly well with heat and humidity. Few cultivars have warranted naming; one, 'Greencourt Lemon', has pale yellow flowers and slightly grayer leaves. Full sun, hardy in zones 4 to 7. Probably the best of the yellow-flowered forms to come along in recent years has been the hybrid 'Lemon Drop'. The plants are mounding and well behaved, and the bright yellow flowers almost cover the plant. It has performed well from Portland, Oregon, to Athens, Georgia. Zones 5 to 8.

Oenothera 'Lemon Drop'

Osmunda cinnamomea fiddleheads arising through epimediums

Osmunda cinnamomea

Osmunda cinnamomea

Osmunda claytoniana

Osmunda
FLOWERING FERN

"Flowering fern" is a misnomer for sure: *Osmunda* has no flowers at all, much less pretty flowers. Rather, its common name is a reference to the conspicuous spore cases and fertile fronds of some of the species. These are some of the largest and most vigorous ferns, and coarser than many others. After all, the genus was named for Osmunder, the Saxon god of war, and what self-respecting Saxon would choose anything but a gung-ho fern? Although obvious differences distinguish the species, all prefer moist conditions and shade.

Osmunda claytoniana

Osmunda regalis

Osmunda regalis spore cases

Osmunda regalis

For the person who thinks he or she can't grow anything, I recommend the cinnamon fern, *Osmunda cinnamomea*. It is most versatile, easy to grow from north to south while still providing the classic fern habit. The fiddleheads are so beautiful when they unfold in the spring, whether by themselves on the woodland floor or coming up through shade-tolerant ornamentals like mayapples or epimediums. The base of each frond bears scattered tufts of cinnamon-colored hairs, hence the common name. The spores are found in the handsome cinnamon-colored fertile columns. Too much heat and humidity yields stunted plants; shade and consistent moisture is required. An excellent fern for the beginning gardener, useful in zones 3 to 7, zone 8 on the West Coast.

When you look into the middle of the interrupted fern, *Osmunda claytoniana*, it looks like a bunch of black hairy strands where the leaves should be. In fact, those are the spore cases that "interrupt" the stem, and where it gets its common name. This spore arrangement in the middle of many of the fronds is unique to this species, and I have yet to meet anyone who isn't fascinated with this interrupted arrangement. Plants are large (up to 3 feet tall and equally wide), and they can eat up significant portions of woodland floor where they are established.

The green fronds, apart from their being interrupted, are like those of most other ferns. Once the spores are shed in early summer, the interrupted area becomes bare. It is the most common fern in the Berkshires of western Massachusetts and easily established in areas of cool temperatures and moist soils. Best for woodland gardens. Plants do poorly in the South as plants dislike heat, and lots of shade and moisture are necessary for best growth. Plants are too aggressive for formal borders. Good for zones 3 to 6, zone 8 on the West Coast.

Osmunda regalis, the royal fern, is the most classic of this classic group of ferns. Where happy, they are some of the largest, most robust plants in the fern family. I love to see them at attention like soldiers reflected along the edge of streams. The light green fronds are compound, unlike the simple fronds of others in the genus. The fertile spores of the plant are borne on the ends of the fronds, rather than separately as in the cinnamon ferns. Plants are large; they can be up to 6 feet tall and 4 feet across, eventually producing a huge tussock of roots, the source of osmunda fiber, long used as an amendment for growing orchids. Absolutely stunning in areas of partial shade and heavy moisture. Needs copious organic matter and cool nights to look its best. Zones 3 to 7, zone 8 on the West Coast.

Oxalis regnellii

Oxalis deppei

Oxalis regnellii 'Purpurea'

Oxalis deppei

Oxalis
SHAMROCK

Oxalis is best known as an awful weed that gets into every nook and cranny in every greenhouse and garden in almost every state. The small yellow flowers produce hundreds of fruit from which the seeds explode like TNT. Its reputation as a noxious weed is the only reputation it has. However, there are many species and even cultivars that more adventurous gardeners can try. Probably the easiest to find and easiest to grow is *Oxalis regnellii*, with its green leaves and white or pink flowers. The foliage of the purple form 'Purpurea' is even better, and the leaves remain quite beautiful in the spring and most of the summer. The pink flowers occur in spring and make a nice contrast to the leaves. Another wonderful woodland plant for handsome foliage is the iron cross shamrock, *O. deppei*, with its red-cross leaves and pink flowers. The leaves are quite beautiful throughout the season. A plant for handsome flowers is our native violet wood sorrel, *O. violacea*. The many green leaves result in a full plant, and early spring violet flowers shimmer above the plants. A white-flowered form, 'Alba', is equally wonderful.

Oxalis violacea

Oxalis 'Copper Glow'

Oxalis violacea 'Alba'

Oxalis 'Gold Net'

Oxalis 'Zinfandel'

Oxalis 'Lucky Gold'

Paeonia 'Balliol' (single bush form)

Paeonia 'Nadia' (single bush form)

Paeonia 'Zu Zu' (semi-double bush form)

Paeonia 'Red Imp' (double bush form)

Several fascinating new cultivars have been introduced lately, with interesting foliage and bright flowers. 'Gold Net' has subtle yellow netting in the light green leaves—sometimes a little too subtle to stand out. Yellow is more common than ever as new plants are introduced. 'Copper Glow' really does glow, and although it is not aggressive, it can move around a little. The flowers are forgettable, but the foliage is truly handsome. The flowers of the purple-leaved 'Zinfandel' are small and yellow but contrast well with the leaves. For flowers, 'Lucky Gold' is one of the best. Plants have performed well in many areas of the country. Oxalis may not be for everyone, but they are certainly no longer just a weed. Full sun, zones 4 to 8.

Paeonia
PEONY

"The colder the winter, the better the blooms." Thus was I taught the First Law of Peonies by my grandmother when I was a young boy in Montreal, and sure enough, every now and then, winters would be milder than usual, and the peonies would produce half the usual number of flowers. The scraggly old plants in that Montreal yard were as ugly as could be, except for a two-week period when they put on their springtime flowers. However, little did I know that when I moved to Athens, the land of the dogwood, but hardly the peony, that I would miss those old dogs.

One does not have to be a zone 3 Montrealer to enjoy peonies: they are excellent south to zone 5, satisfactory to zone 6, but only marginal in zone 7. Since peony performance also declines with high heat in the summer, southern gardeners are always on the cusp as they cheer their peonies on. West Coast-ers benefit from moderate summers and usually enjoy excellent flowering.

Peonies come in two shapes, the bush form and the tree form. Most of my preceding comments refer to the incredibly popular and highly bred bush peonies, which are classified as early-, mid-, and late-flowering, with single ('Balliol', 'Nadia'), semi-double ('White Cockade', 'Zu Zu'), and double blooms ('First Lady', 'Red Imp'). In general,

Paeonia 'White Cockade'
(semi-double bush form)

Paeonia 'Argosy'

Paeonia 'Souvenir de Maxime Cornu'

Paeonia 'First Lady' (double bush form)

Tree peony foliage

Paeonia 'Banquet'

Paeonia 'Golden Hind'

the further south one gardens, early flowering, semi-double (avoid the full double) flowers are best. The number of choices is endless; the best bet is to find a good retail outlet or a good mail-order company and find colors that appeal to you.

The tree peony is more expensive, but its heft and large flowers have resulted in an increase in popularity and availability.

Paeonia 'Daffodil'

Paeonia 'Red Moon'

Panicum virgatum

Panicum virgatum 'Dallas Blues'

Most are hybrids of *Paeonia suffruticosa*. To me, they are a little overhyped. They are often too big for most gardens, and like all peonies, the flowers persist for far too short a time. Sneeze and you miss them, look away and they're gone. That is not to say they are not extraordinary, but their beauty is fleeting. They can grow 4 to 7 feet tall, and the foliage is often more handsome than the flowers. Surely it is more handsome than the foliage of the bush peonies. The massive blooms are usually double, grow to 5 inches across, and are so heavy, they have to be lifted to be admired. Hardiness zones of 4 to 7 are most appropriate. Full sun in the North; afternoon shade is tolerated in the South.

All the clinical information just offered belies the lure and emotion associated with this fine flowering plant. Everybody loves peonies. They are hugely popular as cut flowers, and displaced Northerners struggle to find at least one cultivar for their new homes in Tucson, Atlanta, or New Orleans. Hundreds of cultivars are available through specialty growers, better garden centers, and mail-order catalogs, and collecting peonies can quickly become an expensive obsession.

Panicum virgatum
SWITCHGRASS

The great cry of "low maintenance" has resulted in gardeners embracing ornamental grasses ever more tightly. I have previously talked about the many varieties of *Miscanthus sinensis*; they are the most common and most popular and will continue to be for some time. However, some of the varieties of miscanthus grass have been receiving some bad press lately because of reseeding tendencies. The movement to native grasses has been the result. The native grass

Panicum virgatum 'Heavy Metal' behind 'Goldsturm' coneflower

that has been at the forefront of the native grass movement is switchgrass, *Panicum virgatum*, popular for its low maintenance requirements, reasonably handsome flowers, and excellent fall color. The species itself is a tough filler for well-traveled areas, such as a path for students at the University of Georgia. As good as the species is, the cultivars that have resulted are even better.

Some of the original offerings were large, especially plants like 'Heavy Metal', which can reach 7 feet in height. As a backdrop to *Rudbeckia fulgida* var. *sullivantii* 'Goldsturm', it is stunning. And in the winter, they look like sheaths of hay awaiting harvest. In the North, plants are not nearly as tall but still a golden color in the winter. Another tall form is 'Cloud Nine' with thin leaves and wispy flowers, like a cloud. 'Prairie Sky' is a

Panicum virgatum 'Heavy Metal' in winter

Panicum virgatum 'Cloud Nine'

Panicum virgatum 'Prairie Sky' (left) beside *P. v.* 'Cloud Nine', Cornell Plantations

Panicum virgatum 'Northwind'

Panicum virgatum 'Shenandoah'

Panicum virgatum 'Northwind'

Panicum virgatum 'Dallas Blues'

A field of *Papaver rhoeas*

little more dwarf, as can be seen in a planting at Cornell Plantations. An excellent plant, however, it still grows 3 feet tall.

The strongest upright form originated from Northwind Nursery in Wisconsin and is called 'Northwind'. Unlike the species and other tall introductions, it will not fall over in inclement weather and can even be used to line a path. A terrific plant, highly recommended. Most of the plants I have mentioned are excellent green-leaved plants, but a number of plants with colorful leaves have been introduced. 'Shenandoah' is a medium-sized plant with a purple hue to the foliage that can be useful both in containers and in the landscape. However, in my opinion, plants are not as colorful as the catalogs suggest. I also really enjoy the blue foliage of 'Dallas Blues'. It is 3 to

4 feet tall, and the blue leaves are excellent foils against conifers and other plants in the landscape. However, the best use for the plant I have seen is in the wonderful garden of Liz Klose in Niagara-on-the-Lake, Ontario, where she combined it with 'Margarita' sweet potatoes and begonias in a container on her deck.

Papaver
POPPY

From Flanders Field to the Wizard of Oz, from fresh rolls and bagels to blighted city streets, poppies have been woven into our poetry, literature, and social structure for many years. That they have been memorialized and cursed with equal vigor underscores the longevity and the beauty of some

Panicum virgatum 'Shenandoah'

of the species. Both the Flanders poppy, *Papaver rhoeas*, and the opium poppy, *P. somniferum*, are considered annuals in most North American gardens but will occasionally reseed to produce a "perennial" show. The Flanders poppy is easy and colorful,

Papaver rhoeas

Papaver nudicaule 'Champagne Bubbles'

Papaver somniferum

Papaver somniferum var. *paeoniflorum*

Papaver orientale 'Turkish Delight'

and to see a European field in full finery can bring tears of joy or sadness to the eyes, depending on how quickly John McCrae's poem comes to mind. ("In Flanders fields the poppies blow / Between the crosses, row on row.") It is definitely an age thing. Plants reseed easily, almost anywhere, and soon make a mini-pasture. The opium poppy is so handsome that it cannot be ignored as a garden plant, drugheads be damned. The scarlet flowers of the species are beautiful on their own, but the peony-flowered variety *paeoniflorum* is certainly a different form of this flower. Add to that the handsome blue-green foliage and the everlasting

seed capsules, and we have a plant that can be enjoyed both in the garden and in the vase. What a shame that idiots have messed up such a great plant.

The Iceland poppy, *Papaver nudicaule*, does not suggest sunny beaches and outdoor picnics, but its colorful crepe paper flowers make it worthwhile no matter where you garden. They can be used as a fall-planted complement to the trillions of pansies that are set out in southern and western American landscapes each autumn. Numerous cultivars are offered, usually in mixed colors and nearly always grown from seed, but 'Champagne Bubbles' is the

most common. Spring Fever mix has large bright flowers, and the Pulcinella series is quite spectacular. Big flowers, compact plants, cold tolerance, and bright spring-embracing color are reasons to put these wonderful plants in the garden. The Iceland poppy will not make it through summers in about seventy percent of the country, but so what? As long as you know what to expect, plant and enjoy.

By far the most popular perennial species is the Oriental poppy, *Papaver orientale*, whose bold, colorful flowers enliven late spring. The dark green, coarse leaves appear prickly (they are not), but as tough as

Papaver orientale 'Avebury Crimson'

Papaver orientale 'Marcus Perry'

Pennisetum alopecuroides

Pennisetum alopecuroides in fall

they look, they are wimpy, going dormant as temperatures warm up in the summer. The most common color is red, and the small crimson flowers include 'Avebury Crimson' and 'Marcus Perry', old-fashioned selections to be sure but as beautiful as ever. For other interesting colors in the poppy field, you might want to try 'Polly's Plum' or the salmon-pink flowers of 'Turkish Delight'. Nobody ever accused an Oriental poppy of being subtle.

Oriental poppies do poorly in the South and should be avoided south of zone 6, although some northern zone 7 gardeners will be successful for a few seasons. Where they do well, however, they are spectacular.

All poppies are most comfortable in zones 3 to 5 (occasionally zone 6 for the Oriental poppy), zone 8 on the West Coast. Full sun, good drainage.

Pennisetum
FOUNTAIN GRASS

Of all the grasses—from *Achnatherum* to *Vetiveria*—the fountain grasses have undergone particularly superb breeding, especially in the annual species. Only a few species in the genus are perennial. The most popular is *Pennisetum alopecuroides*, perennial fountain grass, whose graceful flowers hang over the plants like so many

bowing princesses. Plants are about 3 feet tall and make wonderful tussocks—and in the fall the flowers turn a handsome tan color. The available cultivars are quite similar, growing in tussocks and providing dozens of flowers in the spring. 'Hameln' is a mid-sized plant, which looks especially good in the fall, spilling over brick walkways. Dwarf forms like 'Cassian' and 'Little Bunny' are only 12 to 18 inches tall and make nice plantings without the worry of getting too large. I don't know which cultivar is "best," but I love black fountain grass, 'Moudry'. The flowers are dark purple when they start to flower and turn a handsome bronze later in the summer and fall. Plants can reseed,

Pennisetum alopecuroides 'Hameln'

Pennisetum alopecuroides 'Hameln' in fall

so be a little careful where you plant them. I don't consider them invasive, but they can fill in areas quickly.

Pennisetum orientale, Oriental fountain grass, is much underused. The plants grow 3 to 4 feet tall and consist of wispy thin vertical foliage. The tan flowers are thinner and more erect than most of the *P. alopecuroides* flower spikes. 'Karley Rose' is excellent, providing plants with pink to rose flowers, particularly in the cool months.

Recently, some fabulous hybrids have found their way to North American gardens. Through the efforts of my colleague Wayne Hanna at the University of Georgia, Tifton, dark-leaved cultivars that just get better as temperatures get warmer have arisen. The first two were 'Prince' (7 feet

Pennisetum alopecuroides 'Cassian'

Pennisetum alopecuroides 'Little Bunny'

Pennisetum alopecuroides 'Moudry'

Pennisetum alopecuroides 'Moudry' in late summer

Pennisetum 'Princess'

Pennisetum 'Princess Molly'

Pennisetum orientale 'Karley Rose'

Pennisetum 'Princess Caroline'

Penstemon barbatus 'Iron Maiden'

Penstemon pinifolius

tall) and 'Princess' (5 feet tall), both with purple foliage. The newest arrivals, 'Princess Molly' and 'Princess Caroline', are far more compact. No flowers are formed, thus no reseeding occurs. All are cold hardy to zone 7b, perhaps 7a.

Penstemon
BEARDTONGUE

Understanding the names of some of the plants we garden with can be great fun. Take penstemon, for example; its name refers to the five stamens in the flower—and that makes perfect sense. However, if you look inside the flower, only four stamens appear to be there. However, look a little more closely and you will see that the fifth one is there, but looks quite different from the other four. It is properly referred to as a staminode, in case anybody really wants to know such things. Once seen, it makes the genus fairly easy to identify. Also, on many species and cultivars, the thin, narrow tongue-like petal at the base is hairy, accounting for the common name. I guess you have to be there . . .

Penstemons create blocks of colorful flowers and/or foliage and range from tall upright to short ground-cover species, and dozens of eye-popping hybrids. Flowers are mostly in the white, red, purple, and pink range; however, a few species, such as *Penstemon confertus*, also bear quite dramatic yellow flowers. Many are native to Midwest, and species like the gloxinia penstemon, *P. cobaea*, can be found in meadows growing with native coreopsis.

The most cold-tolerant species may be common beardtongue, *Penstemon barbatus*, whose large wide-lipped flowers are slightly bearded on the lower lip. They are easy to cultivate, provide numerous colors, and persist for many years. The name 'Iron Maiden' conjures up a tough old girl, and this introduction is all of that and

Penstemon smallii

Penstemon 'Garnet'

Penstemon cobaea with *Coreopsis palmata*

beautiful to boot. The Phoenix series uses common beardtongue as an important parent, and in 'Phoenix Violet', the white throat truly stands out. The species has also been included as a parent to many hybrids, passing on its larger flowers and additional cold tolerance. Full sun, zones 2 to 7.

The pineleaf penstemon, *Penstemon pinifolius*, with thin green leaves and wonderful tubular, rosy salmon blooms, comes alive with flower power in the late spring and summer. It welcomes full sun but does not appreciate areas of high humidity and summer rain. Hardy in zones 7 to 9. On the other hand, heat, humidity, and rainfall do not

Penstemon 'Firebird'

Penstemon 'Alice Hindley'

Penstemon 'Appleblossom'

Penstemon ×*mexicali* 'Sunburst Ruby'

Penstemon confertus

Penstemon 'Phoenix Violet'

bother Small's penstemon, *P. smallii*, nearly as much. Its flowers are pink-purple on the outside and white on the inside. This species also tolerates shade better than most penstemons, although some direct sun builds stem strength. Partial shade, zones 6 to 8.

The numerous species of *Penstemon* are quite lovely, but it is the hybrids that are stealing the show in North American gardens. Although the parentage of most of them may be traced to the species of this overwhelmingly North American genus, they had to go to Europe, especially England and the British Isles, for finishing. For stunning brights, try 'Garnet', 'Firebird', and 'Pensham'; they will knock your socks off. 'Alice Hindley' and 'Appleblossom'

Penstemon barbatus 'Iron Maiden'

Perovskia atriplicifolia with Saint John's wort

Perovskia atriplicifolia 'Longin'

Perovskia atriplicifolia 'Filigran'

tone those colors down significantly and are a little easier to combine with other colors in the garden. Full sun to a little afternoon shade, zones 5 (sometimes 4) to 8. In consistently warm summer climates, most of the hybrids cannot be counted on for more than a year or so of good performance, sometimes not even that. However, some recent work has resulted in *P.* ×*mexicali* hybrids, such as 'Sunburst Ruby', a cross between Mexican and Southwest taxa. These have been excellent in hot climates, although high humidity is still not to their liking. Full sun, cold hardy to zone 6. The list goes on and on, and a good deal of money will be spent before a short list of favorites can be determined.

Perovskia atriplicifolia
RUSSIAN SAGE

I used to enjoy telling the story of how *Perovskia atriplicifolia*, Russian sage, got its common name: the foliage was so pungent, I was told, that it smelled like the feet of Russian soldiers. But with the Cold War long over, I apologize to all the Russian soldiers whose feet I maligned. (The foliage actually smells like my son's feet, on a good day, but enough on that.) The genus was in fact named for Russian general V. A. Perovsky, and this species is reliable throughout the continent. The plant is as common as dandelions in northern gardens, including every garden in Ontario I have seen, and with good reason: they are tough

Perovskia atriplicifolia with purple coneflowers

as nails and in cooler climates, the flowers are an intense blue and remain that way all summer. I love them in combinations with yellow plants like Saint John's wort, and the combination with purple coneflowers in the Music Garden in Toronto was quite wonderful. They are disappointing in southern gardens: their intense blue fades as summer temperatures increase, and plants tend to flop over. Actually, plants can grow up to 5 feet in height and may flop regardless of light intensity or summer temperatures. A good haircut in late spring encourages branching and reduces height. Regardless of the problems, the silver foliage is handsome, and its fragrance is an additional bonus for those with sinus problems.

A few cultivars are listed, but I don't see a great deal of difference from one to the other. 'Longin' and 'Filigran' are a little more dwarf, and the latter has deeper cut foliage, providing a more lacy appearance. Full sun, zones 4 to 9.

Persicaria affinis 'Superba'

Persicaria bistorta with ornamental onions

Persicaria amplexicaulis 'Firetail'

Persicaria virginiana 'Compton's Form'

Persicaria aubertii

Persicaria
KNOTWEED

Whether these plants should be in the genus *Polygonum* or *Persicaria* (or *Fallopia*—the debate goes on), everyone would agree the knotweeds are probably more cursed than loved, bringing a mixture of beauty and downright belligerence. That the best-known plants are weeds like Pennsylvania smartweed, lady's thumb, and common knotweed tells us that they are indeed adaptable. Several species, however, have been relatively tamed, enough to become part of the garden palette.

When conditions suit it, the low-growing Himalayan fleeceflower, *Persicaria affinis*, can be considered a ground cover. The small leaves emerge purple-green in the spring. As the plants mature, spikes of rosy red flowers appear, covering the planting by early summer. They do well in cool summers and are weedy south of zone 6. 'Superba' will probably be the only selection available. Excellent drainage is essential. Plants perform better in full sun to partial shade; too much shade results in sparse plantings. They perform well in zones 3 to 6. Another quasi ground cover is the large-flowered snakeweed, *P. bistorta*.

The plants consist of wavy green leaves, each with a white midrib, and above them, looking something like pink bottlebrushes, are 4- to 5-inch spikes of pink flowers. They look particularly good combined with purple flowers, such as ornamental onions. The flowers are useful as cut flowers and persist for about a week in a bouquet. Excellent plantings may be found from Pennsylvania to Chicago to Denver, but not in the South. 'Superba' is the most common form. Hardy in zones 3 to 7.

Persicaria virginiana (*Polygonum virginianum*) can be a noxious invasive plant; however, if it is going to be planted, you

Persicaria polymorpha

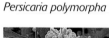

Persicaria polymorpha

Phlomis fruticosa

Phlomis russeliana

might as well enjoy it. 'Compton's Form' is really handsome, and although it might invade, your neighbors will be happy to accept something so beautiful. Another beautiful but questionable choice is fleecevine, *Persicaria aubertii* (*Polygonum aubertii*). It covers fences and other objects well, in the North as abundantly as it does in the South. A fabulous climber, but beware. It will eat entire trees.

Some of the larger species and hybrids have been avoided by knowledgeable gardeners because of their invasive tendencies. However, I can partially endorse 'Firetail', a selection of *Persicaria amplexicaulis*. Plants will rock and roll but in general can be contained much easier than the species or earlier introductions. The plants are about 3 feet tall, and the thin flowers are a fiery red.

My other highly recommended plant is the impressive giant fleeceflower, *Persicaria polymorpha*. Standing 5 to 6 feet tall and equally wide, it looks more like a large shrub. In the summer, it puts on a spectacular display of creamy white flowers for months on end. This is not a small plant, provide room, and get out of the way. I have not seen any invasive tendencies. Zones 4 to 7.

Phlomis
JERUSALEM SAGE

I have gone through my "phlomis stage of life" and had a great time collecting, learning, and watching Jerusalem sage in gardens around the world. There are few available at the garden center, but occasionally one or two will pop up. All have hairy foliage, with some silvering to it, and the flower buds are almost as beautiful as the flowers themselves. *Phlomis* is a useful companion to almost all plants in the garden, regardless of season or stage of flowering.

Phlomis tuberosa

Phlox subulata

Phlox subulata 'Scarlet Flame'

Phlox subulata 'Drummond's Pink'

The yellow forms are bigger but also more compact in habit. They are best represented by *Phlomis fruticosa*, the most popular species, and *P. russeliana*, both known as Jerusalem sage. *Phlomis fruticosa* has 2- to 4-inch-long silvery green leaves and is handsome throughout the season. The green flower buds occur in whorls up the stem, then give way to bright yellow flowers, like lights on a candelabrum. The fruit remains on the plants for many weeks, adding yet another ornamental charm to an already interesting plant. Plants get woody at the base; a hard prune in the spring every two to three years rejuvenates them. Full sun, hardy in zones 4 to 8. Plants tend to reseed, so get ready to share them with others. *Phlomis russeliana* is bigger in every way, with larger leaves and habit, but the leaves are much more dull green than silver-green, and the flowers are a softer yellow. Not quite as hardy, nor as compact of habit. Full sun, zones 5 to 8.

A number of lavender-pinks are known, but I prefer *Phlomis tuberosa*, as it performs well in warmer areas of the country. In general, the plants and leaves are smaller than the yellow-flowered species just described, but the flower color is equally arresting. Plants stand 2 to 4 feet and appear rather lanky. It is more difficult to find nurseries selling lavender-pink phlomis, likely because they are often cold hardy only to zone 7 (6 with protection). Provide full sun and well-drained soils.

Phlox

In 1745, American botanist John Bartram sent a specimen of *Phlox subulata* to England, calling it "a fine creeping Spring Lychnis." No sooner did it land than it became a hit in that land of gardens, and the English embraced it as their own. The genus enjoyed such popularity there that in

Phlox subulata

Phlox paniculata 'David' with purple coneflower

Phlox subulata

1919 Reginald Farrar enthusiastically wrote of it, "The day that saw the introduction, more than a century since . . . ought indeed to be kept as a horticultural festival." So many good garden plants are now available that Messrs. Bartram and Farrar may not even recognize those original plants.

All species of *Phlox* are native to the United States. Bartram could have sent any one of them, so why was such a commotion made over *Phlox subulata*, a plant we call the gas station plant, the outhouse plant, and other ghastly names, but properly known as moss phlox? Let there be no doubt: scorned

as it is, this is a great plant. It covers grand hillsides, sneaks under picket fences, and makes even parking lots less repellent. Dense carpets of color appear in early spring, obscuring the leaves; when the blooms have faded, carpets of green leaves, each an inch long and an eighth of an inch wide, simply blend into the landscape. It may be faulted for its short bloom time, but how extraordinary that time is. The 4- to 6-inch-tall mats come in an astonishing range of colors, with dozens of named cultivars. Some of my favorites include the striking crimson 'Red Wings', 'Scarlet Flame' for a deeper red, and 'Emerald Blue' for a more subtle effect. The flowers of moss phlox have always been relatively small, but 'Drummond's Pink' sports flowers larger than any other. Great plants, easy to grow in full sun and well-drained soils. Hardy in zones 2 to 8.

Some of the finest garden plants belong to the woodland phlox, *Phlox divaricata*, with its handsome coat of lavender flowers and thin, dark green leaves. The shade lover allows us to fill in partially shaded areas in a

Phlox subulata 'Emerald Blue'

Phlox subulata 'Red Wings'

Phlox divaricata with *Phacelia bipinnatifida*

Phlox divaricata with mondo grass

Phlox nivalis 'Eco Flirtie Eyes'

Phlox stolonifera 'Bruce's White'

Mixed display of *Phlox paniculata*

Phlox paniculata 'Miss Mary'

Phlox paniculata 'Shortwood'

Phlox paniculata 'Eva Cullum'

Phlox paniculata 'Nora Leigh'

Phlox douglasii 'Crackerjack'

Phlox paniculata 'Franz Schubert'

Mildew damage on *Phlox paniculata*

rock garden or the woodland. Woodland phlox grow 12 to 15 inches tall and harmonizes well in informal shade settings; it also combines well with foreigners like mondo grass (*Ophiopogon*) in a Japanese setting. If the plants reseed, various shades of blue, lavender, and light purple are sure to appear, and some wonderful cultivars expand the palette to icy whites ('Fuller's White', 'May Breeze') and regal purple ('Louisiana Blue'). Place in partial shade, hardy in zones 5 to 8.

A few other low growers are available, all spring flowerers and all colorful as can be. If you can find *Phlox nivalis* 'Eco Flirtie Eyes', grab it! The same can be said for Douglas phlox, *P. douglasii*, particularly in its selection 'Crackerjack'. The sand phlox, *P. bifida*, has so many flowers in the spring, it is amazing that the sun even penetrates the leaves. All three need full sun and decent drainage. For shady characters, *P. stolonifera* 'Bruce's White' and *P.* 'Chattahoochee' (sky blue) are outstanding. You will enjoy all of these.

Phlox paniculata, garden phlox, is a tough perennial, tolerating late freezes, droughts, and hot summers for many years. Dozens of flowers, averaging about an inch across, are held at the top of each plant in 8-inch-wide clusters. These are plants that turn the summer garden into a veritable rainbow, flowering June through August. Planted in large groups, they provide a vista of color a football field away. Unfortunately, in many cultivars, one of those colors may be the white of powdery mildew. This disease starts on the bottom leaves and can rapidly disfigure the entire plant. I have seen much worse cases of mildew in Montreal than in Atlanta; however, on highly susceptible cultivars, it matters very little where the plants reside. Having said that, new breeding has resulted in many cultivars that are far less susceptible than older ones. Try them out; if they mildew, cull them. Provide good circulation, and thin the emerging plants to four or five strong stems in the spring.

Phlox paniculata 'Delta Snow'

Phlox paniculata 'Little Princess'

Physostegia virginiana 'Vivid'

Phlox paniculata Peacock series

Physostegia virginiana 'Variegata'

With hundreds of *Phlox paniculata* cultivars from which to choose, gardeners can afford to be picky; color of flower, vigor of plant, and susceptibility to mildew are all characteristics to be considered. 'David' has been on the radar for many years for its white flowers and relative mildew resistance, but if I am choosing white, I would choose 'Delta Snow'. She has been in our garden for over ten years, flowers well every year, and has little or no mildew. For pink flowers, the old-fashioned 'Eva Cullum', with her deep rose center, still turns heads, as does the newer 'Shortwood', whose flowers almost cover the plant. However, for eye-popping dazzle, give 'Miss Mary' a try.

Her iridescent rose color certainly catches the eyes. Not all phlox are pink or white; 'Franz Schubert' sports a subtle lavender look. Reports on mildew on this Viennese composer have been mixed. I have never been a fan of variegated foliage on this fine genus, but 'Nora Leigh' is still around so she must be popular with others. Other cultivars are more vigorous than Nora, but her white leaf margins and two-tone flowers are hard to resist. Breeders have been trying to produce low-growing yet vigorous forms of garden phlox for years. 'Little Princess', with wonderful rosy pink flowers, still grows on a 2- to 3-foot-tall frame. The most compact I have trialed is the Peacock series,

growing less than 18 inches tall. The white flowers of 'Peacock White' are probably the best, but all plants in the series have performed well. Place in full sun; plants grow 3 to 5 feet tall unless otherwise stated. Hardy in zones 3 to 8.

Physostegia virginiana
OBEDIENT PLANT

Obedient plant, *Physostegia virginiana*, is a native of the eastern United States and is many things; obedient is not one of them. This elegant plant, with its square stems and handsome pink flowers, is quite beautiful, but its beauty and elegance

Physostegia virginiana 'Variegata'

belie its wandering proclivity. If you don't have sufficient space to allow for a little roaming, don't plant obedient plant. If room is available, however, the 2- to 4-foot plants are excellent companions for late summer- and fall-blooming plants. Dozens of inch-long lipped flowers open from the bottom to the top, and when about a third of the flowers are open, they are perfect for picking and bringing in the house. As a cut flower, they persist for at least a week in tap water, longer if a flower preservative is used.

Some excellent selections of *Physostegia virginiana* can be found in nurseries and mail-order catalogs. 'Vivid' is shorter, more compact, and with brighter pink flowers. The white-flowered cultivars are probably the prettiest; they are a little more dwarf than the pink-flowered selections and flower a few weeks earlier. 'Summer Snow' is my favorite, always making a good show and comporting itself well with others, until it too eats its neighbors. 'Variegata' is the most interesting selection; it produces pink flowers and outstanding white-and-green variegated foliage. The plant is not nearly as aggressive as its cousins, and some people believe that the plants are more handsome when flowers are absent. Plant in full sun in well-drained soils, hardy in zones 2 to 9.

By the way, pick a flowering stem of obedient plant and push one of the flowers to the side, not up or down. It will stay where you push it. So, it is obedient after all.

Physostegia virginiana 'Summer Snow'

Platycodon grandiflorus bud

Platycodon grandiflorus

Platycodon grandiflorus 'Fuji White'

Platycodon grandiflorus 'Sentimental Blue'

Platycodon grandiflorus 'Hakone Blue'

Platycodon grandiflorus
BALLOONFLOWER

Although balloonflower is native to the Far
East, these plants have become American
favorites, thanks mostly to their curious
swollen buds and handsome flowers in
mid to late summer. Slow to emerge, even
given up for dead by rookie ballooners,
they grow rapidly into sizable 3-foot plants.
The flower buds swell and swell, just like
a balloon, finally popping open to reveal
beautiful five-petaled flowers with dark blue
veins. They are particularly useful growing
with lilies or other summer-flowering white
or yellow plants.

Flower form and color vary with cultivar. 'Hakone Blue' and 'Hakone White' are
ugly double forms, but 'Fuji White' is a very
handsome single white form. One of the
problems with balloonflower is that stems
are weak, particularly in inclement weather,
and staking is often required. Because of
this, shorter selections have been bred:
the most popular of the compact forms is
'Sentimental Blue', growing 6 to 9 inches
tall, and 'Baby Blue' is just 6 inches tall.

Platycodon grandiflorus 'Hakone White'

Podophyllum peltatum emerging

Platycodon grandiflorus 'Baby Blue'

Podophyllum peltatum canopy

Both require less maintenance and can be as classy as the real thing. Plants require full sun, or they will flop over. Hardy in zones 3 to 7.

Podophyllum
MAYAPPLE

The common mayapple, *Podophyllum peltatum*, is an absolute must for native plant enthusiasts, but it is a popular shade-loving plants for all gardeners. The eastern native emerges in early spring with dark-tinged foliage. Within a few weeks, the leaves fill in and the purple tinge is lost, forming a beautiful full green canopy. The flowers are formed in April and May but to see them, you need to lift the leaves to find them beneath. They look terrific when planted with almost any other spring plants, even bulbs like spring snowflake (*Leucojum vernum*). Plants roam about freely and are among the very best ground covers for the shade.

Recently species and hybrids with Asian parentage have been introduced, mainly by growers on the West Coast. 'Kaleidoscope', with somewhat cut leaves and purple splotches, is perhaps the best known, but plants are slow and not as vigorous in eastern gardens as on the West Coast. Others with similar genetics are the reddish 'Red Panda' and the fashionable 'Spotty Dotty'. All are interesting, and if they become established, they will make you look like a real gardener.

Podophyllum pleianthum

Podophyllum 'Red Panda'

Podophyllum 'Spotty Dotty'

Podophyllum peltatum

Podophyllum pleianthum

Podophyllum peltatum with spring snowflake

Others are well worth seeking. The pink flowers of *Podophyllum hexandrum* emerge as the leaves emerge and are beautifully handsome. However, my favorite is the Asian mayapple, *P. pleianthum*. The large glossy dark green leaves just keep getting bigger and bigger as spring progresses, and then the flower buds burst open to reveal lipstick red flowers beneath. Plants have been spreading slowly, albeit not nearly as rapidly as common mayapple, but I will take all I can get.

Polemonium caeruleum

Polemonium
JACOB'S LADDER

The genus *Polemonium* ranges from 3-foot-tall plants to dwarf runners, and all grow better in cool rather than warm summers. The blue, white, or pink flowers generally present themselves in early to mid summer. Of the twenty-five or so species, one or two are quite endearing, if not enduring, and a few others are well worth trying.

Polemonium caeruleum, common Jacob's ladder, has about twenty leaves climbing the stem, each leaf representing a rung of the Jacob's ladder "we are climbing." Plants stand 2 to 3 feet tall and produce masses of lavender-blue flowers in the spring and early summer. I have seen excellent stands in Franklin Park, Columbus, Ohio, and in

Polemonium reptans

Polemonium caeruleum 'Bressingham Purple'

Polemonium caeruleum 'Bressingham Purple'

Polemonium caeruleum 'Snow and Sapphires'

Polemonium reptans 'Stairway to Heaven'

Trois Rivières, Quebec, where they grow like weeds. In Athens, they are okay but certainly not weedlike. 'Bressingham Purple' has performed admirably well in the heat as well as in the North. The stems are purple, and the entire plant is a little darker than the species. The flowers are even brighter than those of the species. 'Snow and Sapphires' has narrow pointed leaves, each one bearing a clean white margin. The plants flower, but buy them for the variegated foliage, not the flowers.

Our native plant, *Polemonium reptans*, is a low grower, less than a foot tall. Plants are happiest with afternoon shade, moist soils, and lots of room. They make a handsome ground cover at the edge of the woods. The blue flowers are plentifully produced, followed by fruit that throw out huge amounts of seed, allowing the plants to multiply freely. Similar to the above species, a variegated form has also emerged as a popular new plant. 'Stairway to Heaven' is a selection with green and white foliage, and few flowers. The variegated forms are less vigorous in the garden and more prone to melting out in the summer than green leaf forms. All cultivars are cold hardy to at least zone 4, and heat tolerant to about zone 7 east of the Rocky Mountains, zone 8 west of the Rockies. Full sun, well-drained soils.

Polygonatum
SOLOMON'S SEAL

The genus *Polygonatum* provides a wonderful store of shade-tolerant plants for the garden, many of them among our finest natives. The

Polygonatum humile

Polygonatum odoratum 'Variegatum'

Polygonatum commutatum fruit

Polygonatum commutatum emerging

common name has many a good yarn associated with it; one is that, during the times of the great kings, the roots acted as a glue to heal broken bones, and it was this sealing property that begat the name Solomon's seal. (I don't believe it either.) Of the many closely related species, three have a definite place in the woodland garden.

Polygonatum commutatum, great Solomon's seal, is a wonderfully robust species

(3 to 5 feet tall). I love the way the stems of *P. commutatum* burst through the spring ground, the leaves tucked in and the entire stem resembling a fat green shish-kebab skewer. As the leaves unfurl, the small floating flower buds break open to reveal clean white flowers dangling from each leaf node. After flowering, small black fruit are formed, which often give rise to other plants the next year. When mature, this is

an impressive plant that easily fits into any shade border. So common in the Northeast and Midwest that it is hardly even noticed, this plant richly deserves a place in the shaded woodland.

The fragrant Solomon's seal, *Polygonatum odoratum* 'Variegatum' is the European representative of the great genus and to me is a must-have plant for the garden. Plants grow no more than 2 feet tall, have

Polygonatum commutatum

clean variegated leaves, and still bear those wonderful pendulous white flowers. Both *Polygonatum commutatum* and *P. odoratum* perform well in partial shade with at least two to four hours of bright light. Hardy in zones 3 to 8.

As robust and grand as the previous two species are, *Polygonatum humile*, dwarf Solomon's seal, is refined and charming. Plants grow only 6 to 9 inches tall, still with the characteristic small white flowers formed at the nodes. A rich full planting can be obtained in two to three years, and a better ground cover for a small area is hard to imagine. Plants prefer partial shade, but not as much as the upright Solomons. While I admire and use the upright species, I lust after this one. Partial shade, hardy in zones 5 to 7.

Primula
PRIMROSE

Here is a group of plants that is impossible to hate. That may be said with many flowers, but primroses light up the spring season so brilliantly that people want more. As for me, I do have one major complaint— I can't grow them worth a darn in my southeastern zone 7 garden! When I visit my gardening friends on the West Coast (including Alaska), or overseas, I revel in the magic of spring primroses. Not that the Armitage garden is entirely bereft of this wonderful genus, but the primrose path is easier trodden in climates where hot summers are uncommon. Cold is not an issue if snow cover is abundant. Unfortunately, if you don't live in primrose country in the

United States, you will be hard pressed to find two or three different kinds for sale, even in quality garden centers. Fortunately, some excellent mail-order businesses carry a reasonable assortment of plants. Of the four hundred or so species in the genus, we are sometimes lucky to find one or two at the local garden center and must instead peruse the mail-order seed and plant sources for any satisfaction. Seed is generally not difficult to germinate, and many species may be obtained through specialist seed sources. Essentially all primroses perform better with mild summers, partially shaded areas, and consistent moisture in the soil. Some require boggy soils to do well and wimp out at the first hint of drought or heat, while others are much tougher than they look.

Primula denticulata

Primula denticulata 'Rubin'

Primula denticulata 'Alba'

Primula veris

The drumstick primrose, *Primula denticulata*, is one of the earliest primroses to flower, often appearing at the first hint of warmth, later succumbing to the rigors of heat in much of the country. Looking at the flower reaffirms its common name; these drumsticks occur in shades of lavender, rose-blue ('Rubin'), and white ('Alba'). They are beautiful when in flower, and their foliage simply disappears into the plants that grow up around it. Hardy in zones 5 (4 with protection) to 7.

Primula veris, cowslip, requires similar growing conditions, that is, shady and moist, but cowslips tolerate heat much better. It is a terrific, adaptable, and functional primrose that works well in North American gardens. The dark green leaves are in

Primula florindae

Primula japonica

Primula japonica 'Splendens'

Primula helodoxa

Primula japonica 'Postford White'

Primula bulleyana

Primula vulgaris subsp. *sibthorpii*

Primula vulgaris 'Gigha White'

Primula pulverulenta Bartley hybrids

perfect contrast to the deep yellow flowers, which continue to open for four to six weeks in the spring. One of the best primroses for southern gardeners; heat is far less of a problem, assuming water is available, and plants reseed easily. A primrose path is almost possible, although let's not get too carried away—it is still a primrose. Hardy in zones 5 (4 with protection) to 7.

Some of the most beautiful and architectural primroses of all fall into the candelabra group. The flowers of these several species are arranged on long flower stems, like lights on an exquisite candelabrum. They all require copious amounts of water and in fact are best suited for water

Primula vialii

Primula 'Rowallane Rose'

Primula vialii

gardens, sides of streams, or boggy soils. If such conditions are provided, then plants can tolerate full sun, but afternoon shade is usually appreciated. The best known of the candelabras, the Japanese primrose, *Primula japonica*, is usually seen in a mixture of flower colors. Some monochromatic selections can also be found occasionally, such as 'Postford White' and the rosy pink 'Splendens'. I have seen lovely plantings in the mid-Atlantic states and as far north as southern Alaska.

American gardeners don't have access to as many of the candelabras as their European colleagues; however, if you are successful with Japanese primrose, then all sorts of primrose doors open. I would be like a kid in a candy store and try some that look impossible, such as Bulley's primrose, *Primula bulleyana*, with its vibrant orange flowers. Even the name is terrific. For a more refined effect, I would plant some florinda primroses, *P. florindae*, by the side

of a pond. With its dangling yellow flowers and classic habit, it is a plant well worth trying. My candelabra collection would be incomplete without a few plants of the butter-yellow *P. helodoxa*, the rosy flowers of *P. pulverulenta* Bartley hybrids, or my all-time favorite from Ireland, *P.* 'Rowallane Rose'. These may not take you, your garden, and your neighborhood too far along that primrose path—still, half the fun is in the trying. Plants need lots of water and partial shade. All are heat hardy to zone 6, and most of the candelabra forms will do well far north as long as snow cover remains for most of the winter. Some of the candelabras are like weeds in Homer, Alaska.

Almost everyone who sees Vial's primrose, *Primula vialii*, has to look twice to even recognize it as a primrose, but once the synapses click, the next thoughts are "I must have it" and "Where do I get it?" The purple flowers extend nearly 2 feet into the air and are only vaguely primrose-like. It

Primula ×polyantha mix

Primula vulgaris

Primula ×polyantha 'Danova White'

Primula ×polyantha 'Danova Golden Yellow'

is still an oddball in this country and, to be honest, is on the cusp of oddball-ness most everywhere else. However, if you can find some plants or seeds, give it a try. Like other primroses, plants perform well in moist, shady conditions. Success requires mild summers and winters, moisture, and

a protected area. Partial shade, hardy in zones 5 to 7.

The common English primrose, *Primula vulgaris*, is not all that common in the United States but very common in Europe, where many selections have been made. Short in stature but frost and

heat tolerant, they are usually available in yellows and whites. The most common forms are 'Gigha White' and subspecies *sibthorpii*, which are white or off-white and pink, respectively. They are early, beautiful, and crash at the first sign of heat. The English primrose is also known for the old-

Primula vulgaris 'Double Yellow'

Primula ×polyantha, Compton Acres, England

Primula ×polyantha in New Zealand

fashioned highly bred double flowers, such as 'Double Yellow', which were mostly grown for exhibition and not the garden. Still available, but not nearly as popular as in Queen Victoria's time. Partial shade, hardy in zones 5 to 7.

I suppose that if I take the hopeful primose lover out of me, and look around at what the pragmatic primrose gardener in me can truly succeed with, choices are indeed limited. However, gardeners in places like the United Kingdom and New Zealand often bed out large numbers of hybrid primroses, usually referred to as *Primula ×polyantha*, or polys for short. They are used there almost like annuals, similar to how we use fall mums. These incredibly colorful—okay, gaudy—displays certainly catch the eye. Many of these hybrids are available in a mix of colors and generally for sale in the early spring. At the Trial Gardens at UGA, zone 7b, we have trialed dozens as a complement to pansies and unfortunately have seen mixed results when planted in the fall. The best have been the Danova series, but they are getting better all the time and I am still a believer. After all, how many pansies can we stand?

Pulmonaria longifolia subsp. *cevennensis*

Pulmonaria
LUNGWORT

Lungworts have been around for so long that many gardeners have abandoned them in favor of newer models. However, a well-grown plant can be counted on to produce a blend of blue, lavender, red, or white flowers, but far more important than the flowers is the wonderful and handsome foliage. They are tougher than they look, asking only for some shade and well-drained soils. The plain Jane of the group is *Pulmonaria angustifolia*. The somewhat narrow leaves have no color compared to other species, however, they certainly have beautiful flowers, as seen in 'Mawson's Variety'. They also possess good heat tolerance, performing well in the Trial Gardens at UGA. Happy and hardy in zones 3 to 7 in the East, to zone 8 in the West.

Long-leaved lungwort, *Pulmonaria longifolia*, has long, narrow leaves, which are quite distinct from all other lungworts. The foliage is beautifully spotted, and the flowers are usually lavender to blue.

Pulmonaria 'Trevi Fountain'

Pulmonaria angustifolia

Pulmonaria angustifolia 'Mawson's Variety'

Pulmonaria 'Gaelic Magic'

Pulmonaria 'Gaelic Sunset'

Pulmonaria 'Northern Lights'

Subspecies *cevennensis* (also sold as 'Little Blue') has some of the most ornamental foliage in the entire genus. All the long-leaved selections and hybrids of this species are excellent performers, tolerating hot, humid summers better than other lungworts and providing excellent foliage and habit in most of the country. 'Trevi Fountain' has had lots of great press and is sold everywhere. Hardy in zones 3 to 7.

However, it is the selections of spotted lungwort, *Pulmonaria saccharata*, that are by far the most readily available and popular. The leaves are wider than those of *P. longifolia*, and spotting patterns are highly variable. In fact, they are like fingerprints, no leaf being exactly the same as another.

Pulmonaria 'Regal Ruffles'

Pulmonaria 'Raspberry Ice'

Pulmonaria 'Moonshine'

Pulmonaria 'Argentea'

Dozens of cultivars and hybrids have been introduced, all with very early spring flowers and beautiful foliage throughout the season. The flowers are quite wonderful, but they disappear quickly—buy the plant based on the leaves, not the blossoms. All of the following are likely hybrids, but all have a plentiful dollop of *P. saccharata* in the parentage. The Gaelic series includes 'Gaelic Magic' and 'Gaelic Sunset', which perform well in the heat and humidity and whose foliage always looks good. 'Regal Ruffles' has light green leaves with many white spots. 'Victorian Brooch' glows in the afternoon sun with dark green leaves.

'Moonshine' has so many spots on a silver background, it almost looks like

Pulmonaria 'Silver Shimmers'

Pulmonaria 'Majeste'

Pulmonaria 'Victorian Brooch'

silver. In fact, choices with silver foliage are becoming more and more common. One of the oldest forms is 'Argentea', a great plant which has been replaced with newer forms like 'Raspberry Ice' and the handsome 'Northern Lights'. I love them all but have really been enamored with 'Silver Shimmers' because it makes a large colony almost everywhere I have seen it. However, lots of gardeners have jumped on the wonderfully silver 'Majeste', and it has been quite terrific in our trials. Given the depth and range of offerings, describing lungworts is becoming as difficult as describing coral bells, daylilies, or hostas. All the better for us gardeners! Hardy in zones 3 to 7 in the East, to zone 8 in the West.

Pulsatilla vulgaris seed heads

Pulsatilla vulgaris 'Alba'

Pulsatilla vulgaris

Pulsatilla halleri

Pulsatilla
PASQUEFLOWER

Except to the hard-core alpine and rock garden enthusiasts, the genus *Pulsatilla* is largely unknown. Those in the know grow pasqueflowers for the beauty of their dissected foliage and their handsome purple to white flowers in early spring. Plants emerge as hairy columns, often giving way to flowers shrouded with newly formed foliage—quite a wonderful sight. They often emerge even before the snow has disappeared, and many weeks later, the seed heads continue to add yet another dimension to the plant. In fact, to me it is the waving seed heads that are the most striking part of the plants, persisting for many weeks after the ephemeral flowers have disappeared. Because they emerge so early, the flowers and seed heads persist for as long as the cool weather holds up. I have seen absolutely stunning plantings in the Denver Botanic Gardens (there the pasqueflowers are seeding everywhere) and have even tried them in north Georgia with success. Most gardeners should be able to locate the common pasqueflower, *Pulsatilla vulgaris*, a plant that provides excellent foliage and dozens of deep purple flowers.

Pulsatilla vulgaris emerging

Pulsatilla pratensis

Ranunculus asiaticus 'Bloomingdale Yellow'

The most colorful and the most persnickety is the tuberous-rooted Persian buttercup, *Ranunculus asiaticus*. Usually seen as a pot plant from the greenhouse or as a cut flower grown in cool summer areas, it produces some of the prettiest flowers in the genus. When the tubers are purchased, they should be soaked in water and put in the garden in the fall in mild areas and in the spring in areas of cold winters and cool summers. The deeper they are planted, the less chance for freezing. Plants enjoy cool weather and look their best in early spring; however, they are frost tolerant only to about 28°F. If they don't emerge in the spring, it may be that critters like squirrels, moles, voles, or deer have removed them. Plants will produce many double flowers in the spring, then go dormant in the summer. Selections are similar, but the two most common are the Bloomingdale series and the Sunningdale series. Full sun and excellent drainage are necessary. Hardy in zones 7 to 9.

Another little tuberous species is *Ranunculus ficaria*, which if conditions are to its liking can become terribly invasive. I have seen it take over entire hillsides in New York. One selection of the plant that is not invasive for me (I continue to hope it will grow faster) is 'Brazen Hussy', who lives up to her name in March when the

Pulsatilla vulgaris

Numerous cultivars have been selected, but I have been most impressed with the white-flowered 'Alba', which forms similar seed heads and whose white flowers contrast well with the foliage. If one lives in an area where alpines do well, then it is worth chasing down plants of *P. halleri* or *P. pratensis*, both of which flower early and often. Provide full sun, excellent drainage. Hardy in zones 4 (3 with protection) to 7.

Ranunculus
BUTTERCUP

Buttercups are a study in diversity, for sure. Some are invasive. Some die at the first touch of frost; others emerge through the snow. Some grow from a tuber, like a potato, others from fibrous roots. Although most people think of buttercups as yellow, their flowers appear in a full spectrum of hues.

Ranunculus asiaticus 'Sunningdale Mix'

Ranunculus ficaria 'Brazen Hussy'

Ranunculus repens 'Buttered Popcorn' with bugle weed

Ranunculus ficaria

Ranunculus acris 'Stevenii'

Ranunculus bulbosus 'Flore Pleno'

Rehmannia elata with *Hippeastrum ×johnsonii*

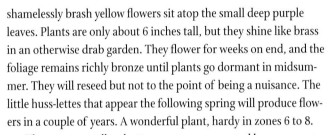

Rehmannia angulata 'Popstar'

shamelessly brash yellow flowers sit atop the small deep purple leaves. Plants are only about 6 inches tall, but they shine like brass in an otherwise drab garden. They flower for weeks on end, and the foliage remains richly bronze until plants go dormant in midsummer. They will reseed but not to the point of being a nuisance. The little huss-lettes that appear the following spring will produce flowers in a couple of years. A wonderful plant, hardy in zones 6 to 8.

The common yellow buttercups are represented by numerous species. The showy buttercup, *Ranunculus acris*, is just that, especially in its selection 'Stevenii'. The double yellow flower of the invasive *R. bulbosus* 'Flore Pleno' is quite lovely, but note the thuggery in its eyes. Creeping buttercup, *R. repens*, is equally invasive. If one is going to use these plants as a ground cover, invasiveness might be a good quality. One of the prettiest selections of *R. repens* is the white and green variegated 'Buttered Popcorn'. In mild winters, the foliage is as pretty as it is in the summer. Hell, it survives below zero temperatures and still looks brand new. It looks terrific with bronze foliage of bugle weed (*Ajuga*) and oxalis. This is such a thug it may be difficult to buy. Be warned—it gallops!

Rehmannia
CHINESE FOXGLOVE

Rehmannia elata and *R. angulata* (Chinese foxglove) are wonderful plants that never fail to elicit all sorts of favorable comments, as well as the all-too-common "What are they?" and "Where did you find them?" They belong to the same family as African violets and gloxinias and are also characterized by hairy stems and light green leaves, which in the case of both species are deeply lobed or toothed, like an oak's leaf. It is hard to tell the two apart unless they are growing side by side but if you are interested, *R. angulata* is smaller (about 2 feet tall) than *R. elata* (2 to 4 feet tall) and not as hairy. The flowers of *R. angulata* bear orange dots inside the lower lip; the larger flowers of *R. elata* have yellow throats and red dots. From late spring to midsummer, they present a handsome look, especially when the large bright rosy purple flowers open. They are bunched in terminal clusters, and when in flower, the plants are similar to foxglove, only shorter. 'Popstar' is a new cultivar of Chinese foxglove, with larger flowers on a more compact plant. Winter wetness can be a serious problem; therefore a raised bed is best for longer-lasting stands.

Rodgersia podophylla

Rodgersia pinnata

Rodgersia pinnata 'Superba'

Rodgersia sambucifolia

All Chinese foxgloves spread rapidly by seed and even in the same season, seedlings will grow and flower, quickly resulting in a reasonably large colony. Although they are native to China, these two species are not cold hardy north of zone 7, and even there, cold winters can take them out. They should be planted in partial shade in a protected area sheltered from the worst of the winter winds.

Rodgersia

Gardeners love large, bold, foliage plants in the garden; the flowers may be secondary to the foliage. The desire for foliage accounts for much of the recent turn to ornamental grasses. *Rodgersia*, however, is also a bold, bodacious plant, one whose foliage provides wonderful contrast to all sorts of flowering plants. That the foliage is outstanding is only part of the appeal; the flowers, like giant astilbes, are also enchanting in midsummer. The flowers are borne well above the foliage and are found mainly in whites, pinks, and reds.

Alas, the tale is not fully told. Beautiful as they are, rodgersias have serious limitations. They are not at all comfortable when temperatures are warm, and once temperatures consistently reach 80°F or more, their

Rodgersia aesculifolia

Rodgersia pinnata 'Rubra' (left) and *R. p.* 'Alba'

Rohdea japonica

foliage looks a little tatty. Furthermore, they are plants best suited for a bog or streamside condition; placing these plants in dry soils is like potting up primroses in Miami. They prefer shady conditions, and a combination of moist soils, cool summers, and partial shade will ensure your chance for success with them. They do well on the West Coast but with proper attention to moisture and shade, they can be wonderful additions to gardens in zones 5 and 6, even though they will be a challenge. Additional mulching is necessary in zone 5; keep them out of the worst winter winds.

For most gardeners, all rodgersias look about the same. The most commonly offered species is *Rodgersia podophylla*, with wonderful bronze palmate leaves and creamy white flowers. The flowers of *R. pinnata* can be tall and white ('Alba'), red ('Rubra'), or the best of all, tall, brassy, and rose-red ('Superba'); its leaves are pinnate and turn reddish bronze in late summer. The architecture of rodgersia foliage is great fun to figure out. The leaves of *R. aesculifolia* and *R. sambucifolia* actually do look like those of horsechestnut (palmate) and elderberry (pinnate), respectively, although they are also easily mixed up.

I am not sure if any one species is easier than the others, but given the dearth of architectural plants, any one is worth a try. What else do you know that is big, bold, and beautiful and wants to be planted in a bog?

Rohdea japonica
SACRED LILY

I never thought I would take up time and space to write about sacred lilies. They are, for the most part, green, slow, and

Rohdea japonica 'Seiki-no-homare' with daffodils

Rohdea japonica 'Striata'

unexciting. Add to that ridiculously expensive and cold hardy only to zone 6—well, what is the point? However, the more I talked to gardeners, the more they salivated over them. And to be honest, they have looked better in the Armitage garden over time—I may even admit to liking them a little.

They have thick, dark green evergreen leaves which, depending on cultivar, may be streaked, variegated, or simply green. The species often changes from a darker color in the spring to bright green in the summer. They grow to about 1 foot tall and $1\frac{1}{2}$ feet wide once mature, but that will take a few years. The flowers are rather forgettable, but short stalks of red berries occur in fall and go through the winter. If you can grow them and you are debating the effectiveness of the money you are about to pay, remember they

Rohdea japonica in spring

Rudbeckia subtomentosa with liatris

are one of the best plants for dry shade, and that fact might just cinch the deal.

If you go online, you will find dozens of cultivars with Japanese names, each commanding an emperor's budget. I have tried only a few, but they all behave about the same. I really like 'Seiki-no-homare' and 'Striata', both of which have white-margined leaves and perform well.

Rudbeckia
CONEFLOWER, BLACK-EYED SUSAN

Of all the genera in the daisy family, *Rudbeckia* is one of the most beloved and popular. Gardeners who can't tell an astilbe from an aster have no trouble confidently inquiring after your black-eyed Susans. For a long visual show with a minimum of upkeep and maintenance, the coneflowers fit just about everybody's idea of a good perennial.

Rudbeckia fulgida var. *sullivantii* 'Goldsturm' remains an incredibly popular coneflower, smothering summer and fall gardens wherever the sun shines. The species itself, *R. fulgida*, which does

Rudbeckia fulgida var. *sullivantii* 'Goldsturm'

not differ greatly from this ubiquitous representative, is found only occasionally in botanical gardens but is strong enough to compete with Russian sage and other aggressive plants. 'Goldsturm' originated in 1937 at Foerster's Nursery in Germany, described as a late summer- to fall-flowering perennial with persistent orange ray flowers surrounding a rounded black disk. Plants grow 2 to 3 feet tall, and large colonies form rapidly, complementing everything from ornamental grasses to rocks. Although they are overplanted, it is with good reason. I admit I am tired

of seeing this thing in every garden and gas station in the country, but I am equally pleased that a plant with this much beauty is enjoyed by so many people who would otherwise have planted five geraniums and watched them die. Other selections, similar to 'Goldsturm', have recently been introduced. One of the finest, with relatively early flowers, is 'Viette's Little Suzy', a terrific performer that flowers at least twice a year. 'Early Bird Gold' is another early-flowering form that has done well in the Trial Gardens at UGA. All require full sun and adequate moisture and are heavy

Rudbeckia fulgida with Russian sage

Rudbeckia fulgida 'Viette's Little Suzy'

Rudbeckia fulgida 'Early Bird Gold'

feeders. Plants hate shade, and don't do well in drought. Hardy in zones 3 to 8.

Rudbeckia nitida and *R. laciniata*, cutleaf coneflowers, can be 5 to 7 feet tall and produce many yellow flowers with a greenish disk. The species are quite dramatic, especially when one comes across a sole specimen, standing like a sentinel. A few excellent cultivars are so large that one plant is sufficient for a good show; they make good eye-popping fall-flowering specimens. They may be listed as selections of one species or the other, but similarities to both species may be found upon close observation. I really like the tall (up to 7 feet) 'Herbstsonne' ('Autumn Sun'), which just may be a hybrid between the two species. Dozens of long drooping sulfur-yellow

Rudbeckia fulgida var. *sullivantii* 'Goldsturm' and *R. nitida*

Rudbeckia nitida

Rudbeckia 'Herbstsonne' ('Autumn Sun')

petals surround a cylindrical green disk, making a glorious show from September through November, dwarfing red dahlias or red cannas. Plants require full sun, good drainage, and protection from winds. Too much shade or exposure to high winds results in the need for staking. Zones 5 (perhaps 4) to 8.

Rudbeckia triloba, the three-lobed coneflower, is native to the Great Plains. This prairie species provides 3- to 5-foot-tall plants absolutely covered with small (1½ inches across) flowers. The bottom leaves are tri-lobed, thus accounting for the common name. Plants are not as perennial as other species, generally flowering themselves to oblivion after two or three years; but they reseed and reappear with

Rudbeckia triloba

Rudbeckia subtomentosa 'Henry Eilers'

abandon, never going away entirely. The yellow to orange ray flowers surround a black to purple disk. A great plant, even when not in flower. Full sun, good drainage, zones 3 to 10. *Rudbeckia subtomentosa*, sweet coneflower, has narrow petals around reddish disks and stands 4 to 5 feet tall. It combines beautifully with gayfeather, *Liatris*. One of the finest new introductions I have seen in the last few years is 'Henry Eilers', a 4- to 6-foot-tall fall-flowering plant that seems to grow almost anywhere and always looks great. Find it, buy it. Full sun. Zones 4 to 8.

Salvia
SAGE

People collect stamps, coins, and cats. Me, I went through a "salvia stage of life." Fortunately I emerged reasonably unscathed. Going through the SSOL is like going through the teenage years: out of control and out of money. Salvias are perfect for the plant collector, but putting the first new salvia in newly prepared ground is like putting the first tropical fish in a newly purchased aquarium. It is impossible to stop at one. It is such a large genus, with dozens of species, selections, and hybrids, that just when you think you have seen the end of them, someone comes along with another.

Meadow sage goes under numerous botanical names; the most common one is *Salvia nemorosa*. Given cool nights and good moisture, meadow sage makes an outstanding display. Plants grow 1 to $1\frac{1}{2}$ feet tall and flower throughout the summer. They don't do too badly in hot summers and high humidity, but when temperatures are cooler, they are wonderfully eye-catching. 'Bordeau' has steel blue flowers, while 'Compact Rose' provides a rosy red color. The most popular may be 'Caradonna', which bears purple flowers on 2-foot-tall

Salvia nemorosa 'Caradonna'

Salvia nemorosa 'Bordeau'

Salvia verticillata 'Purple Rain'

plants. Hybrids which have meadow sage in the parentage are many, but one of the very best is 3- to 4-foot-tall 'Mystic Blue Spires'. We have trialed this plant for years, and every year it is fabulous. It remains one of the best salvias on the market.

Some excellent hardy perennials include lilac sage, *Salvia verticillata*. The flowers are a bit like chandeliers as they grow up the flower stem. The only cultivar available is 'Purple Rain', an excellent plant from zones 4 to 8. Clary sage, *S. sclarea*, is

Salvia nemorosa 'Compact Rose'

Salvia sclarea

Salvia sclarea var. turkestanica

Salvia leucantha

Salvia leucantha 'Midnight' with Caryopteris divaricata 'Snow Fairy'

Salvia leucantha white-flowered form

Salvia leucantha pink-flowered form

Salvia elegans

Salvia elegans 'Golden Delicious'

a fabulous, although smelly, plant that is a big bodacious addition to the border. The species has lavender flowers; the variety *turkestanica* bears whitish flowers. The smell of the flowers can be a little much; the foliage is not a whole lot better.

A lot of salvias are fabulous but perhaps not cold hardy north of zone 7 or 6. However, many gardeners, even in the North, try some of them and perhaps hope they will return. For southern gardeners, all of these are perennial. The very best is

Salvia elegans 'Golden Delicious' surrounding cannas

Salvia 'Hot Lips'

Salvia 'Mystic Blue Spires'

velvet sage, *Salvia leucantha*, with its late fall flowers of blue and white on 5-foot-tall plants. A number of fine selections are available. The best might be 'Midnight' with its full purple flowers; it looks exceptionally good with variegated plants. Exciting new plants include a white form and even a pink-flowering cultivar. They are the future of this plant, and the future is good.

Salvia elegans, pineapple sage, is also hardy only to zone 7, but oh my, the flowers

Salvia involucrata

Santolina chamaecyparissus

Salvia lyrata 'Purple Knockout'

are brilliant. The foliage smells just like pineapple . . . or squash, or lemon or something. It is truly a remarkable plant but flowers in late fall only. If red flowers are not important, try the neat 'Golden Delicious' with its golden leaves. The flowers also occur on this plant, but they are far less important. From a distance, the planting of 'Golden Delicious' surrounding a planting of canna lilies is a fabulous combination.

Salvia involucrata, bulbous pink sage, is actually cherry pink, and the flowers terminate in a swollen knob, not exactly useful for a common name. Plants are large (4- to 5-foot-tall stems) and are very lax and open. In most gardens they'll need at least one pinch, but since they don't flower until late summer and fall, two pinches may be required. It is big and will likely need staking. Full sun, zones 8 (perhaps 7) to 10.

Our native lyreleaf sage, Salvia lyrata, is a wonderfully aggressive weed. Plants normally have green leaves and white spring flowers, but the dark-leaved forms like 'Purple Knockout' are quite dramatic. The purple leaves combine wonderfully well with the white flowers. If summer temperatures are hot, the foliage color may fade. Lastly, I could not leave salvias without including one of my favorite hybrids. 'Hot Lips' has neat red and white flowers on 4-foot-tall plants. They flower in the spring, and if cut back after first flush, they flower just as prolifically all over again. And with a name like that, everyone smiles.

Santolina
LAVENDER COTTON

The raison d'être for lavender cotton is not the plants themselves, but what their gray-green foliage does for their neighbors. That's what makes them so desirable. If you are designing a garden stroll through fragrant foliage, be sure to include this herb. The fragrance is not soon to be forgotten: not awful, but very pungent, a great identification feature. Plants are not particularly tolerant of hot summers and high humidity, and absolutely intolerant of poor drainage. Santolina is not for everybody.

Santolina chamaecyparissus is the most common of the species encountered in gardens. Its many finely divided leaflets are a soothing gray-green with a white sheen beneath, a very effective softener of the intense greens and bright flower colors of summer. When well grown, they make loose leafy balls in the landscape and later in the summer produce rather forgettable yellow daisy flowers. They are

Santolina chamaecyparissus 'Lemon Queen'

Santolina virens 'Lemon Fizz'

Santolina virens

Saxifraga arendsii 'Touran'

often sheared and used as an edging, which is cruel and unusual punishment for any plant. They become woody at the base after a year or so in the garden and may require a hard pruning of old wood for rejuvenation. 'Lemon Queen' has soft yellow flowers and actually makes the plant look good, something the bright yellow flowers on the species do not. Full sun, excellent drainage, zones 6 to 8.

Santolina virens, green lavender cotton, is grown as much for its yellow flowers as its bright green foliage, which resembles that of rosemary. The leaflets are quite small (less than half an inch), resulting in foliage that is more sticklike. Plants do not have the powerful smell of the common species but rather a sanitized aroma. Not nearly as much fun or exercise for the nose. 'Lemon Fizz' is an interesting cultivar. Full sun, excellent drainage, hardy in zones 7 to 9.

Saxifraga
SAXIFRAGE

Saxifraga is a huge genus—some upright, others ground covers; some cold hardy to zone 3, others only to zone 7. One of the better alpine plants available to gardeners is mossy saxifrage, *Saxifraga arendsii*. This is a rock garden plant, performing much better in the North than the South. We trialed it in Athens, and it did well for a year, but the summers were too difficult for it. 'Touran' is a recent cultivar known for its hundreds of spring flowers. It is beautiful in the spring regardless of where plants are grown; they are just green things in the summer. Full sun, zones 3 to 6. Strawberry saxifrage or strawberry begonia, *S. stolonifera*, is a classic ground cover that covers significant ground. The

Saxifraga stolonifera

Saxifraga stolonifera 'Stephanie'

Saxifraga fortunei 'Bronze Beauty'

Saxifraga stolonifera 'Stephanie'

Saxifraga fortunei 'Black Ruby'

Saxifraga arendsii 'Touran'

Saxifraga stolonifera

Scabiosa columbaria 'Blue Note'

Scabiosa caucasica

Scabiosa caucasica 'Vivid Violet'

plants bear runners like strawberries that root when they come in contact with the ground. They are fabulous intertwined around rocks or growing in and around hostas. 'Stephanie' is an outstanding selection, aggressive in its habit and absolutely stunning in flower. They smother the plant, which then gets back to being a great ground cover after flowers are finished. Partial shade, zones 7 to 9.

Saxifraga fortunei, Fortune's saxifrage, consist of many stunning cultivars. Unfortunately, they are useless in areas of warm summers, and the best plants I have seen were in the British Isles, where summers seldom get overly brutal. They are also quite cold hardy; plants such as 'Black Ruby' and 'Bronze Beauty' were beautiful in Calgary, Alberta, zone 3.

Scabiosa
SCABIOUS, PINCUSHIONS

Not as many people have pincushions in their sewing drawers anymore (most people don't have sewing drawers anymore), but as

Scabiosa caucasica 'Perfecta'

Scabiosa caucasica fruit

Scabiosa columbaria 'Samantha's Pink'

Scabiosa columbaria 'Butterfly Blue'

Sedum 'Hot Stuff'

one looks at the flower head of scabious, one appreciates how apt the common name is. (The genus name, on the other hand, is Latin for "scabies," the disease the plant was incorrectly thought to cure.)

Both *Scabiosa caucasica*, common scabious, and *S. columbaria*, dove pincushions, grow 1 to 3 feet tall and are similar in their garden look, environmental response, and availability. Historically, *S. caucasica* has been a mainstay for lilac to purple flowers for the summer garden. The plants consist of pinnately lobed opposite leaves and form large mounds with soft light blue to purple flowers. Many variations of the species occur, from larger lavender ('Perfecta') to the violet-pink flowers of 'Vivid Violet'. We anxiously await the flowers, but let us not ignore the wonderful clean-looking pinwheel fruit. Like an architect's model of a futuristic domed restaurant revolving on a giant leg, such is the fruit of scabious.

Scabiosa columbaria is the most popular of the scabious. They are shorter, more compact, and flower even more than the previous species. 'Butterfly Blue' took the gardening world by storm, but 'Samantha's Pink' is fabulous as well. In a container setting, 'Blue Note' makes a great impression. Both *S. columbaria* and *S. caucasica* require full sun and good drainage and are hardy in zones 3 to 7.

Sedum
STONECROP

I love the sedums for their amazing diversity of foliage, flower, and plant habit, but there are so darn many of them, it is impossible to grow or know them all. Many of the more than three hundred species are succulent and may be upright or low growing, as useful for rock gardens as they are for borders. All sedums perform best in full sun and have moderate water requirements and persistent flowers. Hardiness differs from species to species, but in general plants do well in zones 4 to 7.

The upright sedums and their cultivars are everywhere. They grow 1 to 3 feet tall and may have green, bronze, or purple foliage. Most of them have rosy red flowers and all have thick fleshy leaves. The best-known example of this group by far is *Sedum* 'Autumn Joy' ('Herbstfreude'), one of the toughest and best-known perennials in North American gardens. It is fabulous as a garden plant and is grown by the acre as a cut flower. Others are challenging 'Autumn Joy' for beauty if not for numbers sold. 'Autumn Fire' is pinker than most of the others and is an excellent garden

Sedum 'Autumn Joy'

Sedum 'Hab Gray'

performer. 'Hot Stuff' has bright flowers on a compact, short plant. 'Carl' is a low grower with vivid flowers, while 'Neon' has light pink flowers. One of the prettiest new introductions is 'Mr. Goodbud', whose purple-pink flowers cover the plants. 'Iceberg' is quite unusual in that it has white flowers, although a few pink flowers poke through every now and then.

Other upright forms include the bronze-leaved 'Matrona'. With its large leaves and pink flowers, 'Matrona' has a lot of followers. I am not one of them, as I keep seeing it fall over at the first sign of wind or rain. It is far better in the North than in the South. The dark-leaved forms are indeed better in cooler temperatures,

Sedum 'Autumn Joy'

Sedum 'Autumn Fire'

Sedum 'Carl'

Sedum 'Neon'

Sedum 'Mr. Goodbud'

Sedum 'Iceberg'

Sedum 'Postman's Pride'

Sedum 'Xenox'

Sedum 'Black Jack'

Sedum 'Purple Emperor'

Sedum 'Vera Jameson'

Sedum alboroseum 'Mediovariegatum'

Sedum acre

Sedum rupestre 'Angelina'

and they are great additions to the sedum cupboard. 'Black Jack' is one of the darkest and is quite spectacular even when no flowers are visible. 'Purple Emperor' is equally good and bears lots of pink-purple flowers. 'Postman's Pride' is taller and with dark purple leaves, while 'Vera Jameson', an older cultivar, is also a good flowering form with dark leaves. Rather than purple foliage, 'Xenox' has spectacular bronze leaves. They are all handsome in foliage and fair in flower, but the foliage is the main reason to buy them. Upright forms take on many forms and colors. One popular form is the variegated plant, *Sedum alboroseum* 'Mediovariegatum', and yet another, 'Hab Gray', has bluish gray leaves. It is slow but gets better over time.

Sedum acre

Sedum 'Salsa Verde'

Sedum 'Sea Star'

Sedum dasyphyllum 'Major'

Sedum rupestre 'Angelina' after flowering

Botanically the low-growing sedums differ in many ways, including their flower form, rootstock development, and foliar characteristics. They are all best for rock gardens, ground covers, or simply as low-growing border or edging plants. While they broadly prefer similar conditions, the choice of low growers may be further narrowed when performance, flower color, aggressiveness, or disease tolerance are taken into consideration.

Goldmoss stonecrop, *Sedum acre*, is one of the most aggressive and best-known species in North American gardens. "Goldmoss" is descriptive indeed: when the plants are in flower, the golden yellow flowers entirely cover the mossy foliage. The small quarter-inch leaves overlap like shingles, and the leaves appear scaly. Only 2 to 3 inches tall, plants will move in and around anything in their path, and a

Sedum ternatum 'Larinem Park'

Sedum rupestre 'Angelina'

Sedum lineare 'Sea Urchin'

wonderful soft green ground cover often results. Over time, if Lady Luck is smiling, you will be digging out rather than planting *S. acre*, and the Lady may not be quite as welcome anymore. Hardy in zones 3 to 8.

Probably the finest new sedum to be introduced in recent years is *Sedum rupestre* 'Angelina'. It is wonderful in a rock garden, hugging the boulders as it grows, or as an edging plant: the golden foliage truly

sparkles. It flowers in the summer, but the flowers are ugly compared with the foliage. The finest ground cover I have trialed in years. Sedum is such a diverse group; you will never try them all. I like the 2-inch-tall

Silene regia

Silene virginica

Silene polypetala

Silene dioica 'Valley High'

carpet of 'Sea Star' and the blue foliage of *S. dasyphyllum* and its larger incarnation, 'Major'. In the rock garden, 'Salsa Verde' and the variegated 'Sea Urchin' are two other fabulous plants.

Yet one more low grower is the whorled stonecrop, *Sedum ternatum*. The light green leaves are whorled around the stems, and plants grow about 6 inches tall. 'Larinem Park' sports many small starry white flowers in spring. I love it when I see it among ferns and crested irises. A bonus for these plants is their higher tolerance of shade compared to other ground-covering species. Partial shade, zones 4 to 8.

Silene
CAMPION

These campions provide beautiful and vivid species for containers, rock gardens—any place where color spots are welcome. The flowers may be notched or fringed, often with inflated sepals that look like small bladders. Some of the most brilliant red colors can be seen in our native fire pink, *Silene virginica*, whose flowers dare you to pass them by without notice. The 10- to 20-inch-tall plants do well in cool climates and are occasionally offered to the gardener who enjoys native plants in the garden, but

truth be told, enjoying them in their native habitat makes far more sense. The western relative of the eastern fire pink is royal catchfly, *S. regia*. Plants are taller (2 to 3 feet) but bear the same stunning scarlet flowers. It is a native wildflower but also goes well with phlox and lilies. Both species require partial shade and good drainage, and do well in zones 4 to 7.

A wonderful eastern native is fringed campion, *Silene polypetala*. Plants are only 4 to 6 inches tall, with light green leaves, but the fringed pink flowers are unlike any others in the eastern woodland. They are not easy to grow: even when it appears that a

Silene regia

population has been established, the colony may disappear the next year. If nursery-grown plants are available, however, they are worth a try because of their unique beauty. *Silene dioica*, red campion, is another low-growing species, with pink flowers on 4- to 8-inch-tall plants. Its variegated form, 'Valley High', has green and yellow foliage and produces many pink flowers in spring. 'Rolly's Favorite' is a hybrid with excellent heat tolerance and handsome pink flowers. This has been a good plant.

Stachys
BETONY

The last time most of us felt the ear of a lamb was probably around the last time most of us milked a cow. But if I can't on short notice feel the ear of a lamb, I can at least caress the sheepskin we bought in

Silene dioica 'Valley High'

Silene 'Rolly's Favorite'

Stachys byzantina 'Cotton Boll'

Stachys byzantina

Stachys byzantina 'Countess Helen von Stein'

Stachys byzantina 'Primrose Heron'

Stachys byzantina 'Fuzzy von Stein'

Stachys macrantha

Stachys officinalis

New Zealand. (You know New Zealand: the country that has a population of ten million, three million of them people.) Or I could run outside and caress the leaves of lamb's ear (*Stachys byzantina*). They are nothing alike, but both worth the caress. The handsome gray foliage of *S. byzantina* looks good from a distance and is used effectively both to soften harsh colors and edge brick walkways. But get up close, and you will see that the lamby feel comes from soft white hairs, easily visible on the

Stachys officinalis 'Hummelo'

upper and lower sides of the leaves. The purple flowers shoot up in late spring to early summer, but I think they detract from the foliage. Plants look great anywhere in the spring, but leaves can melt out in areas of high heat and humidity, which now includes almost half the country.

A few selections are fun to try, although not always very persistent. 'Cotton Boll' has very hairy flower buds that seldom open into flowers. They are great fun to try and really do look like bolls of cotton. The primrose-yellow leaves of 'Primrose Heron' look particularly good in the spring, but fade out in the summer and are usually dead by August. Other than that, it is just fine.

'Countess Helen von Stein' ('Big Ears') is the best selection of *Stachys byzantina*

for most of the country; it has significantly larger leaves and fewer flowers than the species, but it is also more tolerant of heat and humidity, its true raison d'être. Better it is, but it is also not nearly as hairy, which kind of takes the fun out of it. The new 'Fuzzy von Stein' takes care of that. This is a great plant, just as heat and humidity tolerant as the countess, but with a little primrose color in the leaves—and lots of hairs. Excellent drainage necessary, partial shade, zones 4 to 7.

Most weekend gardeners know about lamb's ears, but the numbers fall way off when you ask the same group to name any other species of *Stachys*. Actually there are about three hundred of them, but let's not get too picky. *Stachys macrantha*, big

betony, has 1½- to 2-inch-long dark green leaves with scalloped edges; the foliage is roughly hairy, not soft like that of its gray cousin. Whatever the leaves lack is more than made up for by the dozens of violet-pink flowers in late spring and early summer. Plants grow up to 2 feet tall and when in flower can be seen a football field away. I also love 'Hummelo', which is likely a selection of common betony, *S. officinalis*. It is the most impressive of all the betonys; a colony like the one at the Niagara School of Horticulture in Niagara Falls, Ontario, attracts all sort of winged creatures and lots of admiring glances from people. Both selection and species prefer full sun and good drainage, and do well in zones 2 to 7.

Stipa arundinacea

Stipa tenuissima

Stipa tenuissima with *Penstemon* 'Firebird'

Stipa
FEATHER GRASS

Ornamental grasses come in many shapes and sizes, and some of the most popular belong to the feather grasses. The most bodacious and bold is giant feather grass, *Stipa gigantea*, whose 7-foot-tall plumes provide a vertical element missing with lower growing plants. No matter where they are planted, they immediately catch the eye as you walk into the garden. In the summer, the flowers rise to their full heights, and in the fall, they even turn a nicer shade of bronze. Full sun, zones 5 to 8. New Zealand wind grass, *S. arundinacea*, has a beautiful pendulous leaves, clothed in pink and purple, but is hardy only to zone 8, perhaps 7. One of the other great plants that people don't know as well as they should

Stipa gigantea

Stokesia laevis 'Peachie's Pick'

Stokesia laevis 'Silver Moon'

Stylophorum diphyllum

Stylophorum lasiocarpum

is *S. tenuissima* (*Nassella tenuissima*). The plants make a great compact tussock made up of layers of long, thin leaves. They are beautifully handsome throughout the season, and the leaves are bronzed at the ends. They are not at their best by themselves, but boy, they look good with penstemons and other colorful perennials. In the fall, the bronzing is even more pronounced. I love this plant in all seasons and recommend it heartily. Zones 6 to 8.

Stokesia laevis
STOKES'S ASTER

Stokesia laevis, Stokes's aster, is a native of the eastern United States, with small 1- to 2-inch-wide lavender flowers, but the original native has undergone a significant transformation through selection and breeding. Native plant lovers enthusiastically embrace this meadow dweller, while mainstream gardeners use the new and improved models with equal enthusiasm. The flowers open in early to mid

summer and consist of two rows of ray flowers up to 4 inches across, although 2 to $2\frac{1}{2}$ inches is normal. Plants are 1 to 2 feet tall and equally wide. They are tough, do well in full sun to partial shade, and persist for many years as long as winter drainage is good.

The selections of *Stokesia laevis* for the garden are many; my first choice without any doubt is 'Peachie's Pick', with many large (2 to $2\frac{1}{2}$ inches wide) lavender flowers on a compact, vigorous plant. The plants look exceptionally good in spring and early summer. Other lavender-flowering forms occur, but 'Silver Moon' has handsome silvery white flowers. Full sun, good drainage, zones 5 to 9.

Stylophorum diphyllum
WOOD POPPY, CELANDINE POPPY

Woodland native plants keep getting more popular every year, and this one is no exception. Native from Tennessee to Missouri, *Stylophorum diphyllum* is simply a terrific species for the woodland

Stylophorum diphyllum and Virginia bluebells

Symphytum "Goldsmith"

Symphytum asperum

Symphytum ×*uplandicum* 'Axminster Gold'

garden, providing bright yellow spring flowers even in heavy shade. It looks fabulous with Virginia bluebells and other early spring woodland plants: blue and yellow flowers go together like apples and strudel. Early in the spring, as the poppies emerge from their winter rest, light green deeply cut basal leaves and 1½- to 2-inch-wide flowers unfold. A yellow sap exudes from cut parts of the plant, providing great fun for any face- and fingerpainters who happen by. Keep it out of your eyes. Plants reseed, which means that two or three plants can become a significant colony in three to five years. No cultivars are available; the Chinese native *S. lasiocarpum* bears a similar flower and has larger, coarser foliage. Partial to heavy shade, zones 4 to 8.

Symphytum
COMFREY

Plants of the genus *Symphytum* were once used as a poultice, believed, among other things, to speed the setting of broken bones. With such an important healing property, plants became a staple of monastic and herb gardens. About thirty-five species are counted in the genus, and that is about thirty-three too many for most gardeners. Essentially, they have the same look, fill the same shady spaces, and bear similar pendulous bell-shaped flowers on long one-sided inflorescences. But they are loved by many.

Symphytum asperum, prickly comfrey, is coarse to the touch and grows about 3 feet tall. The light blue flowers are formed in the spring and look very much like those of Virginia bluebells. Comfrey is available in some highly ornamental variegated plants. Most sought after are the variegated cultivars of

Symphytum ×*uplandicum* 'Variegatum'

Thalictrum minus 'Adiantifolium'

Thalictrum aquilegifolium

Thalictrum
MEADOW-RUE

Thalictrum species are natural inhabitants of damp, shady areas, flowering in early summer, with lacy foliage that presents a fernlike appearance. In general, the ornamental parts of the flowers consist of colorful stamens and sepals. About 130 species of meadow-rue have been identified, from upright clumpers to 6- to 9-inch ground covers.

Prostrate meadow-rues, most suitable to rock gardens and alpine environments, can sometimes be found in specialty nurseries. The maidenhair fern--like appearance of *Thalictrum minus* 'Adiantifolium' is the best part of the plant and can be enjoyed even if flowering is sparse. The leaves look like those of northern maidenhair fern, thus accounting for the cultivar name. Plants grow in 1- to 2-foot-tall clumps and perform well in zones 3 to 7. The deeper green foliage and numerous lavender flowers of China meadow-rue, *T. ichangense*, are outstanding in late spring and early summer. Plants are only 6 to 9 inches tall and fill in rocky outcrops or other well-drained areas in zones 5 to 7. Neither of these low growers does well in areas of hot summers and high humidity.

the hybrid, *S.* ×*uplandicum*. They include 'Variegatum' and 'Axminster Gold', an extraordinarily vigorous introduction from Canada. *Symphytum* 'Goldsmith' has yellow and white foliage and has become quite popular but does not seem as vigorous or as tough as the others. The variegated plants are eye-catching and must-have plants for

many gardeners. Unfortunately, they are difficult to propagate and thus difficult to locate and quite expensive.

All comfreys require good drainage. They do best in partial shade and burn up in full sun in most areas of the country. Hardy in zones 4 to 7 in the East, to zone 8 on the West Coast.

Thalictrum aquilegifolium 'White Cloud'

Thalictrum ichangense

Thalictrum flavum var. *glaucum*

Thalictrum 'Black Stockings'

Thalictrum aquilegifolium 'Roseum'

Thalictrum flavum var. *glaucum*

The most common of the upright meadow-rues is the columbine meadow-rue, *Thalictrum aquilegifolium*. The foliage is blue-tinted and similar to that of columbine, thus the common and botanical names. Plants are generally 2 to 3 feet tall, but well-satisfied plants can grow 5 feet tall and 3 feet wide. The normal flower color is lavender, provided by sepals and long stamens in the spring. Unfortunately, flowers are not persistent and tend to shatter after a week or so. Sometimes the flowers are dioecious (male or female only); however, the fruit is especially handsome on plants that have female flowers. Cultivars include the

Thalictrum dasycarpum

Thalictrum 'Elin'

Thalictrum dasycarpum

white-flowered 'White Cloud' and the pink 'Roseum'. Partial shade, good drainage, zones 5 to 7.

Thalictrum flavum, yellow meadow-rue, is a robust grower that bursts out of the ground with smooth divided foliage and thick stems. Plants grow tall and thin and are best planted in clumps of three or four. Single plants grow too tall for their width and easily outgrow the space provided. Clumps form rapidly, and panicles of small yellow flowers appear in late spring. Flowers consist mainly of long stamens, which fall like yellow confetti within a few days of opening. Height is generally 4 to 6 feet, and plants are used to great advantage as a backdrop to shorter plants. Variety *glaucum*, the most popular representative of

this plant, presents a winning combination of blue-green foliage and yellow flowers that is even better than the species itself. Full sun, good drainage, zones 5 to 8.

Our native meadow-rue, *Thalictrum dasycarpum*, is another tall (4 to 5 feet) grower with creamy white flowers, dark stems, and coarse foliage similar to that of *T. aquilegifolium*. Plants are hardy to zone 5 and persist for many years. I recommend it without hesitation.

Two recent hybrids have caught the attention of meadow-rue lovers everywhere, and for good reasons. 'Black Stockings' is at least 8 feet tall with handsome creamy white flowers and black stems. 'Elin' grows up to 12 feet tall with dark stems and produces bicolored pale yellow and lavender flowers. These two plants are very impressive but often need staking.

Thymus praecox 'Coccineus'

Thymus
THYME

Thymus is an immense genus of more than 350 species, known equally for their culinary and ornamental properties. All thymes available to gardeners are low-growing spreading plants and, without a label, are incredibly difficult to tell apart. The best way to distinguish thyme from other herbs is to sniff the fragrance of its opposite leaves; remember, however, that thyme not only smells like thyme but also, in some selections, like caraway or lemon. Most are native to the Mediterranean, and therefore excellent drainage and full sun are necessary. Plants lend themselves well to rock, trough, and alpine gardens.

One of the most handsome species is woolly thyme, *Thymus lanuginosus*, whose common name comes from the long hairs on the prostrate stems. Although pink flowers are produced, the plant's fuzziness is its best

Thymus lanuginosus

attribute in dry climates. In warm areas that receive a good deal of summer rain, however, it is a detriment, because water does not evaporate easily from the leaves and plants can melt out badly. Full sun, zones 5 to 8.

Thymus praecox, creeping thyme, is a fabulous ground cover and when the blood red flowers of 'Coccineus' occur, a large planting is an incredible sight. It forms wonderfully thick mats under conditions of cool

Thymus vulgaris

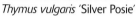

Thymus vulgaris 'Silver Posie'

Tiarella cordifolia

Tiarella 'Black Snowflake'

nights and good drainage. *Thymus vulgaris*, common thyme, is the culinary thyme of the grocery aisle; it forms lavender or white flowers on 12- to 15-inch-tall plants. Several selections of these species are available, including the beautifully variegated 'Silver Posie'. All cultivars do poorly in rainy and humid summers unless planted where drainage is excellent. Full sun, zones 5 to 8.

Tiarella
FOAMFLOWER

The many excellent (and now readily available) selections and hybrids of *Tiarella cordifolia*, an outstanding native plant, have attracted keen interest in the entire genus. Particularly useful for shady gardens, these 6- to 12-inch-tall plants form slow-growing

colonies that bear white or pink flowers in the spring. One of the most impressive uses of this species is in Peirce's Woods at Longwood Gardens, where endless drifts of foamflowers interspersed with creeping phlox (*Phlox stolonifera*) make spring come alive. Placed with other shade plants like cinnamon fern, they create a wonderful river of color. Some of the finest cultivars have

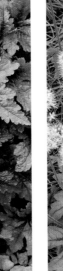

Tiarella 'Neon Lights'

Tiarella 'Stargazer Mercury'

Tiarella 'Stargazer Mercury' display at Al's Garden Center in Oregon

Tiarella 'Spring Symphony'

Tiarella 'Pink Brushes'

Tiarella 'Strike It Rich Pink Gem'

Tradescantia 'Concord Grape'

beautiful foliage, especially 'Neon Lights' and 'Black Snowflake'. The combination of red-veined leaves and white flowers make 'Stargazer Mercury' one of the finest choices, a big hit for retailers who want to show off for their customers. 'Spring Symphony' has been the best cultivar in the Trial Gardens at UGA, and I recommend it for the South.

Improvements have occurred rapidly in those introductions with pink flowers. I love 'Pink Brushes', another excellent plant for hot summers, and 'Strike It Rich Pink Gem' has long flower stems of light pink. The genus provides outstanding characteristics for the garden and has been unfairly stuck in the "shady native"

category for too long. It should be a mainstream plant. Partial shade, good drainage, zones 3 to 8.

Tradescantia
SPIDERWORT

The genus *Tradescantia* commemorates the family Tradescant, in particular the father and son, known as Tradescant the Elder and Tradescant the Younger. As gardeners to Charles I of England in the early 1600s, they received many plants from the colonies. The Younger also traveled to America, bringing back to the Empire such treasures as Virginia creeper and Michaelmas daisies.

Tradescantia 'Sweet Kate'

Tradescantia 'Joy'

Tradescantia sillamontana

Tradescantia 'Sylvana'

Tradescantia sillamontana

Tradescantia 'Pauline'

Our native species *Tradescantia virginiana* remains a staple in American gardening. Its light green straplike foliage is common to all cultivars in the Andersoniana Group, all of which produce dozens of flowers, each opening for a single day. Breeding has concentrated on flower colors, and many are available. Flower color, flower persistence, and compact habit make many of the newer hybrids interesting. Most ('Concord Grape', 'Joy') have purple flowers, while many others ('Sylvana') have rose-red flowers; but some have pink blooms, especially my favorite choice, 'Pauline'. However, not only are the flowers colorful, the foliage of 'Sweet Kate' is a gorgeous chartreuse. The dark blue flowers and yellow foliage make a terrific combination. Afternoon shade and moisture are essential for good performance, but spiderworts don't do well in boggy soils. Be careful of reseeding, as spiderworts can show up all over the place. Hardy in zones 4 to 8.

Other species also have their followers, especially *Tradescantia ohiensis* in its selection 'Mrs. Loewer', which is much taller with thin leaves and light blue flowers. This plant flowers forever and is the very best flowering spiderwort I have ever trialed. It is too big to stand by itself, and needs to

Tradescantia ohiensis 'Mrs. Loewer'

Tricyrtis hirta 'Alba'

Tricyrtis 'Sinonome'

Tricyrtis 'Amethystina'

be planted so other plants keep it upright. Another wonderful plant that far too few people know is the hairy spiderwort, *T. sillamontana*. The young foliage is light green and seriously hairy; the old foliage is dark green to purple. The pink flowers are similar to other spiderworts, and also flower for a very long time. Plants grow only 6 to 9 inches tall. Zones 7 to 10.

Tricyrtis
TOAD LILY

It's obvious that the common name for the genus *Tricyrtis* was not chosen with commercial sales in mind. However, they really do make a great story—all you have to do is ask your friends, "What did your mother tell you about handling toads?"

Almost unanimously, whether they are five or sixty-five, they will answer, "They give you warts!" Turn the flowers over, and sure enough you will see three warts. People love the demonstration, but just try to talk someone into buying a toad lily—not an easy task. That the flowers tend to be spotted and brownish maroon, like a toad, is simply bad luck; no matter how shamelessly one promotes the plant and flower, it is not until you see it in its glory that it can be appreciated. A good deal of effort in breeding has brought toad lilies out of obscurity, and although they all still look

Tricyrtis hirta 'Miyazaki'

Tricyrtis 'Gilt Edge'

Tricyrtis 'Sinonome'

Tricyrtis 'Lightning Strike'

Tricyrtis 'Lightning Strike'

Tricyrtis 'Shining Light'

Tricyrtis 'Variegata'

Tricyrtis 'Gilty Pleasure'

"kind of the same" to my students, the world of toad lilies is just unfolding. Gardeners know they have reached the highest possible gardening plateau when they ask for cow manure for their birthday and peruse catalogs in search of toad lilies. No turning back then. Spouses beware!

'Miyazaki' is a popular selection of *Tricyrtis hirta*, the most common species in this great genus. The spotted flowers are white with a little purple (occasionally lighter) and occur in late summer and fall. I love seeing them arching gracefully over rocks by a pond or other water feature. The flowers of 'Alba' are creamy white with purple spots, making them easy to spot against the green leaves. 'Amethystina' is earlier and has spectacular purple margins on the white spotted flowers. 'Sinonome' has lavender to purple flowers on handsome green foliage and has been one of the best performers we have trialed.

If you want some more interest, beyond that of simply fabulous flowers, try some of the variegated ones. 'Lightning Strike' makes

Trillium decumbens

Trillium underwoodii

Trillium decumbens

Trillium stamineum

an excellent vigorous clump and bears bold green and yellow variegation on the leaves, and 'Shining Light' is even more colorful. For a little more subdued marginal variegation, two cultivars are terrific. 'Gilt Edge' has a thin white margin around each leaf and handsome purple flowers in late summer and fall. If 'Gilt Edge' is difficult to find, 'Variegata' should not be, and although the leaves are a little more narrow, there are few other differences between the two. The both perform well everywhere. If I could grow 'Gilty Pleasure' well, I would have it in my garden in a heartbeat. The leaves, particularly in the spring, shine from a distance, but unfortunately, plants are not big fans of hot, humid summers. Nevertheless, further north, they are quite wonderful. I have tried many toad lilies in both the Trial Gardens at UGA and my own garden—they can be a little frustrating if the leaves get beaten up during the summer. In most areas of the country, partial shade is necessary; afternoon sun is a no-no. Consistent moisture also helps. Zones 4 to 8.

Trillium

Rose trillium, nodding trillium, great white trillium, wakerobin, showy trillium, snow trillium, wood lily, stinking Benjamin, sessile trillium, toad trillium, yellow trillium—these are but a few of the names describing members of the genus. That trilliums prefer woodland conditions, that their flowers appear in early spring and are gone soon thereafter, that plants disappear entirely in the summer—all this doesn't make the trillium sound particularly enchanting. But don't tell a trillium fan that. It is a truth universally acknowledged that if trilliums were native to England, the War of the Roses would have been known as the War of the Trilliums. Trillium lovers are passionate. All reason seems to have left them, and heaven forgive the unsuspecting novice who digs a trillium from the wild. The game of "What trillium is that?" can still get violent among trillites. I must admit to such tendencies in my past, but I am now reformed. I think.

Trillium cuneatum

Trillium luteum

Trillium ludovicianum

Trillium discolor

Trillium grandiflorum

Passions aside, trilliums have a place in the shade garden, and like any other genus, some species are more adaptable than others in a given environment. The easiest way to describe members of this large genus is by describing how the flower is held: either by a short flower stem called the pedicel (pediceled), or attached directly to the top of the plant (sessile), like a king perched on his throne. Each has its own special beauty and charm, but making definite identification is best left to the taxonomists. Exacting propagation techniques make wide distribution of many trilliums difficult; however, if you can't find trilliums in the nursery, take a walk in the

Trillium underwoodii and *Ornithogalum umbellatum*

woods and enjoy nature's treasures. Take a photo, not a plant.

Many of the sessile species essentially look the same, especially to the non-trillite eye. Most of them have maroon flowers and handsome mottled foliage. *Trillium decumbens* is an easy trillium to identify because the long stems grow horizontally along the ground and end with purple flowers perched above silver mottled leaves. The stems are often hidden beneath a carpet of leaves on the floor, and the leaves look like they are sitting on the ground. Plants rapidly form a crowded colony. I think *T. stamineum* (twisted trillium) is one of the neatest trilliums because of its twisted purple petals which lie flat on the leaves, showing off the large conspicuous stamens.

Quite lovely, certainly different. Toad trillium, *T. cuneatum*, is a common plant in the southeast; it has wide leaves, and a good deal of intensity in depth of purple occurs in the flowers. Most trilliums are native to the cool mountain areas in the Carolinas and many northern states like Michigan; however, *T. underwoodii* is native to the South. This is one of the most beautiful plants, with wonderful mottled leaves, especially when it comes through the ground in full bud. The flowers, which are deep purple, open as early as March in Georgia. Another rather weird southern form, Louisiana wakerobin, *T. ludovicianum*, is quite different in that the leaves are barely mottled and the flowers are two-tone, with purple on the bottom and green at the

Trillium undulatum

Trillium grandiflorum 'Roseum'

Trillium flexipes

Trillium rugelii

Trillium pusillum

top. Not all the sessile forms have purple flowers. For sheer beauty, the red and white flowers of the northern painted trillium, *T. undulatum* are hard to beat—and also hard to find. As for me, I have always loved the subtle primrose color of *T. discolor*. They are less than 9 inches tall and quickly make good-looking colonies. Subtle has nothing to do with the color found in the yellow trillium, *T. luteum*, whose long narrow flowers

are butter yellow. The yellow forms show up much better in the shade than those with purple flowers.

As lovely as the sessile forms are, the pediceled species are more popular, perhaps because many have more colorful flowers and are easier to admire in the shade garden. The granddaddy, aunt, and uncle of all North American trilliums is *Trillium grandiflorum* (great white trillium;

zones 4 to 7). Carpeting open woods and regaling all those who view it, whether en masse or one at time, the white trillium is the epitome of woodland natives. As the flowers decline, they often turn a rosy red color, yet another charm to this quite marvelous plant. Plants are so revered in Canada that it was adopted as the provincial flower of Ontario. With its successful carpeting of the northern woodland and its

Trillium grandiflorum 'Flore Pleno'

Trillium vaseyi

Even though it does not attract eyeballs like others do, people love it. As subtle as this trillium is, its opposite is *T. vaseyi*, sweet wakerobin, a large plant with exquisite large purple fragrant flowers. All trilliums perform best in early morning sun and afternoon shade.

There is not a single trillium to dislike; the biggest problem is finding some for sale that will make a decent colony in your lifetime. Grab your jacket, get your hiking boots, and bring your camera to see the wildflowers in your area in the spring. Let nature do the heavy lifting—then support those nurseries that are supporting your habit.

Uvularia
BELLWORT, MERRY BELLS

Subtlety is the hallmark of this genus of woodland plants. Not particularly showy, but admired by those who do not equate showmanship with beauty. All species are shade- and moisture-loving, and all are native to eastern North America. Don't worry what bellworts you can find; they are remarkably similar in makeup and garden performance. In the early spring, you will see small pale yellow flowers hanging from the nodes of the upper leaves. It is the leaves that differ among the species, and although not particularly striking, the differences are notable. In *Uvularia grandiflora* the stem appears to pierce and pass through the leaves—a unique arrangement described by the term "perfoliate." The flowers of *U. grandiflora* are quite pretty and significantly larger than other species. A few cultivars are occasionally offered by mail-order specialists, such as 'Sunbonnet', a bigger, brighter selection. The leaf arrangement of perfoliate bellwort, *U. perfoliata*, is similar, as are the flowers, but these are perhaps a little smaller. Both can spread rapidly throughout the garden,

stunning beauty, this species has probably been subjected to more abuse from picking, gathering, and digging than any other trillium. Somehow it still puts up with humans anyway, making our spring times even brighter. Garden cultivars have been developed such as the double-flowered 'Flore Pleno' and the rosy-flowered 'Roseum'. Many of the pediceled forms are similar, usually discriminated by flower color. A white species, *T. flexipes*, has large nodding white flowers over large green leaves. The southern nodding wakerobin, *T. rugelii*, has wonderful nodding white flowers with its "ears" pinned back and purple pendulous stamens. One of the smallest trilliums is dwarf wakerobin, *T. pusillum*, with white to pink flowers on 3- to 4-inch-tall plants.

Uvularia grandiflora

Uvularia grandiflora 'Sunbonnet'

which is either good or bad, depending on your opinion of the stuff.

The leaves are sessile (that is, no leaf stem or petiole) in the other common species, *Uvularia sessilifolia*. An even more vigorous understory plant, it can quickly colonize an area. The flowers are similar to

Uvularia grandiflora

Uvularia perfoliata

Uvularia sessilifolia

Uvularia perfoliata

Veratrum nigrum

those of *U. perfoliata*. All require shade and moisture and are hardy in zones 4 (3 with protection) to 9.

Veratrum
FALSE HELLEBORE

Veratrum was the ancient name of *Helleborus*, thus accounting for this genus' common name. From a stout black rhizome emerges a plant grown for the wonderful pleated leaves and unique branched flower heads. That all parts of the plant are poisonous certainly tends to limit its use, but only mad dogs and Englishmen would ever think of putting that fact to the test. However, as I read about the poisonous properties of the plant, I am not so sure I want it anywhere near my garden. It turns out it was a frequent addition to poison arrowheads and a favorite poison in European courts, causing all sorts of awful symptoms, usually culminating in a rapid death.

However, when I see false hellebores growing in gardens, I often forget the unpleasant aspects and find myself admiring the plant. European false hellebore (*Veratrum album*), the go-to species for the deadly uses just mentioned, is 2 to 4 feet tall with white flowers. Today, one can read about its homeopathic properties on almost every website dealing with the plant. Toxicity aside, plants are quite beautiful. The black false hellebore, *V. nigrum*, is similar in habit and foliage but has black-purple

Veratrum album

Veratrum viride

flowers in dense racemes. Plants are about 4 feet tall. The flowers of *V. viride* (American false hellebore) form otherworldly branched green panicles. They grow 3 to 4 feet tall and, when in flower, are guaranteed to elicit all sorts of oohs and aahs and a concluding "What is it?" from any and all passers-by. Plants go dormant in the heat of the summer. Partial shade and moisture are needed. None of the veratrums tolerate hot weather; all are found in northern latitudes or in mountainous terrain. Most will be hardy in zones 4 to 7.

Verbascum
MULLEIN

The mulleins are best known for the massive roadside weeds in the Midwest and Canada; usually they are white mullein,

Verbascum bombyciferum

Verbascum bombyciferum

Verbascum 'Helen Johnson'

Verbascum chaixii 'Album'

Verbascum bombyciferum or closely related cousins. They really are quite impressive, particularly the basal leaves, which sit until the 4- to 6-foot-tall hairy flower stems are formed. Some gardeners love that big, bold look and even incorporate "improvements" like 'Arctic Summer' in the garden. Plants are biennials and persist for a very short time. However, a good deal of hybridization has occurred, and amazing colors and forms can be found, resembling that weed hardly at all. We now have deep yellows like the 4-foot-tall 'Banana Custard' and the dwarf 'Gold Nugget' with its handsome yellow flowers with purple centers. Other hybrids such as 'Southern Charm' and 'Helen Johnson' provide strawberry-red flowers on 3- to 4-foot-tall stems. The Cotswold series has some wonderful colors, and plants are often used as cut flowers.

The hybrids are exciting but very short-lived, exhibiting the biennial characteristic in some of the parents. Gardeners in North America have often opted for a number of species such as the nettle-leaf mullein, *Verbascum chaixii*, particularly its white-flowered form 'Album' Plants are a little

Verbascum 'Gold Nugget'

Verbascum phoeniceum

Verbascum 'Cotswold Queen'

more persistent than the hybrids but are not as exciting to be sure. Purple mullein, *V. phoeniceum*, is easily raised from seed and provides purple- and rose-colored flowers on 18-inch-tall plants. Plants reseed quite prolifically and will likely be with you for some time.

As garden plants, mulleins are explosively colorful but, as a rule, do not look great for more than a couple of weeks. It is a great couple of weeks, however, and trying a few of the new hybrids will be great fun.

Verbena
VERVAIN

Verbenas have been a mainstay of perennial gardens since great-grandmother's time and will continue to be one of those plants that comes and goes from the horticultural stage. The argument as to

Verbena 'Aztec Lavender'

Verbena cultivars in the Trial Gardens, University of Georgia

Verbena 'Homestead Purple'

what verbenas are perennial rages back and forth, but if truth be told most of the most colorful new verbenas should be treated as annuals. In the Trial Gardens at UGA (zone 7b), we are stunned by the beauty and the brightness of the introductions, and can't help but talk about some of the new breeding—like 'Donalena Red Pepper' and 'Aztec Lavender'. We could wax poetic about dozens more but alas, most do not overwinter even for us and much less so in the Midwest. One of the surprising exceptions was 'Homestead Purple'. Although it was never considered a perennial when first introduced, plants have proven to be hardy to at least zone 6.

Upright species of verbena include *Verbena bonariensis*, tall verbena, and *V. rigida*,

Verbena bonariensis

Verbena rigida and artemisias

Verbena bonariensis

Verbena bonariensis

Verbena rigida 'Santos'

Verbena rigida 'Polaris'

Veronica umbrosa 'Georgia Blue'

Veronica 'Waterperry Blue'

Veronica prostrata 'Trehane'

Veronica spicata 'Blue Indigo'

rigid verbena. Being upright is not the only characteristic these South American natives share. Both are square-stemmed, bristly hairy, and bear small rosy-purple flowers for a long period of time. *Verbena bonariensis* is 3 to 6 feet high and flowers from early summer throughout the season. Although no cultivars of *V. bonariensis* have been developed, various shades of flower color occur. They look good towering over their companions in a mixed border, as a supporting player in an atypically spiky English cottage garden, and even in containers. Plants are not without problems. Mildew is a serious problem if plants are in wet conditions or too much

shade. They can also reseed prolifically, and after some time, they can look more weedy than weeds. Full sun, zones 6 to 9.

Verbena rigida is similar in texture and color but only about 2 feet tall. The leaves are opposite, also bristly, and likewise susceptible to powdery mildew. It makes a nice contrast when planted to crawl through silver plants like artemisias. The selection 'Santos' has blue-purple flowers; 'Polaris' is lavender-flowered. Be warned, these plants will take over the world in no time; our planting of 'Santos' was beautiful the first year, everywhere the second, and removed the third. Full sun, zones 7 to 9.

Veronica
SPEEDWELL

The genus *Veronica* provides a wide range of height, color, and texture. The low growers work well in rock gardens and raised beds, and benefit from cool nights and good drainage; taller species are used in perennial borders, and some enjoy a well-deserved reputation as cut flowers. Of all the prostrate forms available, I think one of the best is still the 6-inch-tall *Veronica umbrosa*, especially the plant known as 'Georgia Blue', collected by plantsman Roy Lancaster in the western Caucasus. The plant is one of

Veronica prostrata 'Aztec Gold'

Veronica longifolia 'Blauriesin'

the earliest to flower in the garden, opening as early as mid February in zone 7, in late March further north. Plants are absolutely covered with blue flowers, each with a small white eye. Because of the cool temperatures when they flower, they bloom for many, many weeks. Another old-fashioned but excellent low-growing plant is 'Waterperry Blue', similar but with lavender flowers. Low growers like *V. prostrata* can almost be considered a ground cover; plants that roam like 'Trehane' fill in between stepping stones, while those with golden foliage such as 'Aztec Gold' are quite beautiful and becoming more popular. Full sun, zones 4 to 7.

While the low-growing veronicas are useful for the front of the garden, the upright *Veronica longifolia*, long-leaved speedwell, is sufficiently tall to be viewed when placed in the middle or even in the

Veronica spicata 'Baby Doll'

back of a garden. Plants bear upright spikes of flowers on 3- to 4-foot-long stems, each terminal spike consisting of dozens of small quarter- to half-inch-wide flowers. Plants are strong enough and tall enough to be used as a cut flower and are grown as such throughout the world. Evidence of good breeding can be found in blue cultivars such as 'Blauriesin'—still a very popular cut flower speedwell in the world. All selections of *V. longifolia* perform best in full sun in normal soils. Hardy in zones 4 to 8. *Veronica spicata*, spiked speedwell, is still the best-known species of the entire genus. It comes in many colors (blue and lavender are the main colors) and heights, the normal height range one to three feet. The terminal upright flowers begin to open in early summer and often continue for two months or more, especially if spent flowers

Veronica spicata 'Prince's Feathers'

Veronica spicata 'Giles van Hees'

Veronica spicata 'Tickled Pink'

Veronica 'Sunny Border Blue'

Veronicastrum virginicum 'Fascination'

are deadheaded. The dozens of cultivars of *V. spicata* perform well in full sun and well-drained soils. Blue-flowered selections are most common, including the glossy-leaved 'Blue Indigo' and the compact 'Prince's Feathers'. Lavender flowers can be found in 'Baby Doll' and the short 'Giles van Hees'. 'Tickled Pink' is a great name for a great plant with pink flowers.

In a genus with so many species, many hybrids have been introduced. 'Sunny Border Blue' was one of the earliest introductions, but I feel one of the best has to be 'Royal Candles'. Plants are compact, and sport many lavender-blue upright flowers on a compact body. They hold their shape and need only a little deadheading to look their best. I recommend it.

Veronicastrum virginicum
CULVER'S ROOT

This native species should be the darling of American gardeners. Plants grow up to 5 feet tall and can be 3 to 4 feet wide. The

Veronica 'Royal Candles'

Veronicastrum virginicum 'Album'

Veronicastrum virginicum 'Fascination'

whorled foliage is beautiful even without flowers and often sports a bronze hue. Whorls of three to six leaves occur along the stems, and it is this arrangement that is the easiest way to distinguish *Veronicastrum* from the closely related *Veronica*. There is some disagreement among eggheads as to whether the species is strictly lavender, strictly white, or both. I prefer to agree with the lumpers rather than the splitters: white or lavender, I love this plant. The white-flowered variant is the most available color, and it not only makes an excellent garden plant but is highly prized as a cut flower. Plants are best when grown in full sun and provided with sufficient water and fertilizer. A relatively new introduction is 'Fascination', showing off lavender-pink flowers on 4-foot-tall plants. Zones 4 to 8.

Viola labradorica

Viola cornuta 'Jersey Gem'

Viola cornuta Lilacina Group

Viola 'Etain'

Viola
VIOLET

Violets—love them or hate them? obnoxious weeds or spectacular ornamentals? Over five hundred species of this old-fashioned plant have been documented. Many are self-sowing weeds, and gardeners often stay away from anything referred to as a perennial violet. All species perform better in cooler climates than in hot weather: in the North, violets do well in the summer; in the South, in the winter. All violets are excellent in the spring in most locales.

The most difficult thing to determine is the perenniality of violas. No doubt that the dark-leaved Labrador violet, *Viola labradorica*, is cold hardy, probably to zone 3. The mauve quarter-inch-wide flowers may be small but can almost cover up a plant in the spring. The plant essentially sits around in the heat of the summer but is outstanding in the fall, winter (in the South), and spring. The best part of this violet is the purple foliage: almost black in early spring, it lightens only slightly when the plant is in flower. Plants form nice

Viola ×*wittrockiana* 'Yes Coconut Frost'

Viola 'Irish Molly'

Viola ×*wittrockiana* 'Venus Autumn Flare'

clumps but also spread rapidly. *Viola cornuta*, the horned violet, is not as commonly seen in American as in European gardens; possibly the proliferation of bedding pansies and violas has smothered this species. A shame, because it offers wonderful diversity of color and form. The flowers, each 1 to $1\frac{1}{2}$ inches across, are somewhat star-shaped and have a long slender spur, accounting for the common name. It is not as accommodating of weather extremes as other species, but plants generally flower well in the spring, and if cut back after flowering, may bloom again, at least in cooler summers. In the South, plants have a more difficult time surviving the summer and may have to be treated as winter annuals. Dozens of cultivars have been bred in Europe; the purple 'Jersey Gem' and the light violets of Lilacina Group are well worth seeking out. Full sun, good drainage, zones 6 to 9.

There are many hybrids that are beautiful, but their hardiness is a little sketchy. The small flowers of 'Silver Samurai' are fine but not nearly as handsome as its silvery foliage. Plants like the popular 'Etain' and 'Irish Molly' do well in cool climates and are probably

Viola ×wittrockiana 'Velocity Lavender with Yellow Eye'

Yucca filamentosa

Yucca aloifolia

Yucca 'Bright Edge'

cold hardy to zone 6, perhaps 5. These hybrids are excellent in containers and well worth trying, even if they don't overwinter. Of course, we are awash in pansies and violas (*Viola ×wittrockiana*), all sold as throw-away annuals, considered too fragile to overwinter well in cold climates and unable to perform well in warm climates. However, are they perennial? In the South, they overwinter well and are spectacular in the spring but, in general, do poorly in the summer. Hybridizers are breeding heat-tolerant cultivars; the very best is the

Velocity series, which looks good even in Athens summers. While they may overwinter in the North, it still makes sense to buy new ones in the spring, it takes so long for them to look good in that season. So enjoy their beauty, and don't worry too much about their longevity.

Yucca

Yuccas require an absolute minimum of maintenance and provide bold architectural form. Add strong upright leaves and

impressive flowers, and you realize why they have become so popular. Yuccas have a reputation of being drought tolerant and are favorite plants in the Southwest and other arid areas. They also have a reputation of being frost tender; however, Adam's needle, *Yucca filamentosa*, is cold hardy to about 5°F. The spiky foliage is easily noticeable all season, especially with all those filaments throughout the plant. The foliage is sharp and thin, however, and can be quite dangerous, particularly to little children. If children visit, get rid of yuccas. Dense

Yucca filamentosa

Zephyranthes rosea

spikes of white pendulous tulip-shaped blooms occur in mid to late summer. The aloe yucca, *Yucca aloifolia*, grows about 5 feet tall and is a popular plant in areas with mild winters.

Selections of plants with ornamental foliage include 'Color Guard', 'Bright Star', and 'Bright Edge', to name but a few, and they add subtle beauty to all gardens, not only those in the Southwest. These are exceptional plants for areas with too much heat, too little rain, and too much wind. I find myself admiring these more every year. Full sun, good drainage, zones 5 to 9.

Zephyranthes
RAIN LILY

It turns out that sales of *Zephyranthes* aren't setting any records. Hardly anyone knows what they are, but what else is new? They are readily available, they grow well in nearly all parts of the country and into Canada, and they are quite beautiful—so what's the problem? Perhaps that they are not daffodils or tulips may be the problem. It seems when one talks about bulbs, those two dominate the minds and wallets of casual gardeners. To be honest, rain lilies are cold hardy only to zone 7, perhaps 6, and that is obviously a problem in Racine. However, they are easily dug in the fall for those who want to try a few. So let's see if we can change a few minds.

I sure do enjoy the pink rain lily, *Zephyranthes rosea*. The foliage is a bit like that of liriope, seldom showing blemishes from insects or diseases. They flower two or three times a year, especially after a rain, and provide deep red flower buds that open to magnificent chalices of pink. I plant them at the base of some wooden stairs and enjoy them whenever I go in and out of the house. There are many species, and the white rain lily, *Z. candida*, is equally good. The long

Zephyranthes rosea

Zephyranthes atamasca

Zephyranthes candida

narrow tepals surround a yellow center and generally bloom in late summer and as late as October. The earliest to flower is our southeastern native, the Atamasco lily, *Z. atamasca*. They are often seen on roadsides and ditches in Florida and southern Georgia. They are quite large, with pink buds that give way to large white flowers in the spring, quite different from most rain lilies. Plants are more difficult to buy than other rain lilies, but if you live in the Southeast and can find some for sale, definitely give them a try. All rain lilies perform best in full sun but require consistent moisture to really take off.

PART TWO
Selected Plants for Specific Characteristics or Purposes

Aggressive Plants

The following plants tend to grow more rapidly than "normal" perennials, often squeezing out their competitors in a year or two. The difference between aggressive and invasive often has to do with the area of the country and the opinion of the gardener. Aggressiveness is often thought of as a negative trait, but when an area requires rapid filling, this tendency is much appreciated. Many of these plants could also be used as ground covers. Check the text when looking for this trait, as not all species or cultivars in the genus are aggressive.

Ajuga	*Imperata*	*Macleaya*	*Physostegia*
Anemone	*Ipheion*	*Monarda*	*Ranunculus*
Aster	*Lamium*	*Oenothera*	*Saxifraga*
Corydalis	*Lychnis*	*Osmunda*	*Sedum*
Eupatorium	*Lysimachia*	*Persicaria*	*Stachys*
Helianthus			

Plants for Consistently Moist Conditions

The following perennials perform better in consistently moist conditions. These would include but not necessarily be wet and boggy areas as well. Check the text when looking for this trait, as not all species or cultivars in the genus require consistently moist conditions.

Brunnera	*Ligularia*	*Osmunda*	*Primula*
Canna	*Lobelia*	*Persicaria*	*Ranunculus*
Iris	*Myosotis*	*Podophyllum*	*Rodgersia*

Cut Flowers

Everybody loves bouquets. It may be argued that every plant in the garden can be cut and brought indoors to enjoy, but the following plants are considered cut flowers because of their strong stems and reasonably good vase life. Always cut stems in the morning or evening, place immediately in water, and use a cut flower preservative in the vase. Check the text when looking for this trait, as not all species or cultivars in the genus are considered to be good cut flowers.

Acanthus	*Dahlia*	*Gaillardia*	*Lupinus*
Achillea	*Delphinium*	*Helenium*	*Lycoris*
Aconitum	*Dendranthema*	*Helianthus*	*Lysimachia*
Allium	*Dianthus*	*Heliopsis*	*Macleaya*
Anemone	*Digitalis*	*Helleborus*	*Miscanthus*
Artemisia	*Dryopteris* (foliage)	*Hibiscus*	*Monarda*
Aster	*Echinacea*	*Hypericum* (fruit)	*Nepeta*
Astilbe	*Echinops*	*Iris*	*Paeonia*
Astrantia	*Eremurus*	*Kniphofia*	*Papaver*
Baptisia	*Eryngium*	*Leucanthemum*	*Penstemon*
Campanula	*Eucomis*	*Liatris*	*Phlox*
Crocosmia	*Eupatorium*	*Lilium*	*Physostegia*

Platycodon
Polemonium
Polygonatum

Primula
Scabiosa
Stokesia

Thalictrum
Verbascum

Veronica
Veronicastrum

Drought Tolerance

The following plants tolerate drought well, but remember: no plant "likes" to be grown under drought conditions, and performance is always better when some irrigation is provided. Check the text when looking for this trait, as not all species or cultivars in the genus are considered to be drought tolerant.

Aster
Dianthus
Epimedium

Eryngium
Eucomis
Gaillardia

Muhlenbergia
Panicum

Rohdea
Yucca

Fragrant Flowers/Foliage

The following perennials have fragrant flowers or leaves. Fragrance is an intensely personal thing. Some people believe a flower is marvelously scented, while other noses may shrivel up and die at the same smell. Check the text when looking for this trait, as not all species or cultivars in the genus are considered to be fragrant.

Achillea
Allium
Anemone
Artemisia
Aster
Campanula
Clematis

Dianthus
Dianthus
Echinacea
Hemerocallis
Hosta
Ipheion
Iris

Lilium
Lunaria
Lupinus
Monarda
Narcissus
Nepeta
Perovskia

Phlox
Polygonatum
Primula
Santolina
Thymus
Trillium
Zephryanthes

Ground Covers

All plants cover the ground, but some plants do so more aggressively. The following plants, which generally spread by tubers, stolons, or runners, can be used to cover large areas reasonably quickly. As in all discussions, where you live will influence what plants you should select to cover the ground. Remember, there is a fine line between being sufficiently aggressive to be a good ground cover and so aggressive as to be called invasive. Check the text when looking for this trait, as not all species or cultivars in the genus are considered to be good ground covers.

Achillea
Adiantum
Ajuga
Asarum
Astilbe
Astrantia
Bergenia

Brunnera
Campanula
Ceratostigma
Dianthus
Disporum
Epimedium
Euphorbia

Geranium
Hosta
Hypericum
Imperata
Lamium
Lysimachia
Macleaya

Muhlenbergia
Phlox
Persicaria
Podophyllum
Polemonium
Polygonatum
Pulmonaria

GROUND COVERS, *continued*

Ranunculus	*Sedum*	*Thalictrum*	*Tiarella*
Saxifraga	*Stachys*	*Thymus*	*Viola*

Interesting Foliage/Fruit

The following plants are often planted for the ornamental value of the foliage and fruit, rather than the flowers. Check the text when looking for this trait, as not all species or cultivars in the genus are considered to have interesting foliage or fruit.

FOLIAGE

Acanthus	*Euphorbia*	*Muhlenbergia*	*Santolina*
Adiantum	*Eucomis*	*Osmunda*	*Saxifraga*
Ajuga	*Gaura*	*Panicum*	*Sedum*
Allium	*Hakonechloa*	*Penstemon*	*Stachys*
Artemisia	*Heuchera*	*Phlox*	*Stipa*
Aruncus	*Hosta*	*Physostegia*	*Symphytum*
Astrantia	*Imperata*	*Polemonium*	*Thalictrum*
Athyrium	*Lamium*	*Polygonatum*	*Tiarella*
Bergenia	*Lunaria*	*Pulmonaria*	*Tricyrtis*
Brunnera	*Lysimachia*	*Ranunculus*	*Trillium*
Canna	*Macleaya*	*Rohdea*	*Yucca*
Disporum	*Maianthemum*	*Rodgersia*	
Dryopteris	*Miscanthus*	*Salvia*	

FRUIT

Baptisia	*Euphorbia*	*Lunaria*	*Podophyllum*
Clematis	*Hypericum*	*Maianthemum*	*Rohdea*
Disporum	*Kirengeshoma*	*Osmunda*	

Sprawling Habit/Vines

The following vines or plants tend to sprawl if not provided with support. Large sprawling plants can be trained to grow through and over small shrubs or can be supported by neighboring plants. Check the text when looking for this trait, as not all species or cultivars in the genus sprawl or have a vine-like habit.

Aster	*Dicentra*	*Geranium*	*Oenothera*
Campanula	*Euphorbia*	*Heliopsis*	*Silene*
Clematis			

Evergreen/Winter Interest

Although much of the country is covered with snow in the winter, some plants still provide winter interest in the form of architectural features, seed heads, and persistent foliage. Check the text when looking for this trait, as not all species or cultivars in the genus are considered to be good plants for winter interest.

Ajuga	Epimedium	Muhlenbergia	Ranunculus
Asarum	Eryngium	Panicum	Rohdea
Bergenia	Helleborus	Pennisetum	Sedum
Clematis	Hepatica	Phlox	Stipa
Dianthus	Heuchera	Pulmonaria	Tiarella
Dryopteris	Miscanthus		

PLANT HARDINESS ZONES

Average Annual Minimum Temperature

Zone	Temperature (°F)			Temperature (°C)		
1		Below	−50	−45.6	and	below
2a	−45	to	−50	−42.8	to	−45.5
2b	−40	to	−45	−40.0	to	−42.7
3a	−35	to	−40	−37.3	to	−40.0
3b	−30	to	−35	−34.5	to	−37.2
4a	−25	to	−30	−31.7	to	−34.4
4b	−20	to	−25	−28.9	to	−31.6
5a	−15	to	−20	−26.2	to	−28.8
5b	−10	to	−15	−23.4	to	−26.1
6a	−5	to	−10	−20.6	to	−23.3
6b	0	to	−5	−17.8	to	−20.5
7a	5	to	0	−15.0	to	−17.7
7b	10	to	5	−12.3	to	−15.0
8a	15	to	10	−9.5	to	−12.2
8b	20	to	15	−6.7	to	−9.4
9a	25	to	20	−3.9	to	−6.6
9b	30	to	25	−1.2	to	−3.8
10a	35	to	30	1.6	to	−1.1
10b	40	to	35	4.4	to	1.7
11	40	and	above	4.5	and	above

$°C = 5/9 \times (°F−32)$

$°F = (9/5 \times °C) + 32$

INDEX OF BOTANICAL NAMES

INDEX OF COMMON NAMES